ARTISANS
INTO WORKERS

Labor in Nineteenth-Century America

Bruce Laurie

University of Illinois Press
Urbana and Chicago

First Illinois paperback, 1997

Library of Congress Cataloging-in-Publication Data
Laurie, Bruce.
Artisans into workers : labor in nineteenth-century America /
Bruce Laurie.
p.   cm.
Originally published: 1st ed. New York : Hill and Wang, 1989 (American
century series).
Includes bibliographical references and index.
ISBN 0-252-06660-X (paper : alk. paper) / ISBN 978-0-252-06660-3 (paper : alk. paper)
1. Labor movement—United States—History—19th century. 2. Trade-
unions—United States—History—19th century. 3. Artisans—United
States—History—19th century. I. Title. II. Series: American century
series.
HD8070.L38   1997
331.11'0973—dc21   96-52553
                                CIP

P 7 6 5 4 3

ARTISANS INTO WORKERS

To Leslie

Contents

Acknowledgments

Completing this book was easier than starting to write it. The writing was delayed by two unforgettable experiences, a year in residence as Senior Lecturer at the Centre for the Study of Social History at the University of Warwick in 1983–84, and the birth of our daughter, Rebecca, in 1985. My year at Warwick was an endless delight of inspiring classes and seminars as well as many visits to rugby and soccer stadiums and innumerable nights at the Coventry Cottage for beer and political talk. I owe all of this to the courtesy of my Warwick colleagues Edward Countryman, John Davis, Bill Lancaster, Gwynne Lewis, Roger Magraw, Tony Mason, Christopher Read, and David Washbrook. Their hospitality and good cheer made living abroad as easy as moving in with an old friend, and their intellectual rigor made me a better historian. The arrival of Rebecca has made a difference that is impossible to convey.

I have also benefited from students and colleagues at the University of Massachusetts and in the Pioneer Valley. My graduate students Elizabeth Fones-Wolf, Edwin Gabler, Andrew Gyory, William Hartford, Lori Kran, Carlos Pablón, Vivien Sandlund, and Robert Weir helped clarify my interpretation of the Knights of Labor and the American Federation of Labor. Jesse Dizard, a budding scholar in his own right, checked my references. Frank Couvares at Amherst College helped me think through the meaning of the late nineteenth century and encouraged me to call the union practice of the American Federation of Labor "prudential unionism." Fellow historians at the University of Massachusetts Paula Baker and Ronald Story offered much needed encouragement, sympathetic ears, and useful counsel. Leonard Richards provided helpful criticism of Chapter 1. Milton Cantor was his usual witty and sacrificial self. He read the entire manuscript and supplied the kind of criticism one expects of a co-author. It is difficult to express the depth of my gratitude to Arthur Wang and Eric Foner. They read and reread the manuscript with great care and nudged me along when I needed nudging. They gave excellent advice, all of which I appreciated and most of which I accepted. This book is much better for their effort.

Finally, I wish to thank my wife, Leslie, whose unfailing good humor and unshakable support made this book possible, parenthood pleasurable, and marriage a partnership of joy. I dedicate this book to her as small installment on a debt that accumulates daily and can never be repaid.

ARTISANS INTO WORKERS

Introduction

"Why is there no socialism in the United States?" The German sociologist Werner Sombart asked this question in his 1906 study of labor in Europe and the United States. It is one of those historical questions that won't go away. It obsessed John R. Commons and his graduate students who at the University of Wisconsin in the opening decades of the twentieth century established the study of American labor as a proper academic discipline. It still intrigues American historians and it informs this book. By socialism Commons and his students meant both class consciousness and a socialist party speaking for the working class. The American Socialist party was in its infancy when Commons came to Wisconsin in 1904. In the presidential election of 1912 it received nearly a million votes and on the eve of World War I the party was winning over larger numbers of trade unionists. But Commons considered American workers indifferent or averse to socialism by comparison with Europeans, who had formed socialist parties earlier and were more demonstrably class-conscious. In 1928 the American labor movement resembled an endangered species and the political left had shrunk and then had split into warring groups of socialists and communists. In that year Selig Perlman, Commons's most perceptive student, published his synthetic history of American labor which addressed the same question put by Sombart.

Closely following Sombart, Perlman argued that conditions peculiar to the United States imbued social relations and worker consciousness with two fundamental distinctions. First, during the nineteenth century American workers in the name of antimonopoly made common cause in politics with the "producing classes" of farmers and small businessmen. Labor's romance with independent politics defeated the primary function of trade unionism by diverting attention to fruitless third-party political campaigns that necessarily relegated workplace activity to a "sunshine" enterprise, an avocation undertaken between electoral initiatives. Second, in the long run, employers were able to keep their employees satisfied and contented with wage labor. This enhanced the stature of the employer so that his "individualistic spirit" penetrated "the ranks of his employees." Here was the seed of the consensus interpretation of American history that stressed the absence of basic ideological disagreement and the triumph of individualism.

Perlman discussed several features of the American experience that blunted class consciousness and encouraged labor's acceptance of the status quo. A deeply ingrained respect for property rights, "bred into the American community from the very beginning," nurtured "social and economic conservatism" and produced a nation of expectant capitalists. Geographic mobility destabilized working-class communities and disrupted workers' organizations, not the least of which, of course, were trade unions. Mainstream political parties, on the other hand, were more durable and popular than unions. And because (white male) American workers were awarded the "free gift" of the right to vote, they were more firmly integrated into the political order than European workers, who could not exercise the franchise for most of the nineteenth century. In addition, constant waves of immigrants made the American working class "the most heterogeneous . . . in existence—ethnically, linguistically, religiously, and culturally," a Tower of Babel condemned like Noah's descendants to speak mutually unintelligible languages. Growing numbers of the European newcomers, moreover, were Roman Catholics, brought up to believe that "resolute opposition" to socialism was the political demand of their faith.

To Perlman, Catholics figured prominently in the inexorable shift from the impossible and regressive politics of antimonopoly to the realistic and pragmatic craft unionism of the American Federation of Labor. The European-born industrial craftsman as well as some Americans gradually understood there was little to be gained from the reform politics cherished by native-born workers because there were fewer jobs than job seekers. This imbalance in the supply and demand for labor created a "scarcity psychology" that made skilled workmen realize it was vital to protect their jobs. Perlman called "job consciousness" the only appropriate consciousness in the United States. Job-conscious workers saw themselves not as the political companions of petty producers or members of a class with common concerns but as practitioners of individual crafts, a constellation of interest groups with the narrow aims of increasing wages, reducing the length of the workday, and safeguarding their jobs through enforced apprenticeship training and work rules. Such workers could not discard the ideological baggage of the past, however, without an infusion of new blood and farsighted leadership. During the Gilded Age they gained kindred spirits from "old stock" immigrants of Northwestern Europe, both socialist and antisocialist, who repudiated the tradition of the politics of antimonopoly or were unaware of it. The apostolic socialists among them—Samuel Gompers, Adolph Strasser, and other progenitors of the American Federation of Labor—came up with the convincing and "suitable" alternative of "business unionism." Gompers's business unionism took stock of the impracticality of reform politics and socialist politics in America and appreciated the finely tuned pragmatism of the ordinary craftsman. To Perlman, business unionism offered a "perfect fit" between the "peculiar conditions" in the United States and the pervasive "scarcity psychology." The AF of L was the vehicle that carried labor to its historical mission.

Perlman's teleology went unchallenged for over a generation. His students, as well as scholars trained outside the Wisconsin School, perpetuated the distinction between the old politics of producerism and the pragmatism of the new unionism. Philip Taft, Perlman's distinguished protégé, chided his mentor for suggesting a psychology that could not be verified and in any case did not account for the behavior of workers. Nonetheless, Taft stayed squarely within the methodological and thematic confines of the Commons School, limiting his work to organized labor and depicting the AF of L as a historical inevitability. Gerald Grob was not trained by a Wisconsin School scholar, but his study of ideological conflict in the late-nineteenth-century labor movement opens with a paean to Commons and depicts the Knights of Labor and the American Federation of Labor as polar opposites. Even Norman Ware, a contemporary of Perlman and a socialist, refuted the idea of the inevitability of craft unionism but substituted a dualism similar to Perlman's. Ware described workers as either reform-conscious or class-conscious and argued that reform consciousness was imposed upon labor by meddlesome middle-class radicals. Like the followers of Commons, he was concerned with labor organization and paid scant attention to unorganized workers or life off the job. Ware's institutional focus, writes David Brody, tells much about the organized but left us "otherwise ignorant of the history of the American worker."

Not until the early 1960s did historians find a new direction. Brody's study of steelworkers from the 1880s to the 1920s, the first book in the "new labor history," deals with unorganized as well as organized labor, management systems, community life, and other topics traditionally overlooked by what came to be called the "old labor history." In his analysis of Northern labor during the Civil War and Reconstruction, David Montgomery is more directly critical of the Commons approach. Though he deals primarily with the economic struggles and political activities of unionists, Montgomery disputes the rigid distinction between reform-minded and class-conscious workers. The same union men who struck for better wages and working conditions also advocated land redistribution, currency reform, and cooperative production to abolish "wage slavery." Herbert Gutman made an even more radical departure in a series of essays published from the late 1950s to the mid-1960s. Gutman recounted the deliberate and quixotic rebellions of miners and railway workers to illustrate the endurance of anticapitalistic values molded in the prefactory age that sparked labor protest and engendered community support for the workmen of small-town America. In 1974 Gutman expanded this theme into a fresh synthesis that questioned the periodization, institutional orientation, and interpretive pieties of the old labor history. Gutman found no discontinuity in the outlook of American labor after the mid-1880s, no evolution toward business unionism, and no evidence of worker accommodation to the existing order. He instead posed enduring tensions between the preindustrial outlooks and customs of working people and the demands of an increasingly rationalized industrial system. These tensions gave rise to individual and collective protest—absenteeism, slowdowns, spontaneous riots, and organized strikes—between 1815 and 1919 because of the recurring migration into the cities of artisans, farmers, and peasants from the American villages and the European countryside; men and women stubbornly resisted the regimentation of the factory.

By the time Gutman published his synthesis, the "new labor history" had eclipsed the old. It was "history from the bottom up," contrived to evoke the richly textured experience of ordinary people on the job, at home, and in the community. This emphasis derived in part from the impact of social science on history and from growing awareness of the English labor historians, notably E. J. Hobsbawm and E. P. Thompson. No book caused a greater sensation than Thompson's *Making of the English Working Class,* a truly seminal work read by some with the reverence of Holy Scripture. Thompson made a huge impact with the elegant assertion that "class happens when some men, as a result of common experiences (inherited or shared), feel and articulate . . . their interests as between themselves, and as against other men whose interests are different from (and usually opposed to) theirs. The class experience is largely determined by the productive relations into which men are born—or enter involuntarily. Class consciousness,'' he continued, ''is the way in which these experiences are handled in cultural terms: embodied in traditions, value-systems, ideas, and institutional forms.'' This formulation profoundly influenced Montgomery and Gutman as well as their growing corps of graduate students—a new generation involved in the politics of the New Left or at least in the cultural ferment of the turbulent mid-1960s. These young scholars cut their teeth on a youth movement that looked beyond a seemingly affluent and strongly patriotic white working class to the nation's underclass and the ''wretched of the earth'' as the agents of historical change. They were as attentive to the vitality of popular culture and the protests of the dispossessed as they were antagonistic to such ''establishment institutions'' as the trade union. Commons-style labor history appeared hollow and irrelevant to a generation eager to pursue Thompson's conception of class and culture to rescue the ''inarticulate'' from historical obscurity. The old labor history was as suspect as most things of the past.

Community was to the new labor history what union had been to the old labor history. Early works first focused on industrial cities and towns in the Northeast, then on similar places in the Midwest and the Far West. More recently, historians have begun to explore the urban (and rural) South. The steady proliferation of community studies has rounded out the picture of the white industrial craftsman left unfinished by the Commons School. It has deepened our understanding of the wage earner's work habits, domestic life, leisure-time activities, and religious observances. It has also illuminated the everyday existence of those ignored or spurned by unions—the casual laborer, the free black, and the domestic servant, as well as the department-store clerk.

Nonetheless, by the late 1970s, the new labor history began to raise doubts. Some reviewers found that, for all the painstaking research and meticulous attention to methodology, new labor historians had refined but not really overturned the central themes of the old labor history. These conclusions are not entirely unwarranted. Many studies have not ventured beyond Perlman. In his groundbreaking quantitative analysis of geographic and economic mobility, Stephan Thernstrom reported astonishing population turnover for unskilled workers between 1850 and 1880 in Newburyport, Massachusetts. A minority within the small group that stayed behind moved into semiskilled and skilled positions; and many more improved their status by accumulating enough money to buy a small house. Thernstrom's work was infectious. It inspired dozens of comparable studies that typically describe a footloose majority driven from place to place by failure, and a settled, socially mobile minority that never lived the "rags to riches" myth but did climb a few rungs on the job ladder or set aside a nest egg. Thernstrom argued that he had unearthed a source of the weak class consciousness in the United States. "One reason that a permanent proletariat along the lines envisioned by Marx did not develop in the United States," he concludes, "is perhaps that few Americans *stayed* in one place, one workplace, or even one city long enough to discover a sense of common identity or common grievance." As for the few workers that did move up socially and economically, they had a taste of just enough success to prevent alienation and confirm the national faith in a fluid society. Though some scholars greeted these findings as new and compelling, the fact is that Perlman had made a similar claim nearly forty years earlier. Alan Dawley, on the other hand, acknowledges the contribution of the Commons School, if only to show its inadequacy. His study of the industrial revolution in the shoemaking town of Lynn, Massachusetts, argues that the volatility of the population found by Thernstrom "does not preclude the development of class consciousness." The turnover in Lynn did not affect a "permanent minority" of influential shoe workers who sustained local unions and commanded the ranks of the floating majority. Statistical measures of social mobility, he adds, not only begged the question of the impact of social improvement on worker aspirations in Newburyport but flew in the face of evidence from other communities. Such evidence suggested that the successful worker was synonymous with the labor radical and that his achievement "whetted the appetites of those left behind for more." Dawley goes on to fault the Commons School for assuming there was something "inevitable" about the failure of socialism and the success of business unionism. The "equal rights" ideology Perlman considered so debilitating became "increasingly class conscious at the end of the nineteenth century and laid the foundation of the socialist alternative to laborism." Yet, in seeking to explain the impotence of class consciousness and the defeats of labor parties in Lynn earlier in the century, he sounds very much like Perlman. "The establishment of political democracy in the early stages of America's Industrial Revolution," he tells us, gave wage earners "a vested interest in the existing political system before they felt the worst effects of industrial capitalism." He is blunter still in declaring political democracy to be "the nail in the coffin of class consciousness."

The steady stream of community studies published since the late 1970s has led to a second criticism of the new labor history. This monographic scholarship, writes Brody, has exposed complexity and thereby given us pause. It has revealed the "variety of working-class experience—family, ethnicity, mobility, technology, and so on—but the complexity does militate against an easy and obvious synthesis." A more recent reviewer fears that the proliferation of information has outstripped our digestive capacity. Such criticism has become commonplace, for twenty years after the birth of the new labor history we are still no closer to grasping the larger picture or developing an alternative to the Commons School.

In the last few years an earnest debate has begun that turns on two questions first asked by Sombart and then by Commons and his associates: Was American labor less class-conscious in comparison with European labor, and were conditions in the United States exceptional? Sean Wilentz insists we cannot answer these queries without first clearing up confusions embedded in the standard customarily used to assess class consciousness. Scholars on both sides of the debate relate class consciousness to socialism and assume that, because socialism was weaker in the United States, American workers were not class-conscious. Wilentz urges us to discard the socialist touchstone and accept working-class consciousness on its own terms. He finds American workers to have been acutely aware of their class interests during the nineteenth century, for they fought the transformation of their labor power into a commodity to be bought and sold like any other merchandise. They expressed their opposition to capitalism in the language of radical republicanism, which was "nineteenth-century class consciousness, if not a sharply defined proletarianism." Nick Salvatore strongly disagrees. He charges Wilentz with ignoring the vast majority of the unorganized who did not subscribe to radicalism or enlist in the labor wars he recounts. He also argues that Wilentz does not distinguish class conflict from class consciousness; he, instead, conflates the two and thereby exaggerates the strength of class consciousness. Despite the chronic strikes, "only rarely did that experience produce a conscious and sustained self-image of working people as a class in opposition to other classes in society; even more rarely was that consciousness passed on from one generation of workers to another." Salvatore goes further by asserting that even Wilentz's putatively radical workers operated within the political discourse described by the consensus historians of the 1950s.

Which position is more persuasive? It is pointless to deny that most nineteenth-century workers were not card-carrying unionists. Only a third of all industrial workers were organized when union membership reached its nineteenth-century peak just before the panic of 1873. But it is not clear what this means. Stable unions emerged after the mid-1880s. Before their advent, formal membership in unions may be no better a gauge of class consciousness than formal church membership is of religiosity. Some—members of the railway brotherhoods, to cite the most obvious example—can be considered class-conscious only in the loosest sense of the term. It is perhaps even more instructive that not until the mid-1880s did the majority of strikes enjoy union sanction. Most of the bloody disturbances on the railroads between 1873 and 1877 and many of the combative eight-hour strikes in 1886, in other words, were spontaneous uprisings on the part of trade union renegades or workers without unions at all. The percentage of organized workers may not tell us much about the state of class consciousness one way or another for most of the nineteenth century. On the other hand, several studies of nonunion workers are suggestive of the complexity referred to by Brody. Reverent evangelical Protestants, whom Alan Dawley and Paul Faler have called "loyalists" and I have called "revivalists," usually deferred to their betters and assailed "godless" radicals during the 1830s. But New England revivalists in the 1840s, another historian shows, appropriated radicalism for a stinging if ultimately ambiguous attack on competitive capitalism. Revivalists often lived side by side with other workers—"traditionalists," some historians have called them. These young, usually unmarried, and largely unskilled laborers and marginal artisans were a hard-living underclass with a love of liquor and a good street fight. Traditionalists were often disinterested in radicalism, but they were hardly submissive employees or celebrants of individualism. There was not one but several worker cultures with distinctive politics at any point in time.

A multiplicity of working-class cultures, of course, does not rule out the possibility of a dominant culture. This was Perlman's point. Even though he saw a class riven along ethnic (and not cultural) lines, Perlman maintained that job-conscious workers set the tone. For their part, both Salvatore and Wilentz agree that republicanism was the prevailing outlook of the working class in nineteenth-century America. Salvatore is persuaded, however, that "even for the most class aware democratic workers, theirs was in large part a struggle within the accepted political structure to define the *meaning* of such political concepts as citizenship and democracy." While there is evidence for this, there is also good reason to believe that things were not that simple. Salvatore would have been on firmer ground had he elaborated upon his observation that consensus does not eliminate conflict. Indeed, ideological conflict and consensus coexisted throughout the nineteenth century. Entrepreneurial and worker ideology were not frozen categories but flexible constructs in dialectical relationship to one another and to larger economic and political developments. Each received subtly different expression in different contexts. Free labor, the outlook of many Northern and some Southern entrepreneurs before the Civil War, envisioned a dynamic and open economy, a kind of escalator in perpetual motion that would lift sober and diligent workers and yeomen farmers out of their class if unimpeded by unions or government. It borrowed discriminately from working-class radicalism, revering manual labor and incorporating such popular programs as free homesteads and expanded public education. Free labor enjoyed wider and deeper popularity in the North as the antebellum period progressed. It saw the specter of an aggressive "slave power" in the South lusting after Western lands that workers thought to be their birthright and threatening to foist aristocratic rule on a free people. The "consensus" forged during the heat of sectional conflict, however, broke down after the Civil War and not exclusively because of accelerated industrialism. Leading manufacturers in Gilded Age America expressed individualism not through the shared idiom of free labor but through the crude scientism of Social Darwinism, a language workers found vulgar and offensive. That socialism did not come to full flower in the intense class conflicts during the late nineteenth century does not mean that there was consensus. If there was wide agreement on the virtues of individualism, how do we explain the mass strikes, the constant interventions by judges and troops, or the popularity of the Knights of Labor, the most democratic, if not socialist, labor movement of the century and perhaps in American history?

The terms "exceptionalism" and "consensus" are loaded and tend to obscure more than they reveal. They seduce one into accepting simple answers to complex historical problems. Labor in nineteenth-century America was not exceptional, if by that one means anomalous. Each nation is different in some sense; none is exceptional. That American radicals did not copy the British Chartists after the mid-1830s or storm the barricades with the German artisans in 1848 does not mean they were peculiar. It simply means there were distinctive conditions within each nation that shaped the character of class conflict *and* class consciousness.

The Chartists, after all, didn't rebel in 1848 either and when the English working class finally established its own party in the early twentieth century it was more laborist than socialist.

It is my purpose to show that the development of the American working class differed from its European counterpart in two critical respects. First, the ideology of radicalism persisted longer than in any continental nation. Why this was so concerns us below. Here it is enough to emphasize a dualism in the radical tradition before the Civil War and indeed long afterward. At the workplace it encouraged a form of class consciousness, a belief that employers illegitimately accumulated profit from the toil of labor. It justified struggle for immediate gain and proposed the long-term solution of cooperative production. In politics, however, radicalism operated as a force for integration because of its loose compatibility with free laborism and because of the adaptability and social openness of the established parties. The durability of radicalism also inhibited the transition to socialism that took place in some European nations. In France, radical republicanism evolved into republican socialism after 1850; in the United States, its evolution was arrested. In spite of some innovations—support for government owned and operated banks and railways being the most prominent—late radicalism closely resembled its earlier version. This was not solely the mark of radicalism's respect for private property, as some historians, Perlman among them, have argued. Equally important, radicalism never completely repudiated the old republican axiom that active government was corrupt government. It never fully greeted government as a class ally or instrument for class liberation, and as a result could not easily accept the role that socialism demanded of the state. One reason why "there was no socialism" in the late nineteenth century, or to be more accurate, why socialism was comparatively weak, is that radicalism was so persistent.

Second, Gilded Age workers not only ran up against an arrogant and callous class of industrialists fiercely antipathetic to unions. They also encountered ruthless resistance from state and federal government. Judges freely gutted labor laws and stifled job actions with crippling injunctions. Armed militiamen, sometimes bolstered by federal troops, were aggressive and shot down strikers not just during the major strikes but in the course of hundreds of brushfire conflicts. The railway strikes of the mid-1870s, the general strike for the eight-hour day in 1886, the Homestead strike, and the Pullman boycott were not simply dramatic clashes in which each side exchanged blows, ministered to the wounded, buried the dead, and repaired to the bliss of the Victorian home. They were formative events widely discussed, assessed, and reassessed in corner taverns, party headquarters, and union halls. And they proved decisive in the development of the labor movement. The repression ravaged the Knights of Labor and smashed the American Railway Union, the only viable rivals of the AF of L. In addition, the impact of the court orders and police interventions reinforced the AF of L's growing wariness of workers in large-scale industry, since it was they who launched the massive strikes that incited the state. The repression, and not simply an abstract commitment to craft unionism, helps explain why the AF of L turned away from sympathy strikes by craftsmen and ultimately from industrial workers during the 1890s. It was a vital historical experience that helped abet what I shall call "prudential unionism," a growing cautiousness at the workplace designed to ensure the survival of the labor movement.

How far have we diverged from the perspective of the exceptionalist advocates and their critics? Historians writing in the tradition of the Commons School were and continue to be aware of the flexibility of American politics and the limitations of labor politics. They go wrong, however, in dismissing "producerism" or radicalism as the individualism of antimonopoly and in assuming it was uniquely American. Radicalism was more ambiguous: it harbored both individualism and collectivism and before the 1850s it was the universal language of skilled workers on both sides of the Atlantic. That it was not "proletarian" is another matter entirely and not really surprising, given the uneven pace of industrial change. Most workers were not proletarianized at midcentury; that is, they were not yet machine tenders in large factories. Commons and his associates, and many modern-day scholars who differ with them, have also failed to appreciate the significance of government in the making of the labor movement. Perlman, in fact, missed the point entirely. He passed over the antilaborism of government and emphasized the distinctiveness of the federal system, the division of power and authority that rendered it "inherently inadequate as an instrument of reform." It may not have occurred to him that the same government that was so remote before the Civil War and so unresponsive to labor's legislative initiatives thereafter could be so belligerent in defending the interests of employers or so important a force in shaping labor's strategies and tactics.

"Which workers?" one inevitably asks. This book does not pretend to be comprehensive. It seeks to merge the institutional focus of the old labor history with the special social and cultural insights of the new labor history. It is chiefly concerned with organized workers and their politics and more especially with the major labor movements of the nineteenth century—the Working Men's parties and General Trades' Unions in the late 1820s and 1830s and the Knights of Labor and American Federation of Labor in the 1880s and 1890s—but not in isolation. It deals with organized workers in their larger world, their relations to unorganized males, women, and blacks as well as with employers and government. It also attempts to tell us something about the unfolding of capitalism in the countryside as well as the city. And it strives to demonstrate how the making and unmaking of the American working class influenced the country's history.

Insofar as this book examines organized workers and labor movements, it tells a story with the contradictory themes of advance and retreat, of high hopes and dashed dreams. Real gains were made in the course of the nineteenth century. Union men improved their standard of living and significantly reduced the length of their workday. They gained more time and resources for themselves and their families and made life easier for their children. They were also a very productive work force. Despite their work rules and employer complaints about slacking off, union men helped produce the abundance that by the end of the nineteenth century made the United States a leading industrial nation. Yet larger goals eluded them. One need not lapse into judging labor's achievements by some ideal standard of what workers should have been or might have become in order to reach such a conclusion. Northern workers, to be sure, played a major role in ridding the United States of the scourge of chattel slavery but never did eliminate what they called "wage slavery." Nor did they overcome their own sexism, racial intolerance, and cultural chauvinism. If anything, in the 1890s they were more suspicious of women and blacks than they had been in the 1820s. They also gradually embraced a contracting vision of what was possible or desirable. This last and larger failure runs against the grain of the nation's buoyant optimism, the firm belief that things always get better. At the same time the record of unionized labor testifies to the courage and conviction of men and women who dreamed of a different world and struggled mightily to bring it about, to change a system hopelessly stacked against them. Had they wrung their hands in despair, theirs would have been a pallid and uninspiring past. But some of them knew, perhaps better than those of us with benefit of hindsight, that nothing is really predetermined.

Household to Factory

"In countries thinly inhabited, or where people live principally by agriculture, as in America," Noah Webster wrote in 1785, "every man is in some measure an artist—he makes a variety of utensils, rough indeed, but such as will answer his purpose—he is a husbandsman in summer and mechanic in winter. . . ." In these few lines the young Connecticut schoolteacher and future compiler of the nation's first dictionary summed up the economic condition of most late-eighteenth-century Americans. Webster's contemporaries were the epitome of self-sufficiency and versatility, independent yeomen farmers as adept at mending a rake or cobbling a shoe as at plowing a field. He was mistaken, however, in asserting that this "will always be the case so long as there is a vast tract of fertile land to be cultivated." His fellow Americans were beginning to sense the coming of a great transformation that would gradually erode self-sufficiency and remake yeomen, artisans, and their children into workers dependent upon wages.

Three interdependent forces account for this momentous revolution—the market, transportation, and manufacturing. We shall explore each of these in the pages that follow. Before moving on, however, it is helpful to sketch the outlines of these revolutionary agents. The market revolution, which was already under way by the 1780s, discouraged the making of goods for immediate use in favor of producing commodities for exchange in the marketplace. For yeomen farmers throughout the nation and planters in the South, this involved allocating human and capital resources from subsistence agriculture to staple crops. Yeomen might set aside more acreage for corn or wheat; planters might buy additional slaves to work in the tobacco or cotton fields. For rural artisans, the commercial revolution heralded an end to the age of itinerancy when visits to farmhouses to swap finished goods for raw materials were common. For urban artisans, it could mean taking on more apprentices or hiring skilled labor in order to keep shelves stocked for retail sale. Both were drawn into market nexuses in which cash was the medium of exchange and social relations were shaped by economic exigencies. The revolution in transportation went through several phases. First came the construction of roads and turnpikes in the 1790s; this was followed by the building of inland canals in the 1820s, and then railroads in the 1830s. These arteries enlarged the range of the market and fostered the industrial revolution. New means of transportation flooded rural America with articles customarily made at home, stimulating demand in the country and supply in the city. In addition, they made rural labor redundant and freed hands for industrial employment.

Historians no longer equate the industrial revolution with the rise of the factory alone. While the factory was the most visible manifestation of industrialism, it was a relatively small part of the industrial scene before the Civil War. As late as 1860, more wage earners worked in farmhouses and small workshops than in factories, and most used hand tools, not power-driven equipment. The industrial revolution described in the textbooks, with its sooty factories and clattering machines, was only beginning in antebellum America. Indeed, none of these revolutions ran its course before the Civil War. Each developed unevenly and made a deeper impression in the North and Midwest than in the South. The South experienced the commercial revolution and a lesser transportation revolution but did not industrialize to any significant degree.

· · ·

It is useful to return to Webster's yeoman. Celebrated as the backbone of the republic, he was also the prototypical American in his day and indeed long after. Nine out of ten people lived on the land in 1790 and just about eight out of ten were still there in 1860. Of course, there were regional variations. In the lower South in 1860, over 90 percent of the population lived outside urban places (communities with more than 2,500 people), but even in the North two-thirds were still on farms or in villages. On the eve of the Civil War, most Americans lived in the countryside, wedded to a distinctive way of life contemporaries called the "household factory" and some present-day historians refer to as the "household economy" or "household production."

As Webster implied, the early household factory was a flexible productive unit sustained on its own labor and raw materials. Cloth is a classic example. A study of Whitestown, New York, in 1820 discloses that each family turned out an average of forty yards of cloth a year, and the McLane Report, which surveyed workplaces twelve years later, indicates Whitestown was typical. Rural New Yorkers weaved 16.5 million yards of cloth, or 8.5 per capita, in the mid-1820s. Comparable figures for the South are unavailable, but literary evidence indicates that spinning and weaving were essential household activities for yeomen and planter households alike. Indeed, into the 1840s, nimble hands in Northern and Southern homes yielded more yarn and cloth than textile factories.

Farm chores, however, were primary. The representative holding in the Northeast was about one hundred acres, nearly half of which were improved. In the North, verdant pasture and grassland fed small herds, and tilled lands furnished grains and garden vegetables. Woodlots supplied fuel and timber and might include stands of maple trees that provided syrup and sugar. Just as winter's end signaled "sugaring time," so, too, the other seasons dictated work schedules. The work year began with the spring thaw. Fields were cleared, spread with manure, and furrowed by a team of oxen pulling a wooden plow. Planting started in late spring when danger of frost had passed, and the pace of work quickened with the long days of midsummer, which were crowded with harvesting crops of winter wheat and gathering crops from the spring planting. August brought a brief respite before the frantic fall harvest and rush to store grains and put up fruit from the orchard. Winter completed the cycle. The farmer turned to the woods to cut cordwood. The farmhouse, barns, outbuildings, and fences were always in need of maintenance. In the South, vast plantations skewed national figures of the average farm size. Early in the nineteenth century, farms were twice as large and improved acreage twice as great as in the North. Big tobacco and cotton plantations encompassed hundreds of acres and had scores of slaves. Longer growing seasons and dissimilar crops in the South created different work rhythms. But these were differences of degree, not kind.

There were other jobs as well on Northern farms. Livestock and poultry needed tending in all seasons and required special care in spring, when the sheep were washed and sheared and the geese plucked. Flax was reaped in June and prepared for loom and spindle by soaking in water and drying in the warm summer sun. Spinning and weaving awaited the colder months, as did putting up garden vegetables and smoking and salting fish, foul, and meat. Planting and harvesting mobilized the entire family, particularly when frosts or floods delayed sowing or foul weather threatened ripened grain. Damp autumns found the family working corn and wheat fields to save precious crops. But the normal pattern called for a strict sexual division of labor. Men and teenage sons worked field and forest and carried out routine repairs and maintenance. They also made their own equipment and did the slaughtering of the animals. In more leisurely moments, they fished the streams for trout, salmon, and alewives and prowled the woods for deer and small game. Women did the cooking and preserving, not just of game but of all manner of fruit and vegetable. The garden and dairy were as much women's domain as the kitchen, and so, of course, was the work that kept the homestead clean and lighted and the family fed. Plantation women were not exempt from such chores. They had their slaves to do the "worst of the drudgery," the "grimy . . . and never-done aspects of homework," says Suzanne Lebsock, but still worked in the garden and often toiled in the fields.

Farm families fell short of supplying all their needs. For iron, tea, and other commodities of vital importance, they relied upon merchants and the general store, but in a fashion that left the domestic economy largely undisturbed. Instead of purchasing supplies with money, which was scarce in any case, they bartered produce or raw materials. In such villages as Ridgefield, Connecticut, barter involved the entire community. Of Ridgefield's two hundred family heads in 1800, a few were itinerant craftsmen who tramped from farm to farm plying their trades. The butcher slaughtered swine and cattle; the shoemaker fashioned boots and shoes from hides provided by customers; the tailor appeared twice yearly to stitch and sew clothing appropriate to the season. The hatter alone had his own shop, and he gladly swapped felt and beaverskin headwear for hides. In Amherst, Massachusetts, farmer William Boltwood lent Mary Billings a horse for a trip to Vermont in 1799, and the following spring filled her loft with two hundred pounds of hay. Widow Billings was in no rush to square her account, and farmer Boltwood did not seem to care. She retired her debt in two installments, first by supplying a harness and then by delivering a load of stone in 1813.

Farmers of Billings's and Boltwood's generation turned out surpluses of farm and forest products. They reserved a portion for the barter economy and sold the rest for cash to local merchants or buyers in and around cities and towns. The income from cash sales was as precious as water in a very dry season and conserved just as jealously. It was rarely used for necessities that could be had through swapping. Instead, it went for taxes in states that required payment in hard currency, for gifts to children on the verge of marriage, and for the purchase of land to be passed on to sons, yeomen-in-waiting.

The gifts reflected a long tradition of parental obligation. Ever since settlers first cleared the forests and broke American soil, parents took responsibility for giving children a start in life by awarding dowries to daughters and allotments of land to sons. Parents easily met such obligations during the seventeenth century, in spite of large families. Land was cheap and abundant, even though the average household had five to seven children. Sons expected and usually received portions of the family farm or nearby tracts. By the opening decades of the eighteenth century, however, the constant division and redivision of land, coupled with high fertility rates, forced adjustments in this practice. Yeomen in Eastern regions, from Baltimore to Portland, abandoned the convention of dividing the family farm among all sons and willed it to the eldest (or the favored son) and settled the others on land in new and more distant regions. They also began to restrict family size and by the end of the eighteenth century reduced the number of children per family by two. This still left up to five offspring to feed and two to three male heirs eager to work land increasingly hard to come by. In the best of circumstances, sons in the East could count on smaller bequests—or none at all in the worst—and they grew restless as the pull of family and place gave way to yearnings for a fresh start in the trans-Allegheny West. Land was more plentiful in the South but quickly depleted because of the soil exhaustion brought on by single-crop agriculture and planter indifference to investing in soil improvement. Planters, one historical geographer comments, "earned well their reputation as 'soil killers,' " which is why so many pulled up stakes and moved into the Southwest.

This trickle of migration turned into three strong streams between 1780 and 1820. One ran from the upper South into the Gulf states; another from the Chesapeake through the Cumberland Gap into Kentucky, Tennessee, and southern Ohio; and still another flowed across the Berkshires into New York and overflowed into Pennsylvania, northern Ohio, and as far as Michigan. No one knows precisely how many Easterners left New England. If one scholar is correct, in 1820 alone New York State was home to 800,000 former New Englanders: the total figure for the North and border states may have approached two million. But the trek westward did not end in 1820, nor did it come to a halt in the Ohio Valley. Over the next forty years, roads opened up frontier land on the banks of the Mississippi River. Indiana, Illinois, and Iowa, mid-nineteenth-century frontiers, were to their time what the Mohawk and Ohio valleys were to the eighteenth century. The upper Midwest had about four million people by the eve of the Civil War, and most of them

had migrated from the East. Even its reaches of rich and fertile grasslands
failed to hold settlers. It no longer took much to stir the wanderlust of the
American farmer, and the valleys farther west proved irresistible. About
250,000 migrants from Midwestern farms gathered at St. Joseph, Missouri, and other staging points after 1840 for the two-thousand-mile
journey on the Overland Trail to the Pacific coast. Southerners were not
so footloose. By the Civil War, most settled east of the Mississippi in a
belt that ran from the middle of Georgia through Louisiana, the heart of
the Cotton Kingdom.

Migrants to the Ohio Valley or the Far West repeated the experiences
of pioneer farmers but in a different environment. The settlers of New
England and the South had been allotted land free of charge by town
government or colonial authorities. Their progeny in the early National
years had to purchase land either from the federal government, which in
1820 offered generous terms of $1.25 per acre for a minimum of eighty
acres, or from private developers at $2 to $3 for marginal land or up to
$40 for prime acreage. One way or another, most early migrants acquired
plots and began the arduous process of farm building. Those who settled
the Ohio Valley and the Southwest had to hack their farms out of wooded
wilderness. Working at a moderate pace a yeoman could clear five to
seven acres a year, which meant seven to ten years of backbreaking labor
for a farm suitable for a family of six. Pioneers on the flatlands farther
west could establish a workable farm in half the time, as could planters
using slave labor in the Southwest. Grain farmers marketed surpluses
within a few years of settling in, and wasted little time displacing
Virginians and New Yorkers as the nation's chief suppliers of wheat.
Ohioans achieved that distinction by midcentury despite bountiful wheat
harvests east of the Alleghenies in the 1850s.

These patterns of settlement and resettlement left behind a seemingly
uniform population of yeomen farmers in the North. By 1860 the average
holding consisted of 128 acres and regional averages did not vary much.
A mere thirty acres separated New England farms (119 acres) from
Midwestern farms (148 acres). As for the percentage of improved acreage
per farm, New England had the highest (74 percent) and the Midwest the
lowest (57 percent). Figures on the value of farm implements also show
very little regional variation. Midwestern husbandmen, for example, had
only one more draft animal per farm than New Englanders. Statistical
averages, however, mask more complex relations between farmer and
market. Realities conformed more closely to a continuum, with commercial farmers and subsistence farmers at the extremes and a majority of

semisubsistence husbandmen in between. All households allocated some labor to nonagricultural work, but commercial farmers devoted more energy and resources to maximizing profit by cultivating a single crop or raising a line of livestock, using more modern equipment, and perhaps rotating crops. Dairy, staple, and livestock growers along river valleys and around urban areas throughout the East incorporated some or all of these strategies between 1790 and 1820. Such changes, however, were only faintly perceptible before the 1830s. Most yeomen hovered between market farming and subsistence and stubbornly followed general agriculture. Their family factory functioned much as it always had. Change came in the early stages of the industrial revolution, which opened up employment for rural women as operatives in textile mills and outworkers in the shoe and clothing industries. Outworkers far outnumbered operatives and stayed at home doing both industrial work and farm chores. Earnings were scanty but enough to relieve pressures for intensifying farm production for the market.

Southern yeomen and small planters did not have such nonfarm sources of income. The very slow growth of industrialism held down opportunities to garner cash from industrial work. There were only a few cotton mills in the 1830s and they were small firms in the Carolina Piedmont. Tobacco factories, the other major industry, used slave labor. And since the region became a net importer of Northern shoes and clothing, the putting-out system never did take hold. Yeomen and small planters in need of money could only set aside some acreage for staple crops. Wheat farming boomed in western Virginia and in the 1830s cotton patches began to appear on subsistence farms everywhere.

Even if subsistence families were inclined to exploit the market, there were constraints in the 1820s on the development of commercial agriculture. Capital was scarce and tied up in land, shipping, and marine insurance. With the obvious exceptions of cotton and tobacco, foreign outlets were few and domestic markets restricted as long as so many Americans pursued self-sufficiency. Poor transportation also slowed the expansion of commercial agriculture. A road-building spree in the opening decades of the nineteenth century linked hinterlands to market towns and coastal cities in the Northeast, but problems remained. Wagons still lacked capacity and on the best of roads trundled along at two miles an hour or about twenty a day. In addition, freight rates were prohibitive for farmers in the backlands. Philadelphia carriers were among the most competitive in 1816, when wheat fetched a handsome $1.94 per bushel. But the cost of getting it to market was enough to bring farmers to tears: the freight charge equaled the selling price at just under two hundred miles. Upstate New Yorkers did no better. In 1817 their legislators estimated the cost of overland haulage from Buffalo to New York City at three times the market value of wheat.

Few Americans were more aware of this than the market farmers themselves. Once a major force for road construction, they became leading advocates for more ambitious internal improvements following the War of 1812. Merchants and manufacturers joined the outcry for more roads, canals, and river improvements. New York lawmakers took their cue with unparalleled fervor, chartering no fewer than 300 road and turnpike companies that laid down 5,000 miles of gravel roads in the course of the 1820s. While crews etched roads into the countryside, armies of day laborers dug the Erie Canal, which was completed in 1825. It became the pride of the Empire State, a great economic boon, and a catalyst for canal building. Pennsylvania's Main Line, a system of canals and a portage railroad between Philadelphia and Pittsburgh, opened a decade later, just one year ahead of the Ohio and Erie Canal from Cleveland to Portsmouth on the Ohio River. The Illinois and Michigan Canal, which gave the boom town of Chicago a waterway to the Mississippi in 1848, ended a fantastic construction craze that by 1850 produced over 3,500 miles of branch and trunk canals.

What the Erie was to canal construction, the Granite Railroad at Quincy, Massachusetts, was to railroads. Completed in 1826, it ran a mere two miles to Boston Harbor but it had great influence. Anthracite operators in eastern Pennsylvania quickly copied it, but they were soon upstaged by promoters in Eastern port cities eager for rapid transportation ties with the West. First came the Baltimore and Ohio, the nation's first commercial railway, which opened in 1830, and then in 1835 three lines from Boston to its satellites of Lowell, Worcester, and Providence. Five years later there were as many miles of railway track as canal bed. Railroad mileage tripled in the 1840s to just under 9,000 and surged fivefold in the 1850s because of the extension of the Baltimore and Ohio, the completion of the Pennsylvania, and a rush of construction in the Midwest that elevated Ohio and Illinois to leadership in track mileage.

The transportation revolution drastically altered the speed and direction of trade, as well as the cost of shipping. In precanal times the produce of Midwestern farmers was shipped East first by wagon to the shores of the Ohio and then on keelboats down the Ohio and Mississippi to New Orleans for transfer to sailing ships bound for the chief ports of the Atlantic coast. Goods needed by Ohio Valley farmers were moved for a short time from the East by wagon across the Allegheny Mountains, a journey of fifty days. Within thirty years Mississippi steamboats and New Orleans packets made it in half the time and competed with even faster carriers. Northeastern canals delivered Midwestern grains to New York and Baltimore docks in less than three weeks, and by 1850 the region's railways cut the trip to one week. Trans-Allegheny carriers failed to displace Mississippi shippers before the Civil War but did capture a good share of the market. Eastward-bound wheat and flour on the Erie alone reached one million tons in 1840 and jumped fourfold twenty years later. As tonnage soared, shipping costs plummeted from the wagoner rates of $0.30 to $0.70 per ton-mile at the end of the War of 1812 to canal costs of $0.01 to $0.07 by the 1830s. Railway charges fell steadily, reaching parity with canals by 1850.

The South did not completely escape the revolution in transportation, even though canal and railway construction did not keep pace with the North. In 1850 there were under five hundred miles of canal routes and in 1860 just about 11,000 miles of railroad track, or one-tenth and one-fifth of the national totals, respectively. Most railroads, moreover, were in the border states, and very few farther south penetrated the up-country in the Southeast or the frontier of the Cotton Belt. Even in Georgia, which was second only to Virginia in track mileage, no line reached the Piedmont before the Civil War. In 1850 a Rome, Georgia, journalist stated a complaint heard a generation earlier in the North. "The profits of whatever we make," he grumbled, "[have] been consumed in the cost of carriage." This left Southern yeomen isolated from the market economy and doomed to economic marginality and the poverty of subsistence farming. Most owned "little more than the clothing they wore," but remained on the land. Increasingly, they would raise a few bales of cotton for sale in order to accumulate cash for land or supplies, but this did not lead them to commercial agriculture. Up-country artisans still accepted farm goods and reciprocal labor in return for services, and local merchants gladly exchanged cotton and "all kinds of country produce" for supplies. In the late 1840s Thomas Morris, a storekeeper in Franklin County, Georgia, accepted produce or labor in payment for merchandise. In 1847, when Black Belt farmers had to buy provisions with money, yeoman farmer Thomas Scott squared his account with Morris by doing odd jobs for more than a week.

In the North, farm produce, minerals, and other commodities were not the only things that were transported more rapidly and more cheaply. So, too, were people. The transportation revolution accelerated the demographic and social changes already under way. In penetrating the West, it stimulated the flow of young men and women hungry for farmland. Aspiring yeomen who had leased as the first step on the ladder to ownership found it harder to take the step if they lived in close proximity to transport arteries. Higher rents turned them into migrants. A similar fate befell the Massachusetts and New York yeomen who had clamored for internal improvements. Canals and railways allowed competitors in the fertile valleys of Pennsylvania and Ohio to win Eastern markets, forcing farmers into dairying, sheep raising, or off the land altogether.

Improved transportation also opened up Northern agrarians to the market economy. The value of goods produced in farmsteads peaked in the East around 1810 and about twenty years later in the West, just as each area was on the threshold of the transportation revolution. Decline in household production closely followed the arrival of roads, canals, and railways. When the first boats made their trip westward on the Erie Canal in 1825, New York homesteads turned out a total of 16.5 million yards of textiles or nearly 9 yards per capita. Ten years later those figures were halved to 8.8 million yards and 4.03 yards, respectively; by 1855 total production was under one million yards and per capita output was no more than one-third of a yard. Textile production, long the mainstay of the household factory, had virtually disappeared in eastern New York. But the rate of decline was variable. As early as the 1820s, and presumably at the turn of the century, downstate counties bordering the Hudson River had the lowest output and the northern tier the highest. Some twenty years later, when the Erie Canal celebrated its fifteenth anniversary, woolen manufacture did not exist in counties adjoining the canal but persisted in the more remote areas. This process would be repeated in Pennsylvania during the 1830s and later in the West as more efficient means of transportation brought the market to rural doorsteps. As one farmer put it, the cost of "articles [was] so much lower than can be made in the house, it is found more profitable to purchase."

Purchase. Buy. This was the parlance of the market economy, in which the exchange of goods and services for money was taken for granted. It was not the language of the subsistence economy, or the practice of men and women accustomed to face-to-face barter. The systems were in tension, and by the 1840s the market economy was in ascendance throughout the North. Midwestern staple growers turned in hoes for harrows, iron for steel plows, sluggish oxen for faster horses. A decade later they sowed grain with automatic drills, and by the mid-1860s, 90,000 mowers and reapers were in use on the Great Plains. Farmers from western New England to the Ohio Valley had less choice, for merchants had broken definitively with the past by posting signs that read "Cash only." Buyers had to come up with money, which impelled farmers to intensify cultivation, leave agriculture for business, or enter the wage labor force.

Mary Paul was one such person who turned wage earner. Born in 1829, she was the daughter of a central Vermont farm family presumably of middling circumstance. Had she been born a generation earlier Mary would have spent her entire life on the farm. As it turned out, the commercial revolution made her expendable and the industrial revolution provided new occupational choices, opportunities to earn money and perhaps attain some degree of independence. At age fifteen or so, she moved to nearby Bridgewater to work as a domestic and then asked her father's permission to go to Lowell, because she "could earn more to begin with than . . . anywhere around here." Her father consented and at age sixteen in 1846, Mary Paul left for a four-year stint in the factories of the "Spindle City." She would return to rural Vermont for a short spell in the early 1850s and then join friends made in Lowell in a cooperative community in New Jersey before returning to New England in the mid-1850s to work as a housekeeper. In 1857 she married a Lowell marble worker and moved with him to Lynn, where she withdrew from gainful employment to raise a family. Mary Paul was part of a new generation of Northern farm-bred men and women who thought better of lighting out for the frontier and headed cityward for wage labor of one kind or another. Their precise number is unknown, but we get a sense of its magnitude if we look at urban growth before the Civil War.

Between 1820 and 1860 the national population grew from just under 10 million to slightly over 30 million, an increase of 230 percent. At the end of this sixty-year span fewer than one in five Americans resided in urban centers of more than 8,000 inhabitants, but city growth far outstripped growth elsewhere, surging ahead by 800 percent. Immigrants, usually associated with urbanization, played only a minor role in this population explosion. There were only 4 million of them in 1860, well over half of whom arrived between 1846 and 1857 at the tail end of the urban boom, and only one-half of whom settled in cities. Until mid-century, urbanization stemmed partly from natural increase of city dwellers and mostly from in-migration. The cities of Jacksonian America attracted strangers, to be sure, but these were strangers of American origin.

Boston was one such city. In 1830 over nine in ten Bostonians were native-born Americans, mostly from the farms and villages of northern New England. Immigrants from Western Europe and increasingly from Ireland trickled in over the next fifteen years and in 1845 they nearly equaled the proportion of Bostonians born in the city (23 and 36 percent, respectively). The largest group of all, or 40 percent, consisted of village-born New Englanders. Comparable figures for other urban places in this period are unavailable, but fragmentary evidence from a later era indicates that Boston's demography reflected this general pattern. The typical ward in midcentury Syracuse housed two native-born Americans for every immigrant and over half of them were born in surrounding counties. The same was true of Reading, Pennsylvania's Third Ward. Migrants from nearby farms accounted for half its population and an even larger share of the city as a whole.

The rural-urban flow persisted unabated in the 1850s but was overwhelmed by the great tide of immigration to the United States from the United Kingdom, Ireland, and Germany. The breakpoint was 1846–1847, when the number of immigrants rose from 82,000 to over 142,000 and climbed steadily thereafter, reaching the antebellum high of 267,000 in 1851. The yearly tide receded a bit but did not dip below the 1847 mark until 1858. This short eleven-year period brought over 2 million Europeans to American shores. By 1860 immigrants accounted for one-third of the population in the forty largest urban centers. They mirrored the national average in such Eastern ports as Boston and Philadelphia as well as in the inland cities of Albany, Hartford, Lowell, and Utica, and made up one-half of New York City, the major port of entry, and an equal share in Cincinnati, Detroit, and Chicago. Foreigners did not overlook the South, as is commonly believed. In 1860 immigrants accounted for less than 7 percent of all white Southerners but a fifth to a half of the population in the region's major cities. Because so many foreigners were males of humble origins, moreover, they were an even larger proportion of the free white working class in the South. In Richmond and Nashville 40 percent of the free white workers were foreign-born; in Charleston and Baton Rouge one-half were of European origin; and in Mobile two-thirds were immigrants.

All migrants and immigrants wanted to work wherever they ended up. Had they come in such volume before 1815, it is likely that American cities would have been more like present-day metropolises in the Third World that grow without developing industries to absorb newcomers and teem with jobless masses crammed into tin-roofed shanties. The fact, however, is that their arrival coincided with the beginning of the third great revolution of the age—the industrial revolution—which spared them the tragic fate of modern migrants. Jobs were available and efforts at finding work were usually rewarded. The type of employment depended heavily upon nativity, gender, and race. Before the immigration bulge of the late 1840s, white males of native birth dominated the handicrafts in the North and South. Women were found mostly in domestic service and partly in unskilled textile work as well as semiskilled jobs created by the division of labor in the crafts. The comparatively few immigrants divided between skilled Germans and English, on the one hand, and unskilled Irish, on the other. Free blacks concentrated in unskilled labor on docks, waterfronts, and construction projects, though some in Charleston and other Southern cities worked at skilled trades taught by former masters or passed on by fathers. Slaves far outnumbered free blacks in the South, and their occupational profile before the 1850s is still unclear. Some bondmen may have done skilled work in Charleston and in other ports. Skilled slave labor was essential in the tobacco factories and ironworks of Virginia. Greater numbers still were used in what was called "nigger work," jobs considered "servile, dirty, or distasteful," and beneath the dignity of white men. Barbering and butchering were two such occupations, but more common was unskilled work of every description. One man's "nigger work," however, was sometimes another's bread and butter. No black worker, not even the casual laborer, was secure as long as he had to compete with immigrants for jobs. Just as native white workers curtailed the use of slaves in skilled work, so immigrants used force and violence to dislodge many free blacks from unskilled positions.

The huge inflow of immigrants at midcentury transformed the ethnic composition and occupational configuration of the work force in both regions. Native-born whites hung on to the the best-paid handicrafts, or what was known as the "honorable trades." Women and immigrants succeeded white workmen in semiskilled jobs within the declining handicrafts, and Irish women replaced Yankees in the textile industry. Blacks and the Irish shared unskilled work. What had been an ethnically homogeneous working class had become a polyglot group by the 1850s.

Ethnicity, race, and gender were not the only determinants of occupational status; choice of city mattered, too. The textile towns of the Merrimack Valley and the southern Piedmont and the shoe centers of eastern New England offered industrial employment and precious little else. Published figures on the actual distribution of jobs in these and other places must be used with caution because they lump together all unskilled positions (which could come to one-fifth of all occupations) into commerce instead of distinguishing between such jobs in industry and the handicrafts from those in trade. Despite this drawback, it is still instructive that in 1860 only one-third of the labor force in Lowell and one-half in Lynn, two leading manufacturing centers, was found in industry. And they were unique in that respect. Not one of the nation's fifteen major cities came close. The strongest competitor was Newark and only one-fourth of its gainfully employed were industrial workers. More typically in New York City and St. Louis under 10 percent of the population worked in manufacturing. Southern cities were even less industrialized. In Baltimore and New Orleans, the third and fifth largest cities in the nation in 1860 with populations of 212,000 and 168,000, the proportion of manufacturing employees came to 8 and 3 percent, respectively. As the historian George Rogers Taylor once observed, "the great era of the industrial city had not yet arrived."

This comes as no surprise. New textile towns, after all, were superimposed on rural settings and dramatically reflected the industrial revolution. They industrialized more quickly and thoroughly than older metropolitan centers and, much to the horror of some nineteenth-century Americans, seemed to foreshadow the worst of industrial Europe. But critics who imagined a landscape of industrial blight such as in Manchester had it wrong. The factory did not dominate manufacturing before the Civil War. There were two distinct paths to industrial development; one was followed by textiles and the other by the handicrafts. The first resulted in capital-intensive methods centered in large factories; the second in labor-intensive techniques, or the sweating system, carried on in homes and small shops.

The manufacture of textiles embodied a relatively rapid shift from handwork done at home to factories fitted with power-driven equipment. Its American pioneer was not an industrialist at all but Moses Brown, the son of a wealthy Providence merchant. Born in 1738, Brown was the scion of Yankee traders who traced his pedigree to Rhode Island's founders. As a youth he worshipped in the Baptist church and in 1762 joined his brothers Nicholas, John, and Joseph at the helm of the family firm. The youthful entrepreneurs formed a trust with offices worldwide that funneled tidy profits from iron and candles, as well as rum and slaves, into the central office in Providence. The receipts from the trade in human flesh piled up but also weighed heavily upon Moses's conscience. The sudden death of his young wife in 1773 caused him further distress and drove the troubled merchant into premature retirement and then to Quakerism. Brown secluded himself in a kind of Quaker retreat for "peace of mind." It salved his conscience and also restored his enterprising spirit. In the mid-1780s, just before the invention of the cotton gin, he and son-in-law William Almy hatched a scheme of revolutionary proportions for men of commerce. They turned away from merchandising and slave dealing and looked to the manufacture of cloth from cotton picked by those Moses Brown had once sold into bondage. The irony seems to have been lost on him. No matter. He and Almy mustered the reserve army of homestead labor into a force of spinners and weavers under the putting-out system. But the entrepreneurial pair harbored the greater ambition of imitating the British factory system. They experimented with machines for a while before soliciting the aid of someone more familiar with English ways. They found their man in Samuel Slater.

Slater was the son of a Derbyshire yeoman and, in the late 1780s, a management trainee indentured to a local cotton manufacturer. Eager to strike out on his own, he reluctantly took a post with his master when his apprenticeship ended in 1788 but kept a watchful eye for opportunities elsewhere. A year later he came across an advertisement placed in the local press by a Philadelphia manufacturer for an expert in English textile production, and so he boarded a ship for the New World. Landing in New York, he somehow learned of the opening in Brown's fledgling firm. An exchange of letters followed and much to Brown's good fortune the young Briton cashed in his ticket to Philadelphia for one to Providence.

Commissioned to set up an English-style factory, Slater retreated to a workshop, where he developed a mechanical carder and fashioned a faulty spinning frame discarded by Brown into a workable prototype. Within a year he set up a spinning mill, the first of its kind in the North, and three years later moved to new quarters in the Old Pawtucket Mill. The tiny two-and-one-half-story building employed nine workers, all of them children, who carded the raw cotton and spun it into yarn on Arkwright equipment. The business quickly grew to employ one hundred hands and by 1800 marketed thread and yarn throughout New England and as far south as Philadelphia. Mechanics trained at the Old Pawtucket, including Slater himself, started textile mills in the environs of Providence and in the sleepy farming villages of Pomfret, Warwick, and Coventry, Connecticut, as well as Webster and Dudley, Massachusetts. The beat of the industrial revolution picked up with the prohibition on European trade and ensuing war with England between 1807 and 1815, when the number of factories within a day's carriage drive of Providence increased from 41 to 169. Spinning mills simultaneously sprouted up along the Schuylkill River outside Philadelphia and then on small streams draining the southern Piedmont.

Early mills reflected the example of the Old Pawtucket, or what historians call the family or Rhode Island System. This employed families lodged in their own or company-owned houses and engaged in the basic processes of picking and cleaning, carding, and spinning. The yarn and thread that rolled off the machines was sold to merchants or distributed to farm women for weaving into cloth. More and more hand looms were needed as growing numbers of the wives and daughters of Yankee yeomen struggled to keep up with the factory spinners. A traveler in eastern Connecticut reported in 1815 that "every few miles [there was] a factory, from which yarn is furnished to every female available to weave in the vicinity." Weavers were indeed scarce, as Fall River's cotton spinners learned when they opened their city's first mill that year. They scoured farmhouses in southeastern Massachusetts for idle weavers and nearly gave up in frustration before finding some over two hundred miles away at Hallowell, Maine.

It was not for want of trying that weaving was not harnessed to water power. A long line of mechanics and inventors had tinkered with mechanizing the hand loom ever since the flying shuttle appeared in 1738. The Englishman Peter Cartwright unveiled a breakthrough in 1784, but his machine and its design were bound by law to their native land. It took another thirty years for Americans to catch up to Cartwright and push Brown's venture one step further. The key figure in that shift was Francis Cabot Lowell, son of Newburyport, Massachusetts, lawyer John Lowell.

Francis Lowell was not cut out for the humdrum of the counting house. Like Moses Brown before him, he was a visionary fascinated with technology and with the prospects of turning it to profit. He was aware of Slater's achievement but knew it compared unfavorably with advanced factories across the Atlantic that combined power weaving with spinning on a grand scale. He decided to see for himself and made a tour of British textile mills, carefully analyzing power looms in England and Scotland. Lowell returned home with the designs of several looms recorded in copious notes and committed to memory. With the assistance of mechanic Paul Moody, he developed a machine that measurably improved upon its English inspiration. He secured a charter from the General Court in 1813 for the Boston Manufacturing Company, which in 1814 established its first mill on the Charles River at Waltham. Another mill was in place before the end of the decade and between then and 1850 the Boston Associates, as the Lowell clan's business was called, reproduced Waltham again and again, first at Lowell in 1823 and then at Dover, New Hampshire, Saco, Maine, and other places during the 1830s and 1840s.

Patrician Boston's enterprises made Brown's pale by comparison. Their incorporated firms, capitalized at hundreds of thousands of dollars, were managed by a long chain of command. Boards of directors and treasurers based in Boston and staffed by Lowell kinsmen made policy for resident agents at each provincial outpost. The agent directed a supervisor, who in turn managed overseers and their assistants, known as second hands. Such front-line personnel directed a labor force that numbered in the hundreds by the 1830s and differed from English and Providence operatives in age and gender. Boston Associate employees, like Mary Paul, were young, single women coaxed from the farms of northern New England by high wages and paternalistic working and living conditions. They passed from the strict supervision of overseers and second hands to the superintendence of matronly housekeepers in the famous dormitories of the "Waltham System." Keepers were responsible for maintaining "order, punctuality of meals, cleanliness and general arrangements for rendering their houses comfortable, tranquil scenes of moral deportment, and mutual good will." They were essential to Francis Cabot Lowell's genuine effort to answer American critics of the emergent factory system. And for a while it worked. Even Charles Dickens, chronicler of England's "satanic mills" and one of Lowell's many European admirers, found no evidence of the squalor and misery described in *Hard Times*. Within the neat and well-regulated mills of the Boston Associates, however, there were echoes of Manchester, not least of which was the complete integration of production from cleaning the cotton fiber to weaving it into cloth. The Boston Associates centralized all procedures under one roof.

Textile manufacturing in the South lagged far behind the North. Most mills had not progressed beyond spinning coarse thread in 1840, and twenty years later the region had only 10,000 cotton mill workers compared to nearly 40,000 in Massachusetts alone. Power was inadequate and technology as well as managerial expertise had to be imported from the North or England. Comparatively poor wages and salaries compounded the problem of attracting experienced workers and managers, long after the North had cultivated native industrial talent: as late as the 1850s Southern entrepreneurs still depended on outside sources. When in

1848 William Gregg, the region's belated answer to Francis Lowell, opened his notorious Graniteville factory in South Carolina, his management staff consisted of a Scottish superintendent and four overseers from Rhode Island. The progenitors of the industry had banked on underselling Northerners by using slave labor, but this proved difficult at first and in time impossible. In 1790, a year before Slater opened his mill, Hugh Templeton, an obscure South Carolina industrialist, started the nation's first mechanized cotton factory at Spartanburg. Templeton is largely unknown because his firm quickly collapsed. He had rented slaves from neighboring planters and trained them for industrial work but was caught short when they were recalled by their owners for field duty. Industrialists later faced the same problem. Slaves were accessible only when cotton prices fell, as was the case in the 1840s when numerous mills were built in the Southeast. But the rapid growth ended with the cotton boom in the 1850s, which drew slaves back into the fields and inflated the sales price of a prime bondman to over $1,200. By that point the rising rural demand depleted the rental pool and pushed the sales price beyond the means of most industrialists. The privileged few that did use slaves, moreover, risked stigmatizing textile employment as "nigger work" and arousing the ire of whites unaccustomed to working with blacks in close quarters. As a result, manufacturers had to keep work forces lily-white or use slaves sparingly and for the most disagreeable tasks. Gregg followed the latter course by putting a few slaves to work at custodial jobs, which bolstered his white workers' sense of "social and racial superiority," and as Gregg himself put it, assured white women they would "not lose caste by such employment."

White labor presented its own problems. Poor, illiterate, and fresh from the countryside, Southern operatives were quintessential preindustrial workers ignorant of the new "rules of the game" and not avid to learn. All novice industrial workers, of course, brought older customs to factories. As Herbert Gutman demonstrated, farm-bred Northerners habitually left mills to help their families with farm chores, often took days off to hunt and fish, and blithely violated rules and regulations prohibiting reading and drinking on the job. Southern operatives were just as intractable despite their reputation for cowering to the "better people." In 1849 the managers of a Forsyth County, North Carolina, mill painted a window in order to stop the operatives from losing time by gazing out. The workers went on strike until a clear pane was reinstalled. Individual resistance, however, was far more common. There was chronic absenteeism, tardiness, and shirking, the very tactics whites associated with blacks and slaves. Indeed a Georgia overseer believed that white operatives slacked off because they reasoned that to speed up was to place themselves on the same level with "the Negro." He also complained that rampant absenteeism forced him to "send out to the houses and drum in recruits" to keep his mill running. Some disgruntled workers quit and sought other employers in order to bid up rates or relax obnoxious rules. Others simply gave up and returned to the land. One Piedmont manufacturer grew so weary of the truancy and turnover that he advertised in New York for Irish families. More than a few mills went out of business.

Such resistance to industrial regimentation in conjunction with Northern models of factory organization and Southern traditions of paternalism gave late antebellum mills their paternalistic cast. The prototypical mill village of the time was Gregg's Graniteville just across the Georgia border in South Carolina. Gregg's "asylum" for the poor, as he called it, was a total industrial environment designed to mold a reliable and compliant work force from policies that combined features of the Waltham and Rhode Island systems. Gregg hired entire families headed by farmers and textile operatives, and housed them in tiny cottages with small gardens. Methodist or Baptist chapel was mandatory for all and schooling was required of children until age twelve, when they were expected to work in the mills. Gregg personally enforced truancy rules and had employees, as well as buyers of house lots in town, sign pledges of total abstinence. He demanded strict observance of work rules and, as if to stress the importance of promptness, built a huge clock for all to see. Though Gregg bragged in 1858 that only one worker had been let go in the previous seven years, there was an undercurrent of discontent among employees. At Graniteville friends of workers with children told a reporter of widespread objection to the "one great evil" of long hours and indicated that many operatives were awaiting the chance to go back home.

About the time that Graniteville opened, the Rhode Island and Waltham systems in the North began to develop in a similar fashion. Rhode Island-type mills in southern New England and the Middle Atlantic states scrapped the family system, and Waltham-style mills disbanded their boardinghouses. Both employed more adult males, though women made up the majority, and after 1845 or so substituted English and Irish immigrants for native-born Americans. Spinning mills also copied the integrated factories of Waltham and Lowell by installing power looms and hiring weavers to work in the same buildings as spinners. This transition was complete in New England by the 1840s, but was not universally followed elsewhere. Philadelphia and Baltimore producers specializing in finer and fancier yarns kept the spinning and weaving processes apart and ran small mills with skilled mule spinners operating equipment suited to softer threads used for better grades of cloth. They either gave out the yarn to independent weavers working on hand frames at home or sold it to loom bosses who might hire labor at home or gather it into sheds that became workshops. There were about 5,000 such weavers in Philadelphia at midcentury and a substantial number in Baltimore as well. By 1860 most textile hands, however, tended machines in factories averaging over sixty workers each.

Industrial development was similar in the refining of sugar, the production of metals, the fabrication of iron implements, and other pursuits without artisanal traditions. These industries took advantage of the mechanized factory early but not in quite the same way as the textile industry. They were strongholds of highly skilled male workers in a world of their own. Iron making was a rural-based industry initially confined to a belt of mineral deposits that ran from Richmond through eastern Pennsylvania into the Hudson Valley and then northern Vermont. If ore and charcoal (and later coal and coke) were the lifeline of the iron village, the blast furnace was its heart. Its deceptively simple task of making pig iron from an alloy of carbon and iron ore required the seasoned hand of the puddler who tended its fire with the aid of assistants. It took years of training on the job to master the technique of knowing just how to charge the furnace, manipulate the bellows, and work the molten ore into iron. No one questioned the judgment of the puddler or challenged his authority in and around the furnace. He was its master and the maker of the valuable pigs that were turned into wrought iron on-site or at independent forges. This was the work of blacksmiths and other metal tradesmen who wrought the iron by constantly heating and reheating the pigs in cupolas and pounding them with hammers, or later with steam-powered trip-hammers. As the industry crept westward in the 1830s and 1840s toward Pittsburgh and Ohio, more and more furnaces rolled their own wrought iron into shape for the ultimate consumer. Iron rollers were every bit the social and industrial equal of puddlers. Part worker and part manager, these highly accomplished industrial workmen directed teams of underlings using mechanized equipment and earned several times the wages of the best-paid textile hands, if they were white.

In the South some iron manufacturers relied on slave labor. Joseph Anderson's Tredegar Iron Works in Richmond, one historian observed, "was particularly celebrated . . . [as] a test case of the adaptability of slavery to heavy industry." Anderson began to train slaves for skilled berths in 1841 as an economy measure and six years later had occasion to redouble his effort when skilled whites went on strike to protest working with blacks. Anderson replaced the strikers with slaves, and while his labor force grew to 800 from 250 during the 1850s, only 80 were slaves, 30 of whom were common laborers. Anderson could no more afford to own or hire slaves in large numbers than any other Southern industrialist. And even with slave labor, he was unable to undersell technologically advanced, more efficient competitors in the North or England.

With the exception of Richmond, factory workers were not part of an urban working class. Ironworkers, textile hands, and other wage earners employed in new industries collected in small towns located in the countryside. It could not have been otherwise in the pre-steam engine age. Their work required falling water for power or ores and organic fuel, and so labor had to locate along rivers and streams or close to forests and collieries. Lowell, Johnstown, and other places as new as the factories were, of course, where the nation's textile operatives and metalworkers lived. Life was different for the vast majority of workers in the handicrafts.

The crafts had a long and venerable past that began with human history and reached maturity in the guilds of feudal Europe. When transplanted to America, they evolved free from the fetters of the guild system—and in a way that set them apart from the new industries. Classes, in fact, were as alien to the crafts as artisanal skills were to textile operatives. Tradesmen thought of themselves and were considered to be part of a fluid hierarchy that consisted of master craftsmen, journeymen, and apprentices. Masters were proprietors who did everything from waiting on customers to ordering supplies and raw materials and keeping the books, such as they were. They also laid out the work, supervised hirelings, and worked along with their employees. Most were former journeymen, skilled workers paid by the day or the piece depending on the trade. Journeymen were onetime apprentices who usually began their indentures as teenagers and spent three to seven years learning the "art and mystery" of their callings under the stewardship of a master. They could expect room, board, and other necessities, as well as the indulgence of their natural fathers. They were punished by their masters when insubordinate but protected from external authority at all times. Between the ages eighteen and twenty-one apprentices were promoted to journeyman and given a suit of clothes as a symbol of manhood and a set of tools in recognition of their formal entry into the fraternity of the trade. Apprentices-turned-journeymen were for the first time entitled to a wage, even though some were paid modest sums and did not expect to be permanent wage earners. In the best of circumstances journeymen were masters in the making busily accumulating resources in order to set up shop on their own.

Movement through the ranks could not be taken for granted. As early as the 1780s urban masters slighted their moral and educative obligations to apprentices even as they continued to provide them with food and shelter. They took on young trainees without the slightest intention of imparting the nuances and subtleties of their craft and treated them solely as sources of cheap labor. For their part, apprentices were often restive, not afraid to run off with only a rudimentary knowledge of their calling. Their flight, coupled with the first influx of rural-urban migrants between 1780 and 1810, distorted the ratio of journeymen to masters. By the end of the 1790s there were three to six times as many journeymen as masters in Boston and perhaps even a greater proportion in Middle Atlantic cities. If journeymen found their trades crowded and hopes for proprietorship dimmed, they could take at least some comfort in the persistence of their work routines and shop customs. They still plied their trades in surroundings their fathers would have instantly recognized. Workshops were on the street level of two- and three-story buildings whose upper floors housed the master's family. They shared workbenches with another journeyman or two and perhaps an apprentice, and used an array of hand tools that had changed hardly at all over the generations. The shoemaker's kit of awl, knife, lap stone, needle, and thread, to cite but one example, looked pretty much as it had a century earlier. Leather aprons were still the uniform of the day in most trades for journeymen and masters alike, and both groups derived great pleasure from their work. The Newark hatter and future abolitionist Henry Clark Wright put it well when he recalled, "I felt real satisfaction in being able to make a hat because I loved to contemplate the work, and because I felt pleasure in carrying through the various stages."

Wright's satisfaction owed directly to his control of each step in the labor process. In hatmaking and other finishing trades this began with taking an order from a customer and then measuring, fitting and refitting, and working out ornamental details. The journeyman then returned to his bench and made the commodity from beginning to end without much interference from the master and according to a rhythm more familiar to contemporary agrarians than modern Americans (with the notable exceptions of scholars and students). He was task-oriented and worked until a given job or portion of it was completed. This could mean long stints but also spells of idleness because of the irregularity of trade. Journeymen filled up slack times casually doing repair work or chatting with shopmates. No early-nineteenth-century craftsman, however, needed the excuse of slow business to interrupt his work routine. His day was a blend of work, fellowship, and plain fun. New York caulkers and ship carpenters had a kind of coffee break at 8:30 a.m. when building sites were inundated with young women darting here and there with wicker baskets laden with sweets and pastries. They broke again at 11:00 for a dram of beer or sugared rum, and balanced the day with two additional breaks, one for lunch and one in late afternoon for sweets. Printers had similar customs, according to Thurlow Weed, who fondly remembered his days in the trade. Weed and his workmates left presses and compositor's table at 11:00, too, for beer and usually downed several drams later in the day as well. Newly hired journeymen got a quick initiation, for they were obliged to buy beer for the entire shop. Apprentices were not expected to treat, but had to make numerous trips to the neighborhood pub in order to keep the shop jug topped off. If we are to believe a Philadelphia saddler, such obligations were furtive educations in drinking because the lads had the habit of "robbing the mail"—sneaking a sip or two along the way. They were scolded by the older men, as were all artisans who abused spirits. But it was excess and not drinking itself that brought disapproval. Masters themselves seldom passed up the opportunity to quench a thirst in the shop or at the local pub and tolerated drinking as long as journeymen kept it under control.

Lest one get the impression that early-nineteenth-century workshops resembled modern-day taverns at happy hour, it should be stressed that drink was not the only form of relaxation at work. Preindustrial artisans, after all, were literate men who took pride in their forensic skills and even more in displaying them. An observer of eastern New England shoe towns described the men of the "gentle craft" as "foremost among artisans as regards intelligence and social influence." Legend had it that ten-footers, the region's small shops, buzzed with opinion on "political, social, and religious reform." It was even said that preachers in Randolph, Massachusetts, read drafts of sermons to area shoemakers in order to "get pointers beforehand." The New York stonecutter and sculptor John Frazee traced his tendency to "think philosophically" to shop talk. But the curriculum was not always serious. Workers also appreciated lighter fare and seem to have had a special weakness for seafaring tales, folk stories, and other forms of popular fiction.

The casual workplace, however, was in transition. In two great bursts of fifteen years each following the downturns of 1819–21 and 1837–43, most handicraft workshops shed their easy ambience. Shops grew larger, and by 1850, when some twenty to thirty men worked together, their artisanal moorings were broken. Some shops took the path blazed by textile factories, substituting machinery for hand equipment and developing a managerial group. Printing was one. Its growth hinged on the fantastic pace of urbanization and proliferation of educational institutions, which increased the reading public and generated brisk demand for books, newspapers, and literary journals. Some master printers met the demand by borrowing a leaf from the Boston Associates. They purchased stereotyping equipment, which allowed for the duplication of pages without resetting the type, or traded in screw presses for steam-driven presses. They concurrently added more hands and divided the trade into compositors who set copy into type and operators who ran the presses. This not only cheapened skills but invited new methods of passing them on. Few entrepreneurs matched the ingenuity of St. Louis printer Duff Green. In 1834, now a Washington resident and publisher of the staunchly Democratic *United States Telegraph,* he opened a training school for two hundred boys between ages eleven and fourteen. Journeymen wailed that the ''introduction of steam presses and the stereotyping system had thrown perhaps hundreds out of employ, and so reduced the price of press work, that all competition with a hand press is destroyed.'' Green was a relatively easy target: one did not need his imagination or resources to undermine seasoned journeymen. Lesser printers simply hired half-trained youths in place of bona fide tradesmen and graduates of the apprenticeship system. They were joined by women who worked on power-driven presses or at desks to cut and fold press sheets, bind books, and take over other tasks that once comprised the art of book publishing. Compositors represented the last vestige of the trade as it once was. They did precision work by hand, but by midcentury from half to two-thirds of the trade earned their keep in mechanized shops with as many as thirty hands and with new and different managerial arrangements. Newspaper bosses migrated from production rooms to front offices to write and edit copy in collaboration with growing staffs of reporters; the supervision of the manual work was delegated to foremen. For the compositor, this translated into closer direction as well as extra effort in order to keep up with the voracious appetite of the presses. In less than a generation the all-around printer had been reduced to a cog in the large publishing house.

But such a process was not typical of transformed craft production. Entrepreneurs in other trades followed a different route to mass manufacture. They might be former masters, merchant capitalists, or a partnership of the two in the business spirit that animated the Boston Associates in exploiting the decline of self-sufficiency that followed urbanization and innovations in transportation. They ventured there, however, without the capital or technological advantages of the "Lords of the Loom." Men of common birth and modest means, they could not replicate the planned industrial towns of northern New England or afford much space in their cities, where quarters were cramped and terribly expensive. Nor could they substitute machines for handwork given the glacial pace of technological innovation in the handicrafts. Such constraints necessitated production strategies that differed somewhat from trade to trade but fell into the pattern of the sweating system. This system found workers in small shops and homes using hand tools on tasks relentlessly simplified by the division of labor.

By the 1820s the production of ready-made clothing was a bastion of sweated labor. This was not without some irony, for at the turn of the century, when there was not much of a market for inexpensive garments, journeymen employed by custom tailors would make up cheap clothing during slack times. This was reversed by the 1830s. Custom tailors fashioned fine goods during the doldrums of the off-season and spent the busy months in the employ of wholesalers making up coarse wear for the military, Southern slaves, and Western farmers. This segment of the trade expanded until the panic of 1837 and expanded again in the bullish 1850s.

The initial thrust sundered the needle trades into cutters and sewers. Garment cutters were to their craft what compositors were to printing, highly skilled specialists essential to the production process. In addition, they initiated the work in a wildly competitive industry that counted its profit in pennies. Cutters could wipe out the take of an entire season with a bad cut or careless slip of the shears; they exploited strategic advantage into relatively good treatment and comparatively high wages. Teams of two or three in "central shops" worked freehand with shears on several layers of cloth at a time. Larger groups of up to a dozen layered "thickness upon thickness . . . to the number of forty-eight . . . and upon them . . . placed iron patterns of all sizes. The knife does the rest," said a dazzled journalist, "no scissors being employed; and while we stand by, from one counting came out the backs of four dozen shirts."

Cutters methodically carved out sleeves, collars, and other components, which were passed to trimmers, who sewed on buttons and linings. Foremen then gathered the components for distribution to two groups of workers inside and outside the trade. Inside shops were run by boss tailors who agreed to return finished goods to central shops by fixed deadlines. They were subcontractors, not independent operators, beholden to suppliers. No one survived without underselling rivals and economizing at every turn. Even then many fell to the seasonal fluctuations and cutthroat competition, only to be replaced by a seemingly endless line of fortune seekers. They held down overhead by setting up in the attics and cellars of low-rent districts or what contemporaries called "garret shops" or "slop shops." More hard-bitten taskmasters were hard to find. Since there were no machines or improvements in hand tools to speak of before the invention of the sewing machine at midcentury, central shop owners and garret bosses depressed labor costs by slashing piece rates, hiring cheaper labor, and bearing down on workers. Owners of central shops and garret bosses also went beyond the basic division of labor by manufacturing a single line of garments and dividing each task into smaller units, such as basting, stitching, sewing, washing, starching, and ironing.

The rapid cheapening of skills also affected the outworkers. They, too, were semiskilled hands, but of a slightly different order. They made the lightest and cheapest goods for the lowest end of the market, in part because manufacturers were reluctant to entrust expensive grades of cloth to hands beyond their immediate control and in part because the workers were women. The New Haven Shirt Manufacturing Company boasted the largest payroll in its branch of the trade in 1854 when over 4,000 workers were on its books. No fewer than 3,700, nearly all of them women, were hired as outworkers. And this was typical of all large employers. Seamstresses and women tailors enjoyed more autonomy than male shop workers but not much more. Employers insisted on more production and tightened discipline through fines for faulty and tardy work and constant reductions of piece rates. Male workers, some of them husbands of seamstresses, compounded the misery when in the 1840s some brought work home for wives and daughters. The more enterprising among them took on neighborhood women in the guise of "apprentices," blurring the line between capital and labor and raising the adage "every man a capitalist" to a new level of absurdity. The result was a tangle of brutally exploitative relations not only between employer and employee but also between employees themselves.

Entrepreneurs and merchant capitalists in footwear structured their version of the sweating system between the 1780s and 1820s. Their central shops were links in a chain of productive and trade relations that extended from Eastern cities and towns to the plantations of the South and general stores of the emerging West. These shops housed leather cutters who carried on much as their namesakes in the needle trade and packers who prepared the footwear for delivery to the West and South. The cutters sliced hides into uppers and bottoms bound for males and females employed at home under a sexual division of labor. Women sewed the uppers, husbands and sons did the bottoming and lasting, the third and final step in a tripartite division of labor. Bottomers also worked outside the home for garret bosses, who routed the completed shoes to central shops for finishing and packing. Central shops and garrets took on more labor as the century progressed but at different rates.

Massachusetts manufacturers of women's shoes and flimsy slave brogans centralized labor more rapidly than big-city competitors. Micajah Pratt of Lynn, Massachusetts, certainly did so. Born in 1791 to a Quaker retailer, in 1812 Pratt opened a central shop in a rickety wooden building with a few employees. By 1850 he moved into a large, multistory brick factory with over five hundred hands that bore more than a casual resemblance to the mechanized textile mills at Lowell. His factory soon hummed along to the accompaniment of steam engines that powered batteries of sewing machines and McKay stitchers. The former, a modification of Singer's model, was the first power-driven device in shoemaking that resulted in collecting operatives into factories at Lynn. The tandem of factory regimentation and mechanization vastly increased binding capacity, so much so that a single McKay operator could do eighty pairs of shoes to one pair for every handworker. In order to keep the faster machine stitchers properly supplied, manufacturers enlarged their payrolls and redivided the tasks. Job simplification and mechanization had a reciprocal effect on the process: simplification made it possible to use machines and the use of machines intensified the division of labor. Indeed by 1860 there were about forty distinct steps in making a single shoe.

The sewing machine had a similar impact upon the clothing industry even though it entered the factory haltingly or not at all. Large shirtmakers installed foot-powered equipment after 1850 and then reorganized sewers into subgroups of cuff, collar, and sleeve makers, and operatives that stitched the parts together. Similar subdivisions occurred in other branches and among outworkers, who had to purchase their own

machines. Wherever they worked and whatever the technology, tailors
and tailoresses stitched and bound smaller pieces at a faster clip.

But to speak of factories or even machine-directed manufacture before
the Civil War is to read Gilded Age developments into the antebellum
years. Whatever else may be said of Micajah Pratt, he was ahead of his
time. Mechanization did not get under way in the handicrafts until the
1850s, and even then it moved ahead selectively, circumventing some
jobs even while it enhanced the pace of all. Before that time most shoe
and clothing workers labored by hand at home and in garrets.

Variants of sweating took shape in other crafts. Beginning in the 1820s
forces from within and without the building trades diminished craftsmanship in urban housing construction. First came prefabricated windows,
doors, and other parts traditionally made and fitted by skilled carpenters
on construction sites. This proved the thin end of the wedge for
enterprising masters and journeymen. Entry into the craft eased appre-
ciably with the simultaneous appearance of builders and contractors who
put up single homes or rows of tract housing on speculation. They let out
contracts to the lowest bidders in the various crafts, which triggered a
competitive war and search for cheaper labor among master craftsmen.
Masters became framers or installers of precut parts who moved from
project to project and yielded to other specialists when their tasks were
done. Skill and judgment were still demanded of framers who had to cut,
notch, and join huge timbers, but even their future was jeopardized when
balloon framing began in the 1830s. Developed in Chicago and other
Midwestern cities, the balloon frame consisted of vertical studs set about
a foot apart and nailed, top and bottom, to horizontal crosspieces. Having
raised and joined the frame, carpenters nailed on clapboard and dressed
interiors with lathe or sheeting and in a fraction of the time consumed by
other methods.

Other groups of woodworkers, notably cabinetmakers, were also
drawn into the sweating system. All-around journeymen who turned
rough-cut timber into elegant furniture could still be found in the 1850s,
as could accomplished building tradesmen, but their numbers were
shrinking. More and more furniture makers worked in garretlike shops on
single lines of goods for wholesalers in a process best described as a
nonmechanized assembly line. Some cut out the parts, usually by hand
but increasingly on steam-powered saws, that were assembled by another
team, and finished by still another. The twilight of handicraft production
was near at hand throughout the North.

Some crafts also fell under siege in border state cities. During the

1830s, clothing producers in Washington and Lexington went after skills and wage scales as aggressively as Yankee entrepreneurs. In Baltimore hatmakers invoked Northern competition in taking a tougher hand with their workers. "Competition in our city has, during the last ten years, vastly increased . . . ," read their 1833 letter to the press, "and every improvement by which the facilities of commercial communication are increased between Baltimore and our neighboring rival cities, brings that competition nearer. . . . Unless, therefore, we are able to compete with them, we must look sooner or later to a partial loss of our trade." This became the justification for a 25 percent reduction in wages and presumably for hiring cheaper labor. Such employers seem to have looked to women and English and German immigrants, not freedmen or slaves, for tractable labor. Slaves, however, were not exempt from the sweating system.

The development of tobacco processing in Virginia and North Carolina following the 1820s is often considered to be another example of the adaptability of slavery to industry. It is also suggestive of the flexibility of the sweating system. These states counted 4,000 tobacco workers in 1840 and three times that number in 1860, making it one of the leading industries in the South. The major product was chewing tobacco in the form of natural plugs and twists flavored with licorice, sugar, or rum. Some were produced in "county mills," which were extensions of plantations that ran after harvest time. The bulk of the product came from factories in Richmond, Danville, and Lynchburg that had as many as fifty hands in the 1840s and upward of ninety in 1860. Early production methods remain obscure and make it impossible to determine craft integrity, but even by the 1830s the work process was broken down into several steps. Stemmers, first men and later women, stripped the leaf of its midrib; dippers applied the flavorings; twisters and lumpers, the "skilled" hands, shaped the plug; and prizers pressed the twists and lumps on large screw presses. All operations were directed by white overseers with reputations for cruelty that rivaled overseers in the cotton and tobacco fields. Even industrial slavery had its sweatshops.

Most white artisans in the region, however, seem to have escaped the sweating system. They worked much as they had in the past either as itinerants or custom tradesmen doing bespoke work for wealthy planters and merchants. Indeed it is difficult to imagine an economic institution more suited to itinerancy than the plantation of the antebellum South. Larger planters in colonial times, after all, had kept at least some skilled slaves—blacksmiths and carpenters especially—to make farm imple-

ments and maintain buildings and equipment. But rising costs of
bondmen and the premium placed on field work reduced the skilled work
force of the plantation. Planters had to hire skilled labor, and as Eugene
Genovese observes, account books "reveal surprisingly high expendi-
tures for a variety of tasks." They kept carriage makers and wheelwrights
busy making liveries and fixing broken wheels and axles, and hired
carpenters to raise and repair buildings. They were especially dependent
on blacksmiths to sharpen plows, mend equipment, and make tools. We
know little about urban artisans, but we can imagine those in Charleston,
Savannah, and New Orleans providing for the aristocratic tastes of the
rich, creating custom-made imitations of European-style shoes, clothing,
and interior furnishings on casual work schedules. City folk of all classes,
moreover, were a market for traditional masters who supplied such
everyday needs as bread, meat, and light hardware.

Traditional masters were by no means an anachronism in the North.
Urban growth, in fact, gave such employers a lease on life, for no city
neighborhood was complete without its bakery, butcher shop, and
tinsmith. And as long as there were urban dwellers, there was demand for
a variety of accomplished tradesmen. Indeed the trend in the North and
possibly the South as well was toward larger numbers of tiny shops rather
than fewer large ones. In 1850 anywhere from one-half to three-fourths
of the butchers, bakers, and blacksmiths and up to one-fifth of the tailors,
shoemakers, and cabinetmakers in cities worked in establishments with
about five employees each. Masters, moreover, far outnumbered entrepreneurs in every handicraft in the North and probably in the South.

Traditional shops reflected their Jeffersonian antecedents. In sharp
contrast to entrepreneurs, masters shunned speculation or expansion for
slow and gradual accumulations, or what artisans historically referred to
as "competencies." Most could expect to attain a competency until the
1830s or so when the food trades swelled with competitors and entrepreneurial shoemakers and tailors retailed cheap copies of custom styles.
Upward mobility declined as a result, but craft customs endured. Masters
upheld the conventions of boarding and training apprentices and working
alongside journeymen. And men they were, for unless the master's wife
tended the counter, his work force was all male. His journeymen
resembled the versatile tradesman of Jefferson's day who had a thorough
knowledge of his calling and worked in relaxed surroundings. Easy
conversation with fellow journeymen and browsing shoppers, grog and
sweets breaks, and the banter of the shop still enlivened the workday.

Traditional shops had their own social relations among employers and between employers and employees. Masters thought nothing of lending one another equipment or raw materials, or routing a customer to a fellow craftsman. Some pushed cooperation a step further by agreeing to common price lists or collectively adjusting charges to reflect changes in styles and fashions. As for relations with employees, masters relied on custom rather than dictation to arrive at wage scales instead of haggling with their workmen. They also honored the patron-client relations of earlier days, recommending able journeymen to masters and helping hard-pressed employees with wage advances. At retirement they sold shops to favored workers on generous terms.

Such shops deeply impressed Alexis de Tocqueville during his tour of the United States in 1831–32. "What astonishes me," he wrote, "is not so much the marvellous grandeur of some undertakings, as the innumerable magnitude of small ones." Other observers were more taken by the productive units overlooked by the perceptive Frenchman. Edwin T. Freedley studied the nation's workplaces with great care, reporting artisanal methods in vivid detail. "Early printers," he explained with characteristic precision, "made their own ink, as well as their type. This substance was applied to the letters or forms by balls made with sheepskin and stuffed with wool. With these one man *beat,* as it was called, the type, while the other laid the white or half printed sheet on the tympan, preparatory to making the impression." But the men of the craft were minor players in Freedley's industrial drama. His heroes were the entrepreneurs and industrialists who destroyed artisanal ways through the application of machine technology and organization of factories. Nearly two decades and profound economic change separated publication of the first English-language edition of Tocqueville's classic *Democracy in America* from Freedley's hagiographic *Leading Pursuits and Leading Men* in 1854. These depicted very different industrial scenes, but both were correct, for each captured different parts of the spectrum in industrializing America. At one end were the textile mills of Lowell that raced ahead unencumbered by artisanal baggage; at the other were the small shops of city and country that preserved craftsmanship. Between these extremes stood the handicrafts that owed their transitional status to the reorganization of labor under the sweating system. A similar range of orientations characterized rural America as well. The commercial farms in the East and Midwest that adapted machine technology to single-crop agriculture were to their sector what Lowell was to its, just as the general subsistence farms of both regions were the agricultural equivalents of handicraft shops. Modernization of farming and manufacturing was still incomplete at midcentury.

Nonetheless much had changed. The preindustrial world of the self-sufficient yeoman and independent mechanic was fading into obscurity. The acceleration of the commercial revolution pushed barter systems of exchange to the edges of the economy and loosened the ties that had kept generations of Americans on the land. The early rumblings of the industrial revolution saw the old mechanic class become groups of entrepreneurs and traditional employers with diverging interests. Growing numbers of proprietors were no longer master craftsmen but hard-driving employers in a wildly competitive economy. In addition, a working class was in the making, and if its members were not yet factory drudges, they were increasingly dependent on wage labor, gradually stripped of skills, and subjected to hard regimens of taxing work. The beginnings of these changes coincided with the "Era of Good Feelings" during the early 1820s in which social harmony and political agreement were the order of the day. That happy epoch was about to end.

2.

Free Labor and
Radical Labor

The social changes wrought by the economic revolutions during the antebellum period had profound cultural and ideological ramifications. New social organizations and institutions rooted in the sharpening divisions of the workplace gradually supplanted the close-knit social groups of the preindustrial past. As employer and employee drifted apart, each developed fresh outlooks by merging new concepts of political economics with redefinitions of older values. This ideological ferment produced the competing but not wholly antagonistic ideologies of free laborism and radicalism that would shape responses to the industrial revolution.

. . .

Tristam Burges reached a crossroads in 1800. Born in 1770, the son of hardscrabble New England, he was a village cooper by trade who left manual work for the law. He had occasion to reflect on his artisanal past that year when the Providence Association of Mechanics invited him to address their annual meeting. Burges delivered a prepared speech that held deep resonances for an audience of craftsmen. He celebrated the artificer as productive laborer and republican citizen, the "complete mechanic" who embodied command of manual skills with scientific knowledge in a fruitful union of thinking and doing. The man who unites "theory and practice," he said, "who has perfected philosophy by experiment and become more skillful in his own trade, is more sage than Newton." Such a tradesman paid homage to republican simplicity by eschewing excessive acquisitiveness for the more honorable aim of attaining a competency, a deliberate accumulation that secured a dignified retirement. A competency, Burges concluded, meant social independence and a "condition below the dissipation of wealth and above the solicitude of necessity."

Burges's hymn to the self-reliant craftsman cannot be divorced from its institutional setting. Mechanics' institutes took root in the last quarter of the eighteenth century, sometimes evolving out of the extralegal committees that had seized power on the eve of the Revolution. New Yorkers led the way with the General Society of Mechanics and Tradesmen in 1785. Burges's Providence hosts and Boston neighbors organized within a decade, followed by port-city and small-town mechanics as far north as Utica and south to Charleston. These groups reflected the consciousness of a community historically splintered along trade lines and increasingly aware of shared interest. Leaders badgered lawmakers for protective tariffs and internal improvements. Publications and word-of-mouth communication kept members abreast of commodity and capital markets and put jobless journeymen in touch with employers, much like latter-day labor exchanges. Group functions and civic projects called public attention to a class that considered itself the bone and sinew of the republic. The more prosperous institutes erected meeting halls in town centers and turned out in their best finery for the celebrations, festivals, and red-letter days of Federalist America.

Institute members evinced the same reverence for artisanship that suffused Burges's speech. They barred "half-trained" men, "botches," and entrepreneurs who entered trades from the outside by requiring applicants to produce apprentice indentures or collateral evidence of proper training. They also imposed stiff fines for violations of rules designed to discourage abuse or circumvention of the traditional conveyer of skills. Members of the Massachusetts Charitable Mechanics' Association, with headquarters in Boston, were fined ten dollars for taking on underaged youths and thirty dollars for pirating a trainee from a brother in good standing. Members collaborated in other ways for the good of what was widely referred to as "the craft." The overriding objective was enforcing uniform wage and price lists, a tall order frustrated by easy entry to ownership and the erratic performance of the economy. Entrepreneurial owners set their own price lists and wage schedules, and cyclical and seasonal ups and downs caused further havoc. But traditional craftsmen valued cooperation enough to press on. They worked to resolve differences among themselves and in cases of stalemate called in institute officials to adjudicate disputes. The "craft" still mattered.

Mechanics in the Federalist years also enlisted local government in behalf of artisanship. In 1795 the men of Baltimore ended a successful campaign to reform a chaotic apprentice system. Indentures were standardized, masters were ordered to register wards, and jurisdiction was transferred to the County Orphan's Court. The same year Boston mechanics secured a similar statute with a provision authorizing a sheriff or justice of the peace to track down runaways. Mechanics engaged in the preparation of foodstuffs enjoyed broader legal interventions in trade. Bakers carried on the medieval tradition of having municipal authorities set the assize of bread, and bakers went about their work under a comprehensive code that licensed suppliers and restricted stalls to market areas. Late-eighteenth-century mechanics expected the federal government to stabilize the economy and stimulate growth. From their perspective, the Articles of Confederation failed miserably in both respects; the anemic national government could not even halt the dumping of British imports held to be the cause of idle workshops. Traditional fears of strong central government abated to such an extent that mechanics figured prominently in the agitation for the Constitution in late 1787 and were among the most conspicuous celebrants of ratification the following summer. In Philadelphia, birthplace of the new nation, the festivities included a huge procession of artisans who marched according to craft pulling elaborate floats and waving flags emblazoned with revealing mottoes and slogans. The standard of the shipbuilders said it all: ''May commerce flourish and industry be rewarded.''

Such pronouncements support Joyce Appleby's claim that the 1790s mark a historic divide in the republican tradition. This classic body of thought thereafter lost its distinctiveness and was reduced to ''a label to be fought over, a prized appellation to claim for one's views.'' After 1800 it makes sense to refer to specific republican legacies—popular suspicion of active government being fundamental—but not to republicanism as a coherent ideology. Classic republicanism, however, had some coherence. Simply put, it posed an enduring tension between virtue and commerce, the self and the market. Eighteenth-century Americans attached different meanings to virtue but agreed that it signified the subordination of self-interest to the good of the whole. To them, the market stimulated the cupidity that lurked in all men and compromised the self-reliance and moral probity essential for republican rule. They understood the idle rich and dependent poor to be ''parasites'' living off the state or the labor of others, and revered the sturdy yeoman and independent artisan of middling ranks who kept the market at arm's length.

By this standard, Federalist mechanics may be considered republicans only in a qualified sense if at all. They expressed the received abominations of luxury and greed and sometimes spoke of ''nonproductive'' pursuits, a more formal reference to parasites, but did not associate the market with dependence, diminished opportunity, or social inequality, as the Jacksonians did. Early-nineteenth-century mechanics welcomed economic growth as the wellspring for advancement within the ranks of their traditional hierarchy. Inequality was the stuff of meddlesome government, not economic growth.

This distinction between government and the economy proved a durable republican inheritance. As Appleby reminds us, classic republicanism "asserted the predominance of politics over all other aspects of human life. This predominance reflected and perpetuated the subordinate position of all other social institutions. Economic life served purely private household needs." Federalist-era mechanics were only becoming familiar with a different paradigm, a language appropriate to economic affairs, and were only dimly aware of Adam Smith's thinking, the most accessible body of economic thought. Insofar as Smithian economics was appreciated at all, it reinforced the duality between the political and the economic. To Smith, as well as to Thomas Paine, strong government was oppressive, unfettered business activity liberating.

Economic realities, of course, were more ambiguous. In village America, where the old adage "today's journeyman, tomorrow's master" obtained well into the antebellum period, employer and employee shared similar interests and continued to meet on the common ground of mechanics' institutes. Class relations in the South were complicated by the use of slave labor in the handicrafts. White journeymen objected to the competition and some found accommodating employers. Master shipbuilders and others who either owned or hired slaves put them to work on unskilled or menial tasks. Others refrained from drawing upon black labor altogether. The Baltimore Carpenters' Society, a group of masters and journeymen formed in 1791, admitted only those employers who refused to use slaves or accept slaves as apprentices.

Where the early stages of the market revolution cleaved mechanics into groups of entrepreneurs and traditional masters and inundated some trades with journeymen, mechanics were pulled in several directions. Traditional masters first hesitated between joining mechanics' institutes or trade societies and then joined the latter. By the 1820s, trade societies combined fraternal functions with welfare benefits for strikingly high initiation fees and dues. The fees started at ten dollars, an impossible sum for journeymen, who began to gravitate toward organizations confined to their class. Shoemakers, tailors, and printers achieved the highest levels of organization but not exclusively as unionists. Journeymen's societies were torn between factions of class-conscious workmen and "alimoners," a group of compliant journeymen and traditional masters more impressed with social welfare than craft unionism. The unionists prevailed within New York's printers. In 1817 they amended the bylaws of their fraternal society to read: since "the interests of journeymen are separate and in some respects opposite to those of employers . . . when any member . . . shall become an employing printer he shall be considered without the limits of this society." Instincts flowed in the other direction among fellow tradesmen in Boston and Philadelphia, who following the panic of 1819 transformed their union into a friendly society open to masters.

For their part, Northeastern entrepreneurs and manufacturers displayed a sharper sense of class identity. Signs of change appeared during the opening decade of the nineteenth century when institutes relaxed or did away with membership standards. Employers with insufficient craft training or none at all were inducted and together with mechanics on the make produced wealthier and more socially exclusive memberships. Institutes also winked at rules aimed at upholding the custom of apprenticeship, and after 1815 or so rarely intervened to resolve quarrels within trade societies over abrogations of accords. Trade agreements repeatedly broke down under the weight of the market and, except in the luxury trades, quietly passed out of existence by the 1820s.

Jacksonian entrepreneurs paid rhetorical lip service to "the craft" long after they repudiated traditional procedures. They spoke the language of republicanism, denouncing "privilege" and "monopoly" with the same passion as their Revolutionary fathers. They also became conversant in the more modern idiom of Adam Smith, even if in a decidedly selective way. Smithian economics, after all, was to this generation of businessmen what Marxism would later become to workers and intellectuals, a garden of choice theories and propositions to be picked as one saw fit. Some Jacksonians cheerfully overlooked Smith's labor theory of value, others disregarded his abhorrence of tariffs, charters of incorporation, and other political manifestations of favor and privilege. Indeed, what one historian aptly calls the "profoundly liberating features" of Smithian thought were blunted in the hands of Jacksonians. Rising businessmen appropriated Smithian concepts for the foundation of a new perspective that would eventually mature into the ideology of free labor. For adherents of free labor, the good society was the creation of an open and dynamic economy that fostered economic independence for diligent and industrious farmers and workingmen. While their point of view is usually seen as the official ideology of the Republican party, Jacksonian entrepreneurs anticipated the central features of free labor. The ideology of Republicanism originated in the 1830s.

One of the leading proponents of early free laborism was Tristam Burges. A highly respected congressman who left the National Republicans for the Whigs in the early 1830s, Burges traveled a busy lecture circuit that touched businessmen's haunts and charted his own intellectual transformation. He held forth without a hint of his earlier respect for craftsmanship or reprobation of acquisitive individualism. Burges stressed the themes of unlimited opportunity for individual advancement and harmonious relations between employer and employee. Along with Smith he acknowledged that economic progress could be consistent with greater inequality but insisted this was a temporary condition, not a permanent state. He parted ways with Smith, however, in discounting the peculiar needs and interests of labor. Workers would prosper along with everyone else as long as the iron laws of supply and demand worked their will unobstructed by politicians or union men. Labor and capital, he told a group of New York entrepreneurs in 1830, blended into "one great community and brotherhood of labor for mutual benefit."

Revived and reformed Protestantism emerged simultaneously with early free laborism. Much like classic republicanism, orthodox Protestantism fell out of step with the market revolution. The doctrinal rigidity, denial of free will, censure of worldly striving—these seemed out of date amid the swirl of economic dynamism in Jacksonian America. Protestant divines had repudiated orthodoxy in the 1790s, orchestrating the initial camp meetings on the frontier and the first urban revivals of the Second Great Awakening. Reform Protestantism intensified in the city by the 1820s through a rash of revivals conducted by Charles Finney, Albert Barnes, and other restive ministers preaching the Arminian heresies of universal salvation and good works. Theirs was a more humane and flexible deity than the arbitrary God of orthodoxy. Finney held out the possibility of salvation to all who would profess piety and work against sin; he welcomed progress and looked upon social advancement as a token of spiritual regeneration. Finney also held converts to strict standards of personal conduct, or what one historian calls "industrial morality." His Christians adhered rigidly to injunctions against drink, sexual promiscuity, and other libertine habits rooted in preindustrial times and antithetical to the exigencies of the market revolution.

Between the 1790s and the 1850s evangelical fervor spread from the fertile valleys of the North to the region's towns and port cities. It gripped women of all classes from the first camp meetings on the frontier and gradually enraptured men, penetrating the working class during the depression-era revivals of the early 1840s and late 1850s. The revivals in the 1820s and 1830s were a "shopkeeper's millennium" that brought the new Christianity and its righteous morality to the nation's entrepreneurs. One did not have to be an Arminian to endorse industrial morality or impose it on others. Brahmin Boston worshipped a Unitarian God and Southern entrepreneurs a Calvinist deity: nonetheless they required workers to attend chapel and observe rules against tardiness and insubordination on pain of fines or firing. Lesser employers did not consistently observe the new faith either. Some knelt in orthodox pews, some in none at all. Many men on the make, however, found evangelicalism to be consonant with personal ambition, and with more efficient workshops. They hired reborn Christians where possible, prohibited drink on the premises, and enjoined the customary grog breaks that filled neighborhood pubs with thirsty workmen in late morning and again in midafternoon. Some Northerners signed on with the evangelical army captained by merchants and ministers in the war against sin and moral laxity. Their wives and daughters were the foot soldiers handing out leaflets to shoppers and passersby and visiting workers at home. Mechanics' institutes did their part for moral cleansing when, in the 1820s, attention turned from the chronic problem of tracking down runaway apprentices to improving the habits of young men. They established temperance clubs, published homiletic literature, and built libraries, reading rooms, and other escapes from the temptations of the street.

This ideological and religious fervor created not one but several forms of early free laborism that received political expression in the Whig and Democratic parties. Whiggery was the choice of established merchants and manufacturers along with better-off mechanics in the North, and some planters and most industrialists in the South, who were taken by Henry Clay's "American System" of protective tariffs, internal improvements, and fiscally sound banking. Their party also spoke for evangelicals obsessed with moral uplift and social control. It supported public schools with a curriculum that featured heavy doses of religious instruction, as well as penitentiaries and asylums for the removal of the feebleminded and criminal elements in society. Some party stalwarts went beyond the voluntarism of temperance to criminalize the manufacture and sale of spirits and prohibit mail delivery on the Sabbath.

Prohibition and Sabbatarianism, along with education and prison reform, represented what a prominent Northern Whig described as extending "paternal sympathy" to the workers in the land.

That term was anathema to the Democrats. The party of Jackson was a patchwork of social and cultural groups—Southern planters and subsistence farmers everywhere, struggling mechanics, poor native-born and immigrant workers, arriviste merchants and professionals—loosely stitched together by early free laborism and anti-evangelicalism. Its resounding call for "equal rights for all, and special privileges for none" harked back to the old republicans, Paine among them, who decried active government as the font of injustice. "Too many laws and too much government," said a Massachusetts Jacksonian in a refrain repeated ad nauseam from Democratic rostrums, "are among the tendencies of the age against which we must guard." The Democrats were sentinels of the people who stood between government and the "charter mongers and money changers" out to use the state for personal advantage. They denounced tariffs and corporate charters as class legislation, and obstinately fought internal improvements supported by the federal government; some even opposed state construction of roads and canals as excessive. When Democrats tilted leftward in response to the Working Men's insurgencies of the early 1830s, they campaigned for less government, not more: they pressed for the abolition of militia duty and imprisonment for debt. They shrieked "freedom of conscience" and "individual liberty" at Whigs bent on legislating evangelical morality. Democratic lawmakers, much like Jefferson's, governed best when they governed least.

Whig and Democratic views converged at some points. Party leaders on both sides of the aisle rose in behalf of competition, individualism, and wider latitude for the man on the make. "Every avenue to distinction, every path to wealth," went a typical oration, "is open to every citizen alike, and every citizen can make of himself what he chooses." Here agreement ended. Whigs envisioned a kind of corporate order that integrated functionally disparate but mutually dependent social classes. Journeymen were free to reach the top providing they set their minds to doing so. Common men of settled intention and steadiness of purpose moved up the social scale and stood as models of emulation, living testimony that there were no systemic obstacles. Indolence, intemperance, and other stains of character defeated achievement in both the spiritual realm and the material world. Man was responsible for his own fate; success, like salvation, was a matter of free will. On the other hand, personal morality did not assume such importance in the Democratic lexicon. Democrats instead referred to gradations of raw and cultivated talent that gave rise to "just" and "natural" differences. "Distinctions in society will always exist under every just government," asserted Andrew Jackson. "Equality of talents, of education, or of wealth," he stressed, "cannot be produced by human institutions." Bad government hardened "natural" distinctions into artificial ones by granting "gratuities and exclusive privileges." This added up to a vision of a fractious society rent with conflict between its "humble members —the farmers, mechanics, and laborers," as Jackson called them—and the "potent and powerful" who twisted "government to their selfish purposes."

That a Southern planter would consider himself to be a hero to the humble and oppressed is not so curious. All planters were not linen-suited aristocrats contemptuous of bourgeois society, any more than owning slaves was the aspiration of the few. Slavery may have been wasteful and inefficient, but it was, nonetheless, the universal symbol of success in the South; and slaves were a prize avidly sought, if by no means widely achieved. The non-slave-owning majority of mechanics and yeomen clearly resented the planter elite, a sentiment shared and exploited by Jackson, but stood in mortal fear of the racial mongrelization and ruinous competition in land and labor markets they were told would follow emancipation. All talk of ending slavery, which was always limited to pockets of the upper South, stopped abruptly with Nat Turner's Rebellion in 1831. No slave owner, however, ever rested easily. None was confident that the promise of white egalitarianism was enough to ensure the fidelity of the white multitude. Indeed slave owners were of mixed minds on the most effective means of preserving their "peculiar institution." Large planters loyal to Democrats were unalterably committed to an agrarian order that replenished itself through territorial expansion. Industrial promoters in both parties, however, argued for a mixed economy within the context of slavery and regional self-sufficiency. It was they who came up with the Southern expression of free laborism.

Southern free laborism insisted that fostering the mechanical arts and large-scale industry, not territorial expansion, was the key to the survival of slavery and the fealty of poor whites. Not a few free laborites advocated using some slaves in factories, while others preferred employing only white labor. They all agreed, however, that manufacturing would integrate all segments of white Southern society. Planters would enjoy ready outlets for their staples, and merchants would gain new

customers. "Artisan[s] and laborer[s]" would not have to perform the
"nigger work" and would "find ready employment at increased and
remunerating wages." They would be raised out of poverty and given a
larger stake in the system. The "successful worker," predicted a
Southern free laborite, "would aim to become a slaveowner, for the
purpose of alleviating that domestic drudgery which in non-slaveholding
states falls so heavily on the wives and daughters of men of limited
means." There would be a servant in every home and also an underclass
of slaves, said another believer in free labor, that would imbue white
labor with a feeling of "aristocracy" and infuse the mechanical arts with
renewed respectability. The slaves, moreover, could be called upon to
tame unruly workers and enforce class peace. "Capital will be able to
control labor, even in factories," said the textile entrepreneur William
Gregg, "for blacks can always be resorted to in case of need."

More striking still is the popularity Jackson would enjoy on the
nation's subsistence farms and in its small workshops. His histrionic
crusade against the aristocratic Bank of the United States in 1832
accounts for only part of Jackson's celebrity. As several historians have
observed, the Democracy projected an ambiguous and contradictory
image that meant different things to its heterogeneous constituency. To
the man on the make, the party looked to be prying open the market,
extending economic opportunity while containing the middleman. To the
subsistence farmer and urban mechanic, it seemed to be limiting the reach
of the market and preserving economic independence.

It was one thing to rally the many against the few, but quite another to
recognize the class interests of journeymen. Neither political party went
that far, not even the Democrats. Both spoke of the promise of free labor
in the face of emerging unions. To Whigs, union men were "plunderers";
to Democrats, they were "monopolists" little better than large employers
and considerably more dangerous. The laws of supply and demand set
wages and could not be breached, any more than could the sacred
doctrine of "freedom of contract," which gave each man and woman the
right to work as many hours a day as he or she wished. Baltimore workers
learned that this doctrine crossed regional lines. When in 1833 they
appealed to the mayor for support in a drive to establish the ten-hour day,
they were told that "it is the undoubted right of every individual to
determine the number of hours which shall constitute his day's labour."
Besides, wrote Whig polemicist Calvin Colton, "ours is a country where
men start from humble origins and from small beginnings rise gradually
in the world, as the reward of merit and industry, and where they can

attain the most elevated positions, or acquire a large amount of wealth according to the pursuits they elect for themselves.'' Democrats disputed Colton's belief in the way workmen are elevated out of their class, but not with the end itself. For them, as for Whigs, social success was the antidote to social strife.

. . .

Journeymen subscribed to traditional conceptions of social improvement. As late as midcentury, they spoke alternately of achieving independence or securing competencies, not of the constant accumulation of wealth Colton thought possible. Popular understandings of competencies, however, altered with economic progress and varied according to one's status within the working class. Skilled workmen expected considerably more than the unskilled, who could not realistically aspire to much more than a hand-to-mouth existence. We get a rare glimpse of heightened expectations in a letter written by a Philadelphia printer in 1850. Skilled workers, he explained, were no longer content with adequate diets and decent retirements because art and science revealed a ''more exalted and refined'' standard of living that demanded ''a freer and more liberal nourishment.'' He added that the worthy mechanic was entitled to a house ''on a front street, three stories high, [with] bath room, hydrant, good yard, cellar . . . house furniture.'' Beyond these amenities the good life called for enough discretionary income for newspapers, recreation, and membership in a friendly society, along with sufficient savings for an independent retirement.

Competencies were not always elusive. The Quaker City mechanic Samuel King attained his with seeming ease. King completed his apprenticeship in the early 1830s, worked as a journeyman for a few years, and at the end of the decade opened his own business. The ensuing panic that brought down thousands of petty proprietors in King's Philadelphia glanced off the upstart master craftsman. ''He prospered for fourteen years,'' wrote an admiring biographer, ''and by prudent management [acquired] . . . what he considered to be a competency . . . and retired from business with a good reputation [ca 1851].'' His decision to leave the trade at such an early age surprised friends and colleagues, but King had a ready answer. ''I know when I have enough,'' he replied, ''and know how to take care of it.'' Public records do not record King's estate at that time, but it would be surprising indeed if the storefront brush maker had more than a couple of thousand dollars, just about enough for a commodious home and a self-sustaining retirement.

We cannot be certain that King is typical, because of the paucity of research on the careers of antebellum artisans. One study of Philadelphia deals with masters and retailers, not journeymen, but it reveals that small proprietors were more apt to revert to wage labor than expand their businesses. The frequency of downward mobility, in fact, increased steadily between 1820 and 1860. A comparable study of Newark, New Jersey, shows that the proportion of self-employed craftsmen declined significantly in the late antebellum years. In 1840 nearly one in five tradesmen owned his own shop; twenty years later fewer than one in ten did. Occupation is only one measure of social standing. Income level is another and perhaps a more accurate standard for wage earners. Data are a bit better beginning in 1850 thanks to reliable information on annual income. For the years before 1850 we must translate daily wages, the only available figures, into annual incomes. This is complicated by the difficulty of estimating the number of days worked per year. Journeymen lost time due to illness, unstable markets, and seasonal business cycles. A journalist tells us that mechanics were employed off and on in the warm months, and in winter "they are stripped of employment like the trees of the forest, which are divested of their summer sheen." Even summer spelled lean times for shoe and clothing workers, whose busy seasons were the spring and fall. Seasonal employment was one of the hard realities of early working-class life.

Nonetheless it is still possible to get a sense of the changing standard of living for antebellum workers in the North. The evidence would suggest that very few journeymen matched Samuel King's achievement. In the early 1820s shoemakers and tailors earned $6.00 to $8.00 a week, just about $2.00 to $4.00 less than printers, carpenters, and other "honorable" tradesmen. Periodic recessions over the next thirty years, the deepest coming at the turn of the 1830s, depressed wage rates generally, while the intensification of the division of labor eroded scales across a widening spectrum of crafts; shoemakers' earnings plunged to about $1.00 a day. Wages fell following the 1837 panic and crept upward during the 1850s. In 1860 average weekly earnings were one-third higher than in 1850. Wages in the prosperous 1850s made up in part for the past, but workers in the honorable trades fared best. Newark, New Jersey, jewelers, for example, pushed their weekly earnings to $10.25; shoemakers working by hand lagged far behind at $6.00. Footwear workers employed on machines did even worse, taking home under $6.00.

Living standards were initially higher in the "mushroom" cities of the Midwest. Severe labor shortages inflated wages above Eastern levels and a building boom made for cheaper and more abundant housing. "House rent for a mechanic," said a Cincinnatian in 1811, "is about sixty dollars [a year], but most of them soon get houses of their own." This was only a slight exaggeration. In 1820 nearly a third of the city's mechanics were homeowners, possibly the highest proportion in the nation. By the 1850s, however, Cincinnati lost its advantage. "Business and capital," moaned a labor publicist in 1852, "were rapidly centering in fewer hands" and the worker's future was becoming "more and more unfortunate." He was correct on both accounts. The proportion of homeowners plummeted to 6 percent in 1838 and to under 5 percent in 1850. At the same time, the richest taxpayers claimed a larger share of the city's wealth, just as they did in Eastern cities. Upper-crust Cincinnati, which owned 70 percent of the wealth in 1838, owned over 80 percent in 1860.

More journeymen probably lived better in 1820 than in 1850. At the beginning of this thirty-year span an urban family of two adults and three children needed about $330 a year to escape poverty. This required a weekly wage of $8.00 for forty weeks. Since all but unskilled laborers and the most degraded craftsmen commanded such an income, it is safe to conclude that the majority reached this level with wages alone. Thirty years later observers raised the minimum budget to slightly over $500 (over $600 in New York), and at a time when urban journeymen averaged only $300 a year. Luxury tradesmen and new metalworkers surpassed the $500 threshold by enough to put aside savings. The multitude struggled just to make ends meet. Wives bought wheat and other nonperishables in bulk and made the family clothing or patronized secondhand shops in working-class districts. They might save a few pennies on rent by moving into cheaper flats several times a year. The hardship of the English immigrant John Gough was severe but not entirely untypical. Gough, a young bookbinder in the mid-1830s, lived in New York with his mother and sister Mary, a straw-bonnet maker, in a two-room apartment that rented for $1.25 a week. A sudden downturn threw John and Mary out of work and forced the struggling family into a garret at $0.50 a week. Winter found his mother sick, food short, the fuel box empty, and John doing odd jobs to keep the family afloat. He was reduced to scavenging the countryside for firewood and pawning his overcoat for the price of mutton broth for his ailing mother. Not until the spring upturn did he and Mary return to work and John feel secure enough to reclaim his coat.

Gough's tribulations indicate that no amount of parsimony eliminated the need for supplementary sources of subsistence and income. Workers situated outside large cities raised their own fruits and vegetables, hunted fields and forests, and fished streams and bays. Lynn shoemakers were said to have prodigious caches of smoked cod and salmon stored in cellars and drying on racks in the North Shore sun. Some urban workers raised pigs and even cows where space permitted. Those with room to spare usually took in boarders at $0.50 to $1.00 a week, but this seems to have been a luxury because of crowding that accompanied urban growth after 1820. The poorest workers lived in cellars and attics and even the better-paid were crammed into small, three-room homes.

Pressed for additional means of income, most families expected children to work, even if it meant sacrificing their education. This pattern of multiple breadwinners reflected an early urban version of the family wage economy. Child and adolescent wage labor came first in the textile towns, where employers preferred hiring families with youngsters, and then to the countryside with the proliferation of the putting-out system. As we have already seen, farmsteads incorporated outwork on a casual basis without disrupting agricultural regimens. Wives, daughters, and sometimes fathers and sons fit wage labor into the work cycle, binding shoes and making brooms and palm-leaf hats at night and in the dead of winter. For the wives and daughters of most urban journeymen, as well as single women and widows, outwork was a year-round necessity and the chief source of employment. Such needy women were easy prey for merchant capitalists and operators of slop shops, and in some instances for their own husbands, who set up shop with family labor. It was a scandalous system marked by brutal exploitation, fraud, and wages so pitiful that a $1.50 a week was considered doing well. Early-day muckrakers and reformers exposed the abuse and starvation wages that did not "decently sustain life" for unattached women. When added to family coffers, however, sums garnered from outwork made the difference between hopeless poverty and minimal comfort.

Much less is known about the living standards of white labor in the South. Historians have not studied social mobility and have only begun to investigate working-class wages and incomes. The only wage figures available cover unskilled laborers and textile workers, and they reveal what we might expect: Southerners were paid less than Northerners. In the South Atlantic states common laborers earned two-thirds the daily rate of their Northern counterparts in both 1832 and 1850. The annual incomes of textile operatives compared even more unfavorably. In 1850, the first year for which we have any data at all, they took home only 60 percent of the income of Northern textile workers. On the other hand, if the testimony of a Georgia carpenter is any guide, the severe shortage of

skilled labor may have worked to the benefit of some Southern journeymen. In the late 1840s he complained that slave competition knocked
down his wage to $2.00 a day, at a time when fellow tradesmen in the
North were said to pocket only $1.25. Unfortunately it is impossible to
know if he is representative. Nor is it possible to weigh the impact of the
region's economic peculiarities—the retardation of industrialism, the
seemingly large market for luxury and custom-made commodities, and
labor's more immediate access to means of subsistence on the land—on
worker standards of living.

We can be more certain how free black labor fared in the South. No
other group of workers, not even Northern artisans shorn of skills,
suffered such a profound loss of status. The early career of Frederick
Douglass, the fugitive slave who went on to become a leading abolitionist, newspaper publisher, and then diplomat, is instructive. Born in 1817
or 1818 on a plantation in Talbot County, Maryland, Douglass was later
shunted back and forth between households of the Auld family in
Baltimore and the Maryland countryside. In 1836 his Baltimore master
hired him out to a Fell's Point shipbuilder with the understanding that he
would be taught the trade of caulking. Douglass instead worked as a
casual laborer lifting and hauling lumber for the shipbuilders. The crews
were integrated, he recalled. "White and black ship carpenters worked
side by side, and no one seemed to see any impropriety in it," until the
white carpenters suddenly "knocked off, and said they would not work
with colored workmen." The strike not only cleared the yards of the
black artisans but also incited the racist passions of the white apprentices,
who swore at Douglass and then severely beat him. His master then
placed him on another wharf, where Douglass learned how to work with
the "mallet and irons" of the caulker and like many urban slaves was
soon choosing his own employers and keeping some money. A year or so
later in 1838 he escaped to the North and made his way to New Bedford,
Massachusetts. He headed for the docks eager to resume work at his
craft, but "such was the strength of prejudice against color, among the
white caulkers, that they refused to work with me, and I of course got no
employment"—at least not as a caulker. He had to do "any kind of work
I could do," which meant shoveling coal and loading and unloading
ships. The proud tradesman worked as a casual laborer for a few years
until the abolitionist movement gave him a platform for his formidable
oratorical skills, wide political recognition, and ultimately some social
standing.

For ordinary black artisans social deterioration knew no limits. White masters and journeymen in the South, organized into institutes and trade societies, petitioned public officials for licensing laws, capitation taxes, and other statutes to curtail or eliminate black competition. They usually succeeded in the aftermath of rumored or actual slave rebellions when Negrophobia reached fever pitch, and in states with weak planter aristocracies. In the mid-1840s Georgia mechanics pushed through a law banning all black labor from building construction, but this measure was as rare as it was sweeping. Elsewhere planters either fought off proscriptive legislation or saw to it that such laws were not enforced. White workers turned to direct action, and as the mob actions on the Baltimore docks would suggest, they were remarkably effective. Free blacks chased out of skilled work by white violence landed in unskilled jobs on waterfronts and construction sites, as Douglass did. Even these casual jobs failed to provide safe harbor. White workers thrown out of work in the depression at the start of the 1840s and hungry immigrants streaming into cities at the end of the depression set the stage for furious race riots as well as subtle forms of white intimidation in both the North and the South. In Philadelphia racial clashes in the black ghetto in 1841 and 1849 ended blocks away on the Schuylkill waterfront with Irish gangs assaulting black dockers and stevedores and threatening their employers with violence. By the end of the decade, reporters tell us, the Irish had muscled most blacks off the Philadelphia docks. In Deep South cities Irish toughs forced blacks out of dray work and other hauling trades, and in New Orleans they even took over the traditional black work of serving customers in pubs and restaurants. One of the last black waiters in the Crescent City told Frederick Law Olmsted in the early 1850s:

"Im de olest in de home; all de odder ole servant is gone," said the waiter.

"And they have got Irishmen to take their places?" asked Olmsted.

"Yes! and what kind of servant is dey? Ha! all de Irishmen dat I see hadden so much sense in dar heds as I could carry in de palm of my han'."

So it went. Racial violence helped destroy what remained of a black artisan class in both regions by the 1850s. Only in Charleston did free black artisans hold their own.

Free blacks were not always silent victims of white rage. Some fought back with renewed resolve after the mid-1840s. But theirs was a losing battle. Unlike slaves who could rely on the influence and political power of masters and patrons, they could not count on much support from employers. Racism infected all segments of society. It was the rare employer who expressed much sympathy and those that did refused to hire black labor for fear of upsetting white employees. The racial climate improved somewhat in the North during the 1850s as the economy boomed, sectional antagonisms intensified, and some Yankees felt the need to distance themselves from the racial code of the South. Black ship caulkers, Douglass tells us, began to appear on New Bedford docks. Elsewhere white and black stevedores and draymen seem to have declared a truce and worked out territorial agreements and job quotas, which preserved some niches for a privileged few. Most black males were reduced to an underclass of casual laborers, waiters, and ragpickers.

• • •

In the North and in the border states the decline of living standards and the degradation of craftsmanship touched off the nation's first labor movement in the late 1820s. Journeymen and factory hands skeptical of free laborism's faith in broadened opportunity assembled alternatives to the mechanics' institutes, masters' societies, and even mainstream parties. They organized unions on a widening front that drew together in confederations as well as third parties with ambitious manifestos. Politicized labor stood against imprisonment for debt, mandatory militia duty, burdensome taxation, and the use of prison labor, and for mechanics' lien laws and expanded public school systems. Leaders inveighed against "class legislation" in all its varieties, from seemingly innocuous lotteries to the chartering of financial institutions and manufacturing companies.

The beliefs that fueled this movement are best and broadly described as radicalism. It was a loose and variable body of thought subject to the modifications of place, gender, and personal experience. The radicalism of women, factory hands, and small-town artisans diverged in subtle ways from that of the urban journeymen. It was an attenuated radicalism that used customary republican notions of citizenship to challenge the employer's authority over wages, hours, and working conditions. In 1834 striking weavers at Lowell invoked their status as the "daughters of freemen" in protesting a wage cut imposed by "Tory" employers. They took heated exception to being labeled "Factory slaves" and resolved to resist the "grand plan of the proprietors . . . to reduce Females . . . to . . . dependence." Eastern Pennsylvania factory hands likewise poured scorn on "such tyrants as would gladly rob the operatives of [their] rights and privileges as citizens." Protests of this kind were both tacit and direct attacks on work rules one manufacturer considered "absolutely essential" for factory governance, and all considered conditions of employment. One operative thought the regulations to be a signal example of arbitrary rule, a cancer on the body politic. "In spite of all . . . [that] may be said to the contrary," he fumed, "enforcements are not the offsprings of mutual consent."

Neither was "sunup to sundown" toil. Early labor historians understood the twelve- to fourteen-hour day of the Jackson period to be a carryover from agriculture or derived from the British. We now know better. First-generation manufacturers gradually stretched out the workday in order to increase production. Merchant capitalists intensified exploitation by lowering piece rates, for each successive reduction produced corresponding extensions of time on the job. Shoemakers, tailors, and other tradesmen paid by the piece were reported stitching and sewing by candlelight in the 1840s. Preindustrial Americans were indeed accustomed to long hours, but the fact remains that industrial routines were different from agricultural rhythms. Factory hands answered to overseers, bells, and the compulsions of wage labor, not the gentler proddings of nature or the task system of farm work. Indeed no single issue mattered more to Jacksonian labor than reducing the length of the workday and no economic institution appeared so corrosive of the republican spirit as the factory. The New England Association of Farmers, Mechanics, and Other Working Men called the region's mills monuments to "cupidity and avarice" that would crush the independent spirit of "American freemen." One of the few factory hands involved in the National Trades' Union, the first national body of unionists formed in 1834, reviled the factory system as "subversive of liberty—calculated to change the character of a people from . . . bold and free, to enervated, dependent, and slavish."

Skilled workers also adapted the political terminology of republicanism to economic relations, and not just in the East. Midwestern craftsmen, too, measured emergent capitalism by republican standards. Cincinnati tradesmen who formed the Rose City's first General Trades' Union in the mid-1830s described themselves as "citizens of the Republic" united to arrest the "murderous course . . . pursued toward the working classes." It was the bookbinders of Philadelphia who put the matter most succinctly. Locked in a dispute over wages in 1836, they returned a price list drafted by employers with a terse affirmation they would never surrender their "inalienable rights: to affix a price on the only property we have to dispose of: our labor."

Urban journeymen, however, went beyond espousing the political ideals of the American Revolution. They learned a new economic language, new conceptual tools that informed penetrating criticism of the market economy. The source of this awakening lay in a renaissance from below, a remarkable outpouring of political ideas following the panic of 1819. "Never before," writes the historian Paul K. Conkin, "had urban workers encountered such a brilliant and varied spectrum of intellectuals or such a challenging array of proposed programs." Conkin's popular protesters felt intellectual kinship not only with Paine but also with two generations of English political economists in the radical tradition. The late-eighteenth-century agrarian Thomas Spence, who wished to bring about equality of land tenure, was a favorite, along with William Thompson and John Gray, the primitive socialists and advocates of worker ownership of the means of production. The New York Quaker and physician Cornelius Blatchley, though hardly a plebeian, ranged widely over the economic landscape in a series of books, pamphlets, and speeches assailing usury, competition, and land monopoly. Fellow New Yorker Langton Byllesby had an artisanal background but a frustratingly circular career. The orphaned son of English immigrants served a printer's apprenticeship, became a proofreader for a major New York publisher, and opened his own newspaper in Easton, Pennsylvania, in 1824, only to go bust and return to journeyman status in New York. In 1826 he published *Observations on the Sources of and Effects of Unequal Wealth*, one of the first expositions of the impact of technology on unemployment and social inequality and perhaps the first brief for cooperative production by an American. Blatchley and Byllesby shifted their radical emphasis from politics to political economy, but from the vantage point of the polemicist, not the unionist. They spoke for no unions, and apart from Byllesby's call for cooperatives, refrained from urging stronger worker organization. Blatchley, in fact, was a devout Christian convinced of the possibility of social reconciliation through perfectionist communitarianism.

A much larger group of labor advocates combined thought and action. Rhode Island's Seth Luther, son of a Revolutionary War veteran and textile-operative-turned-carpenter, returned home from a tour of the nation in the early 1830s to direct the New England Association of Farmers, Mechanics, and Other Working Men. Brooklyn-born cabinet-maker John Commerford went from a minor post in the Working Men's party of New York to become president of the city's General Trades' Union in 1835. William Gilmore was a Philadelphia shoemaker and another veteran of labor politics who took up the cause of the Quaker City's General Trades' Union. Fellow Philadelphian John Ferral (also Farrell), an Irish immigrant and hand-loom weaver, was one of the few prominent labor leaders of the age to come from the textile industry and from abroad. Most were native-born Americans of Yankee or British stock predominantly in the sweated trades—shoemaking, tailoring, and cabinetmaking the most common vocations, followed by printing and the building trades. Outside New England, nearly all favored the Enlightenment religions of deism, Universalism, or some other form of free thought, merging the late-eighteenth-century faith in self-cultivation with the Jacksonian fondness for voluntary organization. They digested the literature of science, technology, and political economy as individuals and as members of debating clubs and literary societies that held discussions and distributed cheap editions of radical texts. Two of them—Thomas Skidmore and William Heighton—merit special attention.

We still know very little about Thomas Skidmore, author of the agrarian book *The Rights of Man to Property!* Born in 1790 to a declining Yankee farm family in Newton, Connecticut, Skidmore never had much of a childhood or indeed a full adult life; he died at age forty-two in 1832. He was a teacher at thirteen, less out of choice, it seems, than family need, and a few years later an itinerant teacher following a feud with his father that drove him from home. Skidmore wandered through the South and then returned North to settle in New York in 1819, where he opened a small machine shop and, typical of early metal tradesmen, tinkered with inventions. He also partook of the city's intellectual ferment, reading Thomas Paine, the English primitive socialists, and resident radicals Blatchley and Byllesby. Skidmore admired Paine's republican idealism but borrowed more liberally from economic radicalism and especially the labor theory of value. This theory traced the origins of wealth to the work of farmers and artisans—that is, to manual labor. References to it could be found in Scripture—in such passages as "In the sweat of thy brow shalt thou eat bread"—but it took John Locke and the classical economists to give it formal expression. By the Jackson years, it became an article of popular faith, something mechanics and yeomen intuitively knew to be true and some merchants and manufacturers accepted as gospel because of its imprecise and expansive definition of labor. To entrepreneurs, anyone who worked qualified as labor and a producer of wealth; to mechanics, only those who worked with raw materials or on the land deserved such a distinction. Skidmore endorsed the more restrictive meaning, but put his own interpretation on it by arguing that "labor did not, as many believed, have intrinsic value but was only a faculty that could increase the value of property." Labor could also secure rights to property, which for Skidmore meant land. He elevated land over all forms of property and insisted that the natural right to the soil preceded all others, including claims based on use—that is, on labor. The recent past disclosed, however, that developers and speculators had engrossed more and more acreage and thereby deprived ordinary people of their birthright.

Skidmore devised a daring plan for popular reclamation of the land. He summoned New York City artisans to a constitutional convention that would wipe out inequality in a stroke. The new constitution would void all titles and debts, provide for a survey of real and personal property, and then redistribute proportional shares to each man when he reached the age of twenty-one. Tenure extended for the life of the individual and reverted to the state at death for redistribution to the next in line. Skidmore's New York partisans, who helped found the Working Men's party in 1829, never amounted to much more than a corporal's guard. Expropriation came across as draconian, too drastic even for embattled workers open to almost any change in existing arrangements. The proposal also suffered from the personal quirks of its author: Skidmore was a stern and impatient man with a pride of authorship fellow Working Men found insufferable. He was soon forced out of the party and his program dropped but not entirely rejected. The agrarian ideal never completely lost its grip on the popular imagination. Working Men's parties in the 1830s endorsed land reform in some fashion, and George Henry Evans of New York, a former follower of Skidmore, later concocted a more moderate scheme that would command an audience in the 1840s. Evansism would become a plank in the Republican party platform of 1860 as the Homestead Act, which proposed giving any citizen 160 acres of public land on the condition that he work it for five years.

If land reform remained secondary in Philadelphia, it is because William Heighton never thought it particularly important. Heighton's background is little known. We know that he was the son of a poor English tradesman born in the Midlands shoemaking center of Oundle, Northamptonshire, possibly in 1800, and that he left with his family for the United States around 1812, eventually settling in Southwark, the southernmost borough of Philadelphia. There he joined the ragged throng of shoemakers eking out an existence making cheap footwear for merchant capitalists. He left the Quaker City for parts unknown in the early 1830s but not before leaving a profound impression on its working class. In 1827 he founded the *Mechanics' Free Press*, official organ of both the Mechanics' Union of Trade Associations and the Working Men's party, the nation's first union confederation and labor party, respectively. Heighton shared early radicalism's preference for rationalism and an unrelenting animus against organized religion. He mercilessly baited the clergy in the columns of the *Mechanics' Free Press* and belonged to several rationalist groups. He and fellow "infidels," as they called themselves, revered Paine the deist and republican, but turned to the English radicals for their political economics. The self-taught shoemaker made his mark not so much with caustic editorials as with three public speeches delivered in 1827 and 1828, the first of which, entitled "An Address to the Members of Trades Societies and to the Working Classes Generally," is credited with lighting the spark that ignited the labor movement in Philadelphia and, if we can believe contemporaries, elsewhere as well. Robert Owen, co-founder of the New York's Working Men's party and an educated man of worldly experience, considered the "Address" more enlightening than "all the writings on political economy I have met with." Taken together, Heighton's speeches constitute an extraordinarily consistent and comprehensive synthesis of early working-class radicalism.

The labor theory of value was for Heighton what the doctrine of natural rights to the land was for Skidmore. No other labor advocate of the age breathed such life into its abstract categories of "producer" and "nonproducer." He made radicalism accessible in crafted speeches refreshingly direct and delivered in a style that combined the invective of the class partisan with the power of the skilled pedagogue. His first address moved systematically through the idiosyncratic and collusive misdeeds of what Heighton identified as six classes of nonproducers: "The Legislative, the Judicial, the Theological, the Commercial, the Independent, and the Military." Theologians, for instance, violated their *"special duty"* to enlighten the people because they accumulated "in abundance through the Medium of SALARIES" the products of *"other people's labour"* and conspired to keep productive labor "in ignorance and mental blindness." But Heighton consistently singled out the machinations of the commercial class, a diffuse group encompassing "monopolizing companies; master manufacturers, and the proprietors of machinery, brokers and shavers; wholesale and retail merchants or dealers; and in short, ALL of every description who accumulate wealth or obtain a subsistence by PROFIT; the exclusive original source of which is *the labours of the working class."* Heighton acknowledged two distinct groups of workers: "productive" and "official." All radicals recognized the first and along with the Philadelphia shoemaker understood it to consist of manual workers supplying "tangible articles of wealth"— yeomen, master craftsmen, and journeymen. The category of "official labor," which was Heighton's invention, embraced unskilled workmen who transported and prepared commodities for popular use. "Those employed in these . . . operations," he stressed, "are as useful and necessary to the happiness of the community as those actually employed in productive labor." This departure would help distinguish the Philadelphia labor movement for welcoming unskilled labor.

But Heighton was no mere social taxonomist. The burden of his argument was to account for the paradox of want amid plenty, why the producers and transporters of wealth wound up with so little and the accumulators made off with so much. Heighton pointed to developments in the different but related spheres of politics and the economy. Applying lessons learned from Paine and shared by fellow radicals, he argued that accumulators had pulled off a gradual and quiet counterrevolution following 1776 by seizing the machinery of state and rigging legislation to promote private gain. They extracted charters of incorporation for banks and manufacturing companies that profited from labor's toil and strangled the small proprietor. They took advantage of the nation's liberal lands laws by gobbling up huge tracts for speculation and thus slammed shut the escape hatch of shop-weary workers. And they purchased bonds floated for internal improvements and public utilities that returned princely sums from tax levies that fell heaviest on productive laborers. Corrupt lawmakers were partly to blame for this stream of "aristocratic legislation," but Heighton uncovered the "root of the evil" in the maldistribution of knowledge and class awareness, a theme he reiterated again and again. "WANT OF INTELLIGENCE," he thundered, was labor's crippling disability, just as "superior information," armed accumulators with "superior power." Here, too, Heighton revealed his debt to Paine and the Enlightenment's faith in the potency of knowledge.

Heighton simultaneously ventured far beyond Paine in probing the character of economic relations. He discussed the ruinous force of competition from the standpoint of the producer and society as a whole. He quoted extensively from John Gray's "Essay on Human Happiness" to argue that nature imposed two constraints on the capacity to produce: *"the exhaustion of our productive powers* and *the satisfaction of our wants."* The advent of the market revolution, however, unleashed the

mischievous force of competition that turned the world of Adam Smith on
its head. As Gray put it:

> The *quantity* of wealth which a working man receives, is always the
> *least* that his labour can be purchased for; and the reason why he does
> not obtain twice the quantity he obtains at present is, because if he, an
> individual, were to demand it, and refuse to work for a less[er]
> quantity, he would be thrown out of employment altogether, by another
> individual offering to do the same work for the new quantity given—or
> in other words, by another individual *competing* with him.

While Gray went on to show how competitive pricing depressed the
revenues of merchants and landlords, Heighton dwelled on the plight of
labor. The handicrafts, he affirmed, inexorably declined from "the surest
means of a gradual and certain accumulation" to "precarious" undertakings avoided by young men for careers in the more remunerative
branches of exchange. Retailing and merchandising expanded with rivals
hustling to outdo one another in a lusty war for survival that inevitably
affected suppliers in the crafts. Masters and entrepreneurs had to cut
wages and bear down on hirelings, or fold up and take their place at
workbenches.

Even technological improvement, which Heighton acclaimed as a
means of ending excessive work and burdensome manual tasks, became
a "source of the most abject poverty, wretchedness and starvation."
Machines glutted markets with *"cheap* articles of wealth, until the
demand is oversupplied; work becomes scarce . . . labourers . . . thrown
out of employment, and the wages of those who still obtain it . . .
reduced to the very lowest term."

Who would check this ominous drift? Eighteenth-century republicans
had instinctively summoned the fiercely vigilant freestanding citizenry;
Jacksonian radicals were not so optimistic. They feared that "this system
of individual interest and competition," as Heighton called capitalism,
neutralized its opposition; it diminished upstanding producers to grovel-
ing dependents compelled to defer to their betters, and more troubling
still, deadened spirits as it laid waste to craft skill. Impoverished workers
condemned to the monotony of repetitive tasks were at risk of being
drained of the inquisitive zeal and incentive for self-improvement
characteristic of Burges's "complete mechanic." They might seek relief
in frivolous amusement, or even drink, to radicals the worst form of
self-abuse. A veteran shoemaker with a longer perspective on the demise
of his craft put it well in lamenting that "the strain on a man doing just

one thing over and over again must necessarily have a wearying effect on him; his ideals, I believe, must be lowered." Adam Smith, of course, predicted much the same thing, if in stronger language, of the division of labor. The worker deprived of the need to use his skill "naturally loses . . . the habit of such [intellectual] exertion, and gradually becomes as stupid and ignorant as it is possible for a human creature to become," but he also contributes to "universal opulence which extends itself to the lowest ranks of the people" as a result of higher productivity. Heighton and fellow radicals, however, saw no such compensations for labor in the bastardization of craft work. Poverty, not prosperity, was the fate of the workman.

This outlook should not be confused with socialism. Skidmore and Heighton underlined different aspects of inequality, but respected private property and looked to bring about a wider and more equal distribution. No radical of this generation dreamed of public ownership or had much use for the forceful government of socialism. The platforms of the first Working Men's parties, though more comprehensive than those of succeeding labor parties before the 1870s, were manifestos for smaller government. Radicals never did shake off the old republican fear of state activism. Nor did they recognize the classes or the dynamics of economic exploitation later put forth by Marx. They saw their world as divided between producers and nonproducers rather than more specifically between employees and employers. Mechanics who worked with their hands qualified as producers and friends of labor. The minority of manufacturers and enterprising mechanics, moreover, were not normally seen as the sole or even primary oppressors of workers. They competed with and were often considered secondary to merchants, financiers, or, more generally, "the wealthy." Even Heighton went out of his way to absolve some employers, explaining that "many . . . are in some degree excusable . . . for thus accumulating; for instance a large portion of master craftsmen . . . [who] deal with accumulators [bankers and merchants] more powerful than themselves."

When radicals referred to producers, moreover, they meant white male artisans. No early radical accepted Heighton's category of "official labor" or saw a community of interest with unskilled workers and factory hands. They perceived such groups as social inferiors, reflections as well as symbols of dependency. In addition, workers outside the handicrafts often bore the stigmas of race and gender. Radicals were strangely silent on the race question, neither openly taunting abolitionists nor resorting to the racist diatribes of Democratic politicians. They simply ignored

Afro-Americans, if not women. They may not have fully accepted the emerging bourgeois paragon of the virtuous woman, keeper of the fireside and moral guardian of husband and children. As Christine Stansell writes, radicals wanted their women "in the home" not "to shed their sacred influence . . . but to submit to the benign authority of a republican patriarch." But even this was an ideal not easily realized. Radicals, after all, could not afford idle wives and daughters any more than most other workmen. As wage earners, moreover, they had firsthand knowledge of the hardships female outworkers and textile operatives faced. They excoriated employers who took advantage of women and in the most extreme cases supported the struggles of female workers. But understanding ended there: radicals saw no public role for women.

· · ·

Despite these limitations, radicals provided a strong alternative to early free laborism. What the entrepreneurs who unfurled Whig and Democratic banners understood to be economic opportunity, radicals condemned as greed, avarice, and "legal robbery," convinced, as they were, that one man's gain was another's loss. They distrusted the self-made men in control of mainstream politics; the homilies of evangelized businessmen and their clerical allies were singularly offensive to them. They scoffed at those who preached that frugality and sobriety overcame inequality built into the system, that misfortune was one's own fault. "Not all the fervent intercessions of prayer," Heighton wrote, "nor all the influence of pathetic exhortation, can ever arrest the progress of sin while the system of . . . competition is supported." Radicals applauded Democratic assaults on evangelicalism and "class legislation," but for different reasons. Democrats lambasted corpulent bankers and silk-stocking manufacturers for squeezing out competition; radicals denounced accumulators for being exploitative and doing producers out of the "full product of their toil." They cheered wildly when Andrew Jackson killed Nicholas Biddle's monster bank in 1832, but felt let down when he sheathed his sword after a single blow. They had anticipated a more sweeping assault that would bring down the village wildcatter with the urban grandee.

The irony is that radicals found hope in the devastations of the market revolution. The economic processes that uprooted the yeoman and turned masters into journeymen swelled productive labor into a majority with the capacity to act upon a radical agenda. Journeymen would not succeed, however, by spontaneous action or militant strikes directed by disciplined unions, even though trade societies were seen as necessary. Nor could they expect much from the informal discourse and shop talk of earlier days that sustained plebeian politics from one generation to the next. Workers had to be organized and schooled in the causes of inequality, shown another way through lyceums, reading rooms, and a press of their own making. Theirs had to be a broad approach that was at once economic, political, and cultural.

3.

Movement Culture and Received Culture

Philadelphia was not only the adoptive city of one of Jacksonian America's magisterial working-class intellectuals, William Heighton. It was also the cradle of the nation's labor movement, a movement that would go through a political and then a union phase. The formation of the Working Men's party of Philadelphia in 1828 touched off a political rebellion that saw Working Men's parties, People's parties, and Working Men's Republican Associations storm the political barricades in scores of cities and towns in sixteen states. As labor politics faded at the turn of the 1820s, workers took their cue from New Yorkers who in 1833 banded together in the General Trades' Union of New York. Within two years federations of craft unions agitated urban centers along the East Coast north of Washington and throughout the Midwest, only to be stopped in their tracks by the panic of 1837. In the ensuing seven-year depression evangelical ministers and ethnic politicians stepped into the void left by unionism, while the huge increase in European immigration during the late 1840s and 1850s reinforced intraclass discord. Unionism revived and class conflict persisted in late antebellum America, but both were subordinate to the politics of ethnicity and free labor.

How do we account for the ebb and flow of the labor movement? The historian Lawrence Goodwyn has offered a conceptual frame of reference for probing the anatomy of what he calls the "movement culture" of American Populism that may be applied to worker insurgencies. To Goodwyn, and to anthropologist Sidney Mintz, culture is a kind of social resource, a constellation of beliefs, practices, and organizations that deny or confirm conventional arrangements of "status, power and identity." Cultures may therefore be either oppositional or accommodative; they may dare the status quo or confirm it. Oppositional cultures become movement cultures when they develop organizations and ideologies for mobilizing the dispossessed in the name of democracy or equality.

Goodwyn's movement cultures evolve through four distinct phases. They begin with producer or consumer cooperatives that nurture collective economic activity. Recruitment is next, followed by the establishment of educational and agitational groups that disseminate beliefs consistent with the collective endeavor. The movement then becomes politicized through an independent party informed by a democratic agenda. As Goodwyn is quick to point out, however, the progression from one stage to the next is not always smooth. Movements may defeat themselves by skipping one or more of these processes, recruiting members, for instance, without educating them, or jumping into third-party politics without cultivating a constituency. Popular insurgencies may also divide from within over racial, ethnic, or ideological discord, or they may limit their reach by overlooking or excluding benighted groups. At the same time movement cultures face opposition, both co-optive and repressive, from the "received culture," the "rules, manners, power relations, and memories" that secure the existing order.

. . .

The radical founders of the labor movement also had to overcome received cultures. There were journeymen in the myriad tiny shops that retained the fraternal social relations of quieter times. The St. Louis iron molder Henry Brokmeyer learned his trade in just such a workplace. Brokmeyer's employer no longer boarded apprentices or journeymen, as did many small shopkeepers, but he still took a personal interest in them. He and his foreman patiently walked Brokmeyer through the various methods, from building sand molds to pouring metal, and carefully inspected his output. They firmly reprimanded him for his mistakes, complimented work well done, and as one expects of confident tradesmen observant of craft custom, discouraged the exuberant student from working too hard and rushing too much. When Brokmeyer was promoted to journeyman, he carried on with hardly any supervision and counted boss and foreman among his closest friends. They would gossip on the job and treat one another to beer at the corner tavern. A hunting holiday became a paid vacation when the boss handed over two weeks' pay, "a handsome way," wrote an elated Brokmeyer, "of saying thank you, Mr. B—for the trip." Henry Brokmeyer did not have much time for unions or labor agitators.

Neither did workers in the employ of paternalists. The paternalism of Lowell did not affect men, for male workers were not required to live in the dormitories or attend chapel. But they did have to submit to the likes of Dirk Boott, the haughty Anglophile and first agent of Lowell, who screened out potential dissidents, routinely fired ten-hour men and Democrats, and brooked no insubordination from anyone. Linus Child, Boott's successor, was even more imperious. Machinists and spinners were so anxious to please, it was said, that they left the Democrats for the Whigs and canvassed for the party on company time and money. They also addressed him as "the Squire" or "Squire Child." Rituals of deference were even more deeply ingrained in Southern textile hands. Such workers may have been slow to adjust to industrial work rhythms but most appreciated the chance to work at all and looked upon employers as benefactors who bailed them out of rural poverty. "I am thankful," said a woman spinner, "to be as well off as I am."

Small employers, loath to interfere in the political life of employees, had natural allies in evangelical workers. Devout Christians, to be sure, were not uniformly submissive or gulled into church by scheming bosses. More ambitious workmen took to worship on their own accord, even though some employers "insisted upon seeing" their hands "in church," as one historian of the Second Great Awakening observes. "I don't give a d—," said a worker on the roll of a proprietor under attack for favoring churchgoers. "I get five dollars a month more than before I got religion." Church membership held other advantages for artisans on the way up. Socially prominent parishioners might endorse their wares in the local press, lend start-up capital at discount, or agree to form silent partnerships. Needy workers also derived benefits from church affiliation. John Gough, the reverent Methodist of English lineage who arrived in New York City from upstate with a "dollar only in . . . [his] pocket" in the early 1830s, looked up an influential minister, who got him a job as an errand boy and then apprentice bookbinder at the church press. Gough worked his way up to journeyman but respected his employers and never stepped foot in a union hall.

Evangelized women also abjured the necessity of class conflict. Many of them, to be sure, violated the "Cult of True Womanhood," a direct outgrowth of the new Protestantism, by taking a public stand against the unchristian abominations of slavery and intemperance, and in some instances, against their own confinement. Most women moral reformers, however, were of middle-class origins, and even then theirs was a partial rebelliousness that stopped at the workshop door. Very few if any found fault with the market revolution or the exploitation of female labor.

In the South slavery and pervasive racism subsumed class divisions within the ruling race. White Southerners understood that the slave embodied capital and labor in one and that to attack slavery was to attack private property, the linchpin of capitalism in the South as well as the North. Every now and then a dissident voice was heard. In 1838 a Georgia mechanic warned planters that white workmen could bring down slavery by becoming "masters of the polls in a majority, carrying all before it." While few workers favored abolition, there were no unambiguous defenders of the system. Some may have accepted the free labor cant of a slave in every household, just as some Northern workers believed they would rise out of their class. Most realized that slavery was both a labor system, which protected them from objectionable work, and a caste system, which kept the races separate, locked the blacks in their place, and fostered a semblance of social equality among whites. Slavery attenuated the glaring social distinctions within the master race and created the illusion of "white egalitarianism."

Slavery also proved troublesome to white labor. Industrial slaves endangered white livelihoods, and as free laborist William Gregg was quick to point out, chattels could be used to defeat whites in times of labor unrest. John Anderson, principal owner and superintendent of the Tredegar Iron Works, showed what Gregg had in mind when in 1841 he began to upgrade the skills of his slaves both to cut labor costs and to muffle his white workers' talk of unionism. Six years later in 1847 he summarily fired the whites who went on strike to prevent the introduction of the slaves into the rolling mill. "Such combinations," said Anderson in an argument often heard, "are a direct attack on slave property," and could not be tolerated. The Whiggish *Richmond Times and Compiler* likewise condemned the work stoppage as a "frontal assault" on the "rights and privileges of the master, and if acknowleged . . . will soon destroy the value of slave property."

White workers in the South found themselves enmeshed in a system that both helped and harmed them. Small wonder that beyond the question of abolition their response was ambiguous. In the border states, where slavery was losing its ideological grip, white journeymen sometimes unionized or fought for better wages and working conditions. In the Deep South unionism was as weak as slavery was strong. Throughout the region industrial slavery drove masters and journeymen together in an alliance that sought to drive slavery from the workshop and factory so as to confine it to the plantation and household. Even then, slavery determined the tactics of its critics. Strikes rarely produced results, and as the Tredegar strike indicated, they could also backfire. Political action aimed at restricting or barring the use of slaves in the mechanical pursuits was less risky but seldom successful because of the political power of the planter class. White workers were left to cope with profound racial and class resentments they simply could not resolve.

Received cultures do not always originate in society's upper reaches or in its middle. For evidence of this one need look no further than the libertine street life of the antebellum city with its raucous gangs and fire laddies, bustling markets, sleazy bars, and tippling houses. These were the resorts of the lower middle class and the poor—grocers and street vendors, sweated tradesmen, casual laborers, and, above all, apprentices who made a religion of hard drinking, avenging insults to manhood and neighborhood pride, humiliating rival gangs and fire companies. Such belligerence could extend to overbearing employers. The mayhem and riot that flared up along canal routes and on city docks were often occasioned by strikes in which aggrieved ditchdiggers and coal heavers took out their frustrations on foremen and, if need be, strikebreakers. Violence hid a militant class consciousness that reflected an acute sense of social difference but not an alternative social vision.

Politics constituted another aspect of received culture. The so-called second party system of Whigs and Democrats closed the curtain on the pre-party age in which family and faction shaped political affinity and the rich and wellborn stood for office without opposition. Politics had been a gentleman's game played out at the highest social reaches before a disinterested public. All that came to an end in the 1830s with the ballyhoo engendered by mass parties, feverishly partisan presses, and fiercely loyal followings activated in heated contests by the party "machinery." The industrial metaphor is appropriate. Whig and Democrat adapted market practice to politics by advertising candidates and hawking platforms with the hyperbole of the entrepreneur. Voter turnout soared to 80 percent by the 1840s and not because of the political climate alone. While many artisans had exercised the right to vote in spite of property qualifications, the movement for white male universal suffrage between 1815 and 1840 greatly enlarged the electorate. Here lay a source of the social configuration of the parties and the comparatively low level of working-class consciousness. American workers achieved the franchise without a struggle at the dawn of the industrial revolution before class relations deteriorated or social divisions hardened. In Europe workmen had to fight for the right to vote, and that fight turned into a class war that extended into the industrial revolution. The politicization of class struggle on the Continent sharpened the social consciousness of all classes and increased the likelihood that enfranchised workmen would support the party of their class. In Europe political and class lines were parallel, while in the United States, where such political conflicts were largely unknown and class loyalties correspondingly weak, parties crossed class boundaries. Party organizations cut deeply into the social structure and thwarted the politics of class. In the late 1820s and early 1830s, of course, the American worker was not yet integrated into the mainstream parties because both were new and only developing into mass organizations. Partisan affinities were still in formation, but workers had to be lured from the politics of nascent free laborism and convinced of the politics of radicalism.

The movement that challenged these received cultures flowed out of the agitation for the ten-hour day in the late 1820s. In summer 1827 Philadelphia journeymen, on the heels of an unsuccessful strike for shorter hours by construction workers, flocked to a meeting called by William Heighton. At Heighton's urging they formed the Mechanics' Union of Trade Associations, the nation's first citywide federation of local unions. Though the MUTA began as a union, the delegates at a January 1828 meeting endorsed a resolution drafted by Heighton calling for the organization of the Working Men's party. This precedent, plus rumors that employers considered extending the workday, stirred New York City radicals to follow suit within a year. A Committee of Fifty, appointed at a rally in the Bowery and headed by Thomas Skidmore, discussed strike strategies but continued to meet when the threat passed. A midsummer gathering voted to enter the 1829 municipal elections under the Working Men's standard. In New England the long workday had vexed labor since the mid-1820s. Twice in five years, in 1825 and again in 1830, Boston construction workers were beaten in ten-hour stand-outs and then turned to an independent party in 1830. As in New York and Pennsylvania, the Boston movement radiated outward from city to country, dotting village and small-town New England with Working Men's parties that coalesced into a statewide organization for the 1831 elections. While the Massachusetts Working Men's party did not survive the year, the hours question simmered. A fall 1831 meeting in Providence of ten-hour men that denied capital's "absolute and unconditional right" to set the terms of work scheduled a second conclave in Boston the following February that spawned the New England Association of Farmers, Mechanics, and Other Working Men, a broadly based union with electoral ambitions.

"From Maine to Georgia," wrote a New Jersey labor journalist in the midst of the turmoil, "we discern symptoms of a revolution, which will be second to none since '76.'' The parallel with the Revolution was weak. These soldiers were not revolutionaries-in-arms, and they did not always march to the same drummer. Rural and small-town organizations were labor parties in name only, shadowy groups hastily patched together on the eve of elections and in disarray after a single campaign. Many were headed by political "outs," opportunists in search of constituencies, or entrepreneurs playing at politics or using Working Men's podiums to launch political careers. The Working Men of Erie County, Pennsylvania, was the brainchild of National Republicans and latter-day Whigs in overalls promoting the "American System." Elsewhere maverick Democrats brushed aside by party regulars latched on to the Working Men but retired after a race or two. Some urban parties suffered equally from the loss of summer soldiers. Boston's laborists were indistinguishable from National Republicans; Newark's were interchangeable with Democrats.

Most metropolitan parties, however, enjoyed an authentic artisanal influence. Journeymen staffed committees and directed field staffs, even though nominees included entrepreneurs and petty professionals endorsed by mainstream parties. Party manifestos combined modest with sweeping reforms. Most asked for the abolition of imprisonment for debt, mandatory militia duty, and the use of prison labor, for a cheaper legal system and more equitable tax laws, and for mechanics' lien laws that assured workers first rights to employers' payrolls. Some called for improving the quality of urban life by extending water and sanitation services already enjoyed by the rich to neighborhoods of the poor. What made the Working Men radical were planks designed to bridle monopoly and speculation and preserve the small shop and independent farm. Some stumped for wider access to the soil, none more aggressively than Skidmore's partisans in New York; all railed against charters of incorporation for banks and manufacturing companies. Since radicals deplored ignorance as much as monopoly, they also demanded "republican education." New Englanders were content with free public schools for all in place of the dual system of separate classrooms for the rich and poor. Philadelphians showed more originality with a plan for comprehensive education that included kindergartens and technical institutes along with common schools funded by stiff taxes on liquor dealers. Robert Dale Owen's forces in New York were even bolder in proposing the "state guardian system" of publicly supported boarding schools that Owen had attended as a youth in Switzerland.

Working Men ran lively campaigns that anticipated the pageantry of the developing party system. They canvassed working-class wards, distributed handbills and voting tickets, and held open-air rallies that recalled the spectacles of Revolutionary times. Crowds sometimes numbering in the thousands heard worker orators assail the effects of the market revolution, the growing distance between those who worked with their hands and those who did not. The Working Men of suburban Philadelphia deplored the polarization into "two distinct classes, the rich and the poor; the oppressor and the oppressed; those that live by their own labor, and they that live upon the labor of others." Colleagues in the city center attacked authoritarian school directors who treated students like "convicts of the work-house, having to submit to the tyrannized government of masters." Seth Luther, leader of the New England Association, knew adult despotism from the inside. The former textile hand condemned the region's factories as "palaces of the poor, a cruel system of exaction on the bodies and minds of the producing classes."

Yet Working Men were a meteor in the political sky. In Philadelphia they polled well in 1828 and even better in 1829, tripling their initial vote to over 30 percent of the total. They had achieved a balance of power in 1829, but were a spent force by 1831. New York City "Workies" made an auspicious entry in the 1829 race by capturing a third of the vote for the state assembly and coming within a dozen ballots of sending Skidmore to Albany. No sooner had the cheering stopped than factional discord sundered the fledgling party. The moderate followers of Noah Cook, always uneasy with Skidmore's "General Division," first allied themselves with Owen's "state guardian" faction to expel the agrarians, and then turned on the Owenites. As a result, the 1830 race saw three pretenders to the Working Men's colors, each stronger in conviction than popularity. The 1832 race, in which the Cook faction merged with the National Republicans and the Owenites with the Democrats, ended the role of the Working Men. Luther's New England Association, which entered the Massachusetts gubernatorial contests in 1833 and 1834, never collected more than 5 percent of the vote statewide and did best in rural towns.

Several factors conspired to undo the Working Men. Inept organization and the mischief of interlopers hampered urban and rural Working Men equally. First-timers and political neophytes headed all parties, and sometimes this told in embarrassing ways. In 1830 upstate New Yorkers called a convention to be held in Albany in preparation for the gubernatorial race, but neglected to inform downstate brethren who had inaugurated the Working Men's movement. When the Gothamites did show up, the convention had to choose between rival delegations of Cook loyalists and Owenites. It tapped the Cook men after a stormy session and then nominated Tammany renegade Erastus Root for governor, but Root soon backed out and left the divided party without a candidate. Regional differences also hurt because rural distrust of the city could not be overcome. Backwoods and textile New England were at one in cursing speculative middlemen and acquisitive factory owners, but the Working Men's party was more in tune with the sensibilities of cash-poor subsistence farmers than with textile operatives or artisans. At a time when urban workmen hit the hustings for strengthened public services, rural insurgents fought for less government and lighter tax bills. Workers who read the Massachusetts Working Men's broadsides must have been amazed in 1831 when the party chose wealthy sheep rancher and textile entrepreneur "Squire" Henry Shaw to run for governor. The New England Association, successor to the Working Men's party in the region, showed more acumen but not much in nominating Samuel Cresson Allen for governor of Massachusetts in 1833 and 1834. The eccentric minister and erstwhile Federalist polled no better among workers than Shaw had.

Although conventional parties were new, they boasted more experienced political talent, commanded superior resources, and wielded more authority outside as well as inside the political arena. National Republican journalists teamed up with evangelical ministers to smear the Working Men as "infidels" and "Jacobins." Employers were said to have threatened to dismiss employees sympathetic to the Working Men, and as a result, fumed the *Mechanics' Free Press,* some workers were "driven *through fear of losing their places,* to bow to this galling yoke." Democrats pursued a co-optive strategy that peaked in the heralded "Bank War" of 1832 but began earlier when urban party activists scurried to undercut the Working Men. In the late 1820s city Democrats appropriated the language of radicalism and advocated debtor relief, militia reform, and other measures borrowed from the Working Men's platforms. Such tactics lent legitimacy to the Democratic party as the voice of the common man and siphoned off votes from the Working Men.

Seen in the context of "movement building," the political phase of the labor movement proved deficient in the leaven of a movement culture. Unions and cooperatives that could have served as centers of recruitment and agents for instilling class loyalty remained underdeveloped except in Philadelphia; even there the Mechanics' Union of Trade Associations, parent of the Working Men's party, withered as leaders turned their energies to politics. The movement's pungent press and evocative campaigns gave wider vent to radicalism but waned because of voter apathy. Labor spokesmen, absorbed in the party, failed to build organizations for an effective movement culture. In dooming independent politics, the Working Men also left a bitter and enduring political memory. Labor advocates who assumed control of the union phase of the labor movement in the early 1830s, and many former Working Men themselves, soured on third-party politics and vowed to keep trade unionism free from partisanship. This gave the received political cultures of orthodox parties the opportunity to consolidate popular constituencies.

The failure of labor politics followed by worsening standards of living delivered the early 1830s to trade unionism. A rash of wildcat banks unleashed in part by Jackson's destruction of the U.S. Bank flooded the market with paper money, setting off a sharp inflationary spiral. From 1834 through 1836 the general price index climbed 25 percent, but the cost of necessities outstripped even this high rate of inflation. In 1836 Eastern grain merchants got nearly $12 a barrel for flour that had fetched only $5.00 two years earlier, and landlords who let space for $25 a year were demanding $40. Journeymen also faced greater insecurity, not from mechanization, but from the relentless division of labor. In addition, employers tightened up shop discipline and ignored wage standards customarily set by journeymen. The labor press rang out with complaints of "usurpation of authority."

Baltimore hatters and New York carpenters were the first to react. Both left their jobs in wage disputes in 1833 that a decade before would have been isolated events unworthy of much attention. But unity incited by the Working Men's movement carried over into workshops and called forth a wider response. Journeymen in both cities, then in the process of organizing their own unions, dug deeply into their pockets. New York tailors and masons raised $300 for the carpenters' strike fund in an unprecedented demonstration of brotherhood. Rising class awareness led New York printers to call a meeting to consider bolder action. Several gatherings and one month later, in August, New Yorkers inaugurated the General Trades' Union, the decade's first citywide confederation of tradesmen. Similar central unions took hold in Philadelphia, Boston, Baltimore, and Washington and then in Louisville, Cincinnati, and other trans-Allegheny cities. By the end of 1834 over a dozen urban centers had general unions.

The trade union phase of the labor movement had a narrower geographic reach but a deeper and wider following within the working class than its political predecessor. No unions admitted women and

Philadelphia's alone would welcome the unskilled, but all grew beyond their original base in the sweated trades. Such privileged workmen as jewelers and goldsmiths along with impoverished hand-loom weavers unionized and joined hands. By 1835 the General Trades' Union of Philadelphia counted no fewer than fifty-three locals (three and one-half times the number of the old Mechanics' Union), one more than its New York counterpart. No other federation came close, but even city centrals in the burgeoning frontier cities of Buffalo and Cincinnati had a dozen member unions. While estimates vary on the proportion of organized workers, it is likely that between one-fifth and one-third of urban journeymen belonged to unions, the highest in antebellum history.

These general unions did not differ much. Loosely modeled on the structure of the federal government, they consisted of two deliberative bodies and an executive. Monthly conventions of delegates elected by member unions on a proportionate basis heard debate and made policy. Convention delegates also elected officers who served for a year or six months and set up ad hoc and standing committees. The committee on finance, with one representative from each affiliate, approved all appropriations. The costs of operating borne from capitation taxes as well as emergency levies and voluntary contributions went into war chests to assist unions on strike and to support newspapers, libraries, and lyceums along with guest lecturers. Far from being appendages, these cultural and educational activities formed the core at this stage of the labor movement. Monthly lectures and debates, periodic rallies and demonstrations, and an edifying labor press that reported news and reprinted radical tracts—all these spoke to a revitalized movement culture with a new emphasis. Whether labor politicians realized it or not, their foray into independent parties had exposed both the limits and the vulnerability of political radicalism. Apart from Skidmore's agrarianism and Owen's "state guardianship," which never gained much currency, radicalism sounded very like the free laborism of the Democratic party. Political radicalism presented few fresh policies Democrats did not endorse or would not claim as their own, Jackson's war on the U.S. Bank being the most poignant example. The combination of radicalism and unionism, however, nudged worker and politician further apart since unions were only for workers and most political figures were critics of unions. The new autonomy told in two ways: it fostered an upsurge of militancy on the job and then instigated a search for options to capitalist institutions that transcended anything political radicalism had to offer.

That worker militancy arose over the ten-hour day is easily understood.

No issue elicited such intense feeling or garnered wider support than the length of the workday: if radicals, evangelicals, and everyone in between could agree on nothing else, they craved more leisure time. But no objective proved more elusive. Strikes had come up short, and the Working Men's parties, fueled though they were by ten-hour fervor, never incorporated the shorter workday into their manifestos. The only form the ten-hour demand could take in such a political context was a legal limitation on the hours of work, and no one, above all working-class carriers of the republican torch, could imagine such a solution: legislation that benefited workers was still class legislation. Nonetheless, ten-hour feeling outlived the Working Men. It ran highest in Boston, the scene of two unsuccessful strikes for ten hours by construction workers in 1825 and 1830. Baltimore workers agitated the cause in 1833 without much success, and two years later Boston journeymen regained the initiative. In spring 1835 Hub City journeymen prepared to try again, this time with the backing of the sixteen societies of different crafts within the General Trades' Union, but encountered unanticipated resistance. They admitted "friendly" master craftsmen to the GTU, only to discover that sympathy had its limits. The masters stacked a committee ordered to investigate the possibility of a general strike and wrote a temperate report recommending action by individual trades. The journeymen persisted and went ahead with plans for a general work stoppage in a monthlong organizing effort driven by rallies and shop meetings. Some strikes were already in full swing when Boston tradesmen assembled at Julien Hall in early May. Resolutions proclaiming labor's natural right to "dispose of our time in such quantities as we deem and believe most conducive to our happiness" provided a fitting introduction to the featured speaker, Seth Luther. In a passionate address crammed with republican allusions, Luther denied it was the place of "any man or body of men . . . to require . . . that we should toil as we hitherto have done under the old system of labor." The new system of republican labor that promised moral uplift and self-cultivation, he assured a spellbound audience, was within reach.

Reprinted and widely distributed throughout the Northeast as the "Ten Hour Circular," Luther's words set off an explosion of strikes that would not be duplicated until the labor turbulence on the railroads in 1877. The journeymen of Salem, Hartford, and cities as far west as Cincinnati either stopped work or served employers with demands for ten hours. In Philadelphia, Luther's message arrived as Irish day laborers marched through the city chanting "six to six!"—catchphrase of the short-hours movement. The "Circular" became the talk of the pubs and workshops, further exciting emotions aroused by the laborers' show of strength. Workmen dashed from shops and construction projects to join a line of march that swelled with each block and reached mammoth proportions by nightfall. Their spontaneity led to a rapid succession of union meetings that emitted a flood of strike resolutions and then massive open-air meetings directed by Trades' Union officials. Some journeymen proclaimed triumph within a week but walked picket lines with comrades still on strike. By the end of June at least twenty trades were picketing and perhaps twice that number were back on the job satisfied with ten-hour schedules. It was a glorious Fourth of July, a cause for toasting what John Ferral called "our bloodless revolution," not only for Quaker City workmen but journeymen everywhere—except Boston. It was ironic that the city where it all began witnessed no celebrations: Boston masters and merchant capitalists prevailed for the third time in ten years.

The general strike was not exclusively a male drama. Women textile hands in Philadelphia, Paterson, and New England villages apart from Lowell mounted strikes that resulted in compromise settlements for eleven-hour days. Nor were these the only job actions of the women who worked at loom and spindle. Dover, New Hampshire, and Pawtucket, Rhode Island, operatives had earlier left their machines to reverse changes in work rules and wage reductions: the most notable rebellions broke out in textile mills at Lowell, in 1834, to thwart a rate cut, and then in 1836 to fend off an increase in board. The first ended in defeat for the women, the second in compromise, but neither was supposed to have occurred at all, not under the gentle hand of paternalism that was Lowell's trademark. The causes of unrest lay in the very system contrived to shield allegedly frail operatives from the harsher aspects of modernizing production. The prepared meals and decorous rooms of the boardinghouses for Lowell women may have been better than their sisters in the needle trades had, but they were no defense against the whims of the market, much less the authority of the Boston Associates, owners of the Lowell factories. When cotton prices collapsed in 1834, the Boston men did not hesitate to slash wages a thumping 25 percent or boost rents two years later. On the other hand, the relatively narrow compass of mill recruitment reunited neighbor and kin: the intimacy of the boardinghouses solidified friendships and sealed new ones that created unity in periods of protest and labor tension. Millhands also shared a profound sense of indignation rooted in common republican beliefs. To them, manufacturer and foreman resembled the court favorites of King George III or, worse, the plantation tyrants of the South. In the 1836 strike they censured this "kind of slavery" and marched through the streets of Lowell singing:

> Oh! Isn't it a pity, such a pretty girl as I—
> Should be sent to the factory to pine away and die?
>> Oh! I cannot be a slave,
>> I will not be a slave,
> For I'm so fond of liberty
> That I cannot be a slave.

Wage slavery in the North! This is one of the first references we have to what would become the battle cry of Northern workers by the Civil War and continue into the latter half of the century. Such workers likened dependence on wages to the predicament of chattel slaves in the South. Wage slavery was a powerful image but a sectional one rarely invoked south of Philadelphia. It was too easily mistaken for abolitionism to be heard in the Cotton Kingdom.

But neither noble sentiment nor the solidarity of sorority was enough in Lowell. Being unskilled and single, the operatives were more easily replaced than male artisans and more mobile than married workers of both genders. They could return to their homes to wait out strikes or hard times; they could move on; or, as was often the case, they could marry and leave gainful employment. Turnover for unmarried women was high, the average stay at Lowell was about two years, and thus the informal work groups that sustained job actions were weak.

Seamstresses and shoe binders employed at home or in garrets ran into even greater barriers to effective organization. Most were indigent widows and young girls earning a fraction of a textile worker's income; they were mired in the loosest labor markets. An army of idle and desperate hands bid down wages, dampened the courage of the employed, and could be pressed into service as strikebreakers. Since most working women in the shoe and clothing trades were employed in urban homes or farmhouses under the putting-out system, they were, in contrast to the operatives, widely dispersed, difficult to reach, and strangers to one another. Those that did catch the contagion of unionism in the mid-1830s managed to create only fleeting organizations more akin to strike committees. In Philadelphia they won the support of male shoemakers and tailors in the GTU who volunteered to work with their strike committees and arrange fund-raisers. Most journeymen, however, looked upon women's entry into craft work as unwelcome incursions and stated their antipathies in condescending terms, if not in the idiom of the "Cult of True Womanhood." New York's tailors greeted the Tailoresses' Society, a union of 1,600 needle workers, with the discouraging assertion that women's "physical organization . . . and moral sensibilities" best suited them for domestic chores. The National Trades' Union, a conclave of urban unionists that met once a year from 1834 to 1836, elaborated on this view in a report on female labor in 1836. While earnestly recommending unions to all female workers, the report also predicted a dark future made darker because women's labor and mechanization would "entirely supersede the necessity of male labor." Its blunt conclusion was that wage work for women "must be destroyed by gradual means." Between the constraints of labor markets and the opposition of males there was not much opportunity for women's unionism.

Male unionism, of course, was another matter. There was no better advertisement for trade unionism than the general strikes of 1835. Those revolts put fight into tradesmen with weak union traditions or none at all. Horseshoers, brush makers, and others got together for the first time and entered the General Trades' Unions. Established unions overflowed with new members, poor immigrants as well as some evangelicals, and locals took the first steps toward coordinating activities between cities. National gatherings of printers, shoemakers, and house carpenters discussed strengthening apprenticeship, fixing uniform wage scales, and establishing traveling cards that gave migrating craftsmen who belonged to a union in one place automatic membership in another. Not much came of these meetings as unions bent their energies to keeping up with inflation in a spate of strikes for wage advances. In 1836 New York craftsmen went out at least ten times, Philadelphia's artisans struck even more often—all with the help of Trades' Union subsidies and extraordinary acts of solidarity from individual unions. Tailors and hand-loom weavers, many of them Irish earning subsistence wages, took up collections for striking bookbinders and others in the more remunerative callings. Such favored craftsmen returned the favor when the weavers took to the streets.

The strike wave of 1836 set off a reaction. New York City and Philadelphia entrepreneurs regrouped into trade societies that vowed to bust strikes and destroy unions. New York entrepreneurs had better luck if only because of the interventions of courts and police forces. In late winter a New York court found in favor of master stonecutters who had sued journeymen for damages resulting from a strike; several months later merchant tailors had twenty journeymen convicted of conspiracy.

Between these courtroom battles trouble erupted on the New York waterfront, where dockers and riggers paraded to call attention to demands for better pay. The police arrived on the scene and paused long enough to scuffle with both groups before heading off to the site of yet another stand-out, this by unskilled laborers a few blocks away. They coaxed the laborers back to work and returned to the waterfront to arrest militant dockers. When the strike continued the mayor ordered out the militia, and though the soldiers drilled at City Hall far from dockside, the prospect of armed intervention sent the men back to their jobs. Waterfront workers on the Schuylkill in Philadelphia also ran afoul of the authorities in the spring of 1836. Coal merchants, frustrated over failures to attract strikebreakers, called on Mayor Swift, who not only clapped the leaders into jail but set bail at $2,500. The severe treatment meted out to skilled and unskilled labor in both cities brought angry responses from Trades' Unionists. A New York rally said to have drawn an astounding 30,000 protesters condemned the repression. Philadelphia demonstrations were smaller but just as defiant, and in at least one sense, unprecedented. Trades' Unionists voted to admit the dock men into their ranks, marking the first formal alliance of skilled and unskilled labor.

While the streets and public squares in larger cities teemed with restive workmen, trade union radicals stepped back to assess their movement. They did so with a mixture of pride and concern. On the one hand, the scattered trade unionism of 1833 had turned into a broad movement with an impressive record. Mutualism had improved living standards, checked employer authority, and delivered the crowning achievement—the ten-hour day. On the other hand, radicals worried that the militancy of 1835–36 risked becoming an endless cycle of strikes that deflected attention from the larger purpose of social reconstruction—arresting the competitive frenzy and constructing alternatives to the institutions of capitalism. In the summer of 1836 radicals began to warn against dissipating energies and squandering resources on work stoppages. As a report of the National Trades' Union put it, "a more permanent" solution had to be found.

That solution was cooperative production. During the second half of 1836 labor journalists and lecturers enthusiastically recommended worker-owned shops and forcefully argued their case at the annual convention of the National Trades' Union. Several delegates spoke in favor of cooperation on the convention floor and a few managed to weave it into a committee report on the causes of inflation. The report acknowledged fluctuating currencies issued by wildcat banks but transcended this axiom of middle-class radicalism by singling out the imperatives of the industrial revolution, "the division of workingmen into employers and journeymen." "If therefore," it continued, "the mechanics sold their labor directly to the consumer, speculation would cease, and they would receive the full product." Cooperation would also reverse the erosion of artisanship, the dilution of skills, by affording mechanics "absolute control over the disposal of . . . [their] labor." This version of cooperation was not the individualist piety that made "every man a capitalist," as some historians have maintained, but a collective project to achieve social equality and worker control.

The discovery of cooperation marked a major tactical departure. Radicals, after all, had warred against the market economy with the feeble politics of antimonopoly. Now they were armed with a cause that offered a closer, if by no means perfect, fit between means and ends, a different means of structuring productive relations. They also had a new didactic instrument, for cooperation was more than an abstract ideal: it could be practiced, it could deepen collective experience. In addition, cooperation might broaden the base of radicalism by appealing to cautious workers disturbed by conflicts with employers. To these workmen, cooperation was balm for the social wounds inflicted by the strikes of the immediate past.

On the other hand, cooperation was no panacea. It had no relevance to unskilled labor or to textile and metallurgical workers in advanced industries that required substantial capital outlays. Its strongest supporters were craftsmen in small workplaces using simple technology in producing for local markets. These workmen still had to come up with capital, and this need exposed another shortcoming of radicalism. Radicals did not consider banks, which were unlikely lenders in any case, and given their view of government, they did not consider a public creditor. The only option was the voluntary effort of labor itself.

Radicals devoted the second half of 1836 to publicizing the virtues of collectively owned workshops. They used the lecture hall and labor press to explain the advantages over entrepreneurial enterprises, and helped unions to set up cooperatives. The gradual appearance of numerous worker-owned shops suggests that cooperation had become the major thrust of the movement culture, the pivotal point that turned members from strikes to the "more permanent" solution recommended by the National Trades' Union. Nonetheless, resources were needed to sustain these enterprises and assist in forming others. It remained to persuade delegates to amend central labor union constitutions so that funds earmarked for strikes could be diverted to support cooperative ventures. Unionists discussed such proposals in early 1837, but the financial panic that plunged the country into a seven-year depression not only cut short the debate but tilted the movement in a different direction. Radicals, in what can only be described as an ideological retreat, railed not against capitalism but against financiers and speculators. They condemned the "money changers" before immense crowds until the despair of extended unemployment set in during 1838. Rally grounds emptied, general unions disintegrated, and the few unions that did survive turned into friendly societies dispensing funds to jobless members. The labor movement died with a whimper.

· · ·

Reports of deepening hardships filled the press. In a few short years irregular employment and unremitting wage cuts erased the advances of unionism. But 1840, midpoint of the depression, worker earnings dipped from a third to a fifth of 1836 scales: journeymen who had commanded $10 and $6.00 a week were getting $7.00 and $4.50, respectively. A Cincinnati tailor who "found it impossible to gain a livelihood" in 1840 was pressed even harder by additional rate cuts over the next two years. Some workmen took out frustrations on one another. In early September 1841 a mob of desperate workers in Cincinnati went on a weekend rampage of the city's black ghetto. Nearly a year later Philadelphia's Irish laborers and hand-loom weavers assaulted a procession of blacks commemorating Jamaican Emancipation Day. To be sure, these were not the first race riots. White and black had clashed as early as 1812 in Baltimore and as recently as the mid-1830s in several incidents in Atlantic coast cities, including Washington. In Baltimore white ship carpenters and their apprentices had driven black journeymen and unskilled workers out of some shipyards. But unlike the flare-ups in the past, those in the early 1840s were orgies of brutality that stretched over several days, claimed several lives and scores of injuries, and left black ghettos in charred ruins. Philadelphia's white rioters put the torch to an Afro-American church and temperance hall and obstructed firefighters as the blaze consumed more than twenty additional buildings. The city's hand-loom weavers simultaneously fought employers, who had lowered piece rates by 40 percent, and showed no mercy for fellow tradesmen still at work. Striker turned on strikebreaker in intermittent street fights through 1842 and into 1843.

While the Irish lashed out at blacks and against one another in the

second half of the depression, native-born white workmen turned inward
and away from radicalism. They sought solace in the received culture of
evangelicalism, and emerged from that experience in the mid-1840s more
impressed with nativism and free labor. This outburst of nativism,
followed as it was by the immigration bulge from 1846 to 1857,
fragmented journeymen into clusters of ethnic groups. Given this
climate, it comes as no surprise that the 1830s proved the high-water
mark of a cohesive working-class radicalism. In the 1840s wage earners
remained hopelessly divided.

Ominous signs of cultural balkanization first appeared in the evangelical paroxysms of the Second Great Awakening between 1840 and 1843.
Obscure ministers in storefront churches and urban missions funded by
lay groups looked past the traditional middle-class following of the
Protestant church to urban journeymen. Not even the seamiest neighborhoods deterred these eager divines. Bibles in hand and often accompanied
by plebeian churchwomen in black broadcloth, they preached the gospel
on street corners and pursued converts in workshops, garrets, and even
tippling houses, braving the insults of drinkers half amused and half
outraged. Revivals that droned on for days at a time enraptured workmen
down on their luck and a step away from the soup kitchen. Ministers
convinced penniless workmen that Christ brought on hard times as
retribution for worldly sin, but held out better days and salvation for those
who would mend their ways. Church membership skyrocketed.

Evangelized workmen were by definition practitioners of total abstinence. All teetotalers, however, were not churchgoers or sectarian
Protestants. Labor activists in the 1830s had promoted abstinence even as
they ridiculed the official temperance movement. Growing awareness of
the harmful effects of drink, employer enforcement of temperance in
workplaces, and the obvious need for frugality in the depression further
discouraged consumption of spirits. The trade-based beneficial societies
that flourished in the early depression demanded total abstinence for
admission. No secular group, however, matched the popularity of the
Washington Temperance Society. Founded in 1840 by six Baltimore
artisans and self-described ''reformed drunkards,'' the Washingtonians
became the rage of working-class America within two years. Official
estimates counted 200,000 members in 1841 and 3 million two years
later. Even if these figures are exaggerated, there can be no question that
Washingtonianism exerted a strong influence on the popular imagination.
In 1843, there were probably two to three times as many members of

Washingtonian lodges in major industrial centers as there had been trade unionists at the height of the union movement seven years earlier.

Washingtonianism was not strictly a journeyman's movement. Members included petty entrepreneurs and master craftsmen as well as unskilled laborers in a kind of popular bloc galvanized by the despair of hard times and the millenarian zeal of revivalism. With good reason, one scholar calls the movement a "secularized revival." Much like the evangelical church, this temperance crusade accommodated popular needs and tastes. Washingtonians scoffed at the punitive policies of temperance regulars by rejecting prohibition and the idea that drinkers were misfits. They ministered to the hardened drinker, not the casual user, and extended a sympathetic hand to him. "Expressive meetings" heard emotional testimony from reformed inebriants, "secular missionaries" exhorting others to break their habit. Women's auxiliaries organized Martha Washington lodges, dispensed food and clothing, and, where possible, arranged employment to lift a brother back to his feet. Lodges also sponsored a breathtaking array of amusements, substitutes for the pub and tippling house in the form of libraries and reading rooms, picnics and processions, and theater groups and singing societies that adapted such popular entertainments as minstrel shows to self-reform. This was no bourgeois movement.

Experiences of Washingtonian stalwarts and confessions of ordinary members at "expressive meetings" make it clear that it was no labor movement, either. Very few leaders had histories of trade union involvement. Popular lecturer John Gough, driven to a New York pawnshop for cash in 1834, was even worse off several years later, having buried his mother and watched a fire consume his workplace. The misfortunes exacerbated a drinking problem and the panic threw him out of work, but Gough turned to temperance, not unionism or political radicalism, for help. Fellow Washingtonians likewise attributed their conversion to personal loss, financial distress, or both. John W. Oliver, another national leader, had been a master printer until the "financial difficulties of 1837" leveled him "to . . . journeyman." Gough, Oliver, and others conveyed a message of deliverance wholly at odds with political radicalism or class antagonism. A Baltimore activist is reported to have told a gathering, "Take care of intemperance, and providence will take care of the currency." In the North liquor had replaced monster bank and grinding employer in the demonology of the Protestant worker.

Evangelicalism and temperance fervor cooled with the onset of recovery in 1844. Ohio Washingtonian Samuel Cary also felt that Washingtonianism had lost its popular soul, complaining that nothing was left but "the pledge." But both movements left workers imbued with a new spirit that received two basic expressions. Small-town workers hewed to Christian laborism, big-city colleagues to militant nativism. Each outlook muted class consciousness and paved the road for the Republican party and the ideology of mature free labor.

The New England Workingmen's Association reflected the first of these tendencies. The Association took shape in 1844 as a loose coalition of local unions and labor reform groups in eastern and central Massachusetts. It became a platform for middle-class reformers peddling such pet programs as land reform and Fourierism, a form of utopian socialism. Working-class contingents included Washingtonian lodges that merged with unions or as in Worcester, Massachusetts, sent their own delegations to Association conventions. The Worcester men had assembled a separate Washingtonian society of "True Reformers" when in 1843 middle-class prohibitionists took over the Worcester lodge. A year later they went to the founding convention of the New England Association pledged to "arrest the progress of capitalists in the reduction of the price of labor." Even Washingtonianism had its social tensions.

The biting rhetoric of the Worcester men convinced many labor historians that the New England Association was a house divided between militant, class-conscious workers and fuzzy-minded, middle-class reformers. To Norman Ware, it was William Field Young, the Fitchburg, Massachusetts, harness maker and editor of the Association's *Voice of Industry*, who spoke for labor; Young's recent biographer demonstrates he was no more of a militant than his region's sentimental reformers. Too youthful to have taken part in the labor movement of the 1830s, Young nevertheless was aware of its radical legacy. He used the labor theory of value for blistering polemics against the region's "false and anti-republican" factory system, its "Monied Despotism," and its "corrupt politics." His social vision, however, disclosed an evangelical passion that took the sting out of his radicalism. He saw the depression-era revivals as harbingers of a millennium "big with tendencies for the future." For Young, industrialism pitted the children of light against the children of darkness, not producers against accumulators. His hazy "Christian republic," rooted in biblical injunctions to honest toil, would come about through the peaceful diffusion of Christianity rather than class warfare. Young was a literalist when it came to scriptural teachings on charity and turning the other cheek. An editorial that began with an attack on capitalists "feasting upon the labors, bones, and sinews of God's poor" ended with "Father forgive them for they know not what they do."

Young was hardly idiosyncratic. Fall River and sometimes Boston artisans also invoked the revealed truth of Scripture as they drew back from social confrontation. So did the women operatives at Lowell, who in 1846 vowed to see through their struggle until "slavery and oppression, mental, physical, and religious shall be done away with and Christianity in its original simplicity . . . re-established." The preceding decade had been cruel for these women. They had stayed at the looms during the ten-hour strikes and in the early 1840s worked long after most artisans went home for the day. Some toiled after sundown when production rooms were fitted with oil lamps at the end of the decade, and most worked harder. Lowell weavers who ran a single loom at about 100 beats a minute in 1840 had to operate four machines at 140 beats four years later. The initial stages of the speedup gave rise in 1844 to the Lowell Female Labor Reform Association, a charter member of the New England Association and staging point for the ten-hour movement at Lowell. Female Labor Reform leaders Huldah Stone and Sarah Bagley, who worked with Young on the *Voice of Industry,* shared their colleague's Christian spirit. Like Young and in sharp contrast to area operatives a decade before, they spurned a work stoppage to win the ten-hour day. They tried without success to remind mill agent and minister of Christian obligation and, left without an option, beseeched lawmakers for a ten-hour statute. Petition drives in 1845 and 1846 prompted legislative hearings on mill conditions but failed to disabuse officeholders of the belief that such a statute would violate freedom of contract. As operative protest subsided in Lowell, it picked up in New Hampshire and Pennsylvania. Both states passed ten-hour laws that gave with one hand and took with the other, stipulating ten hours to be a legal day's work while allowing individual employees to contract for overtime.

Short-hours sentiment was not unknown in the South. A Georgia law passed in 1853 cut the workday to "sunrise to sunset, the usual and customary time for meals being allowed," an apparent reference to a ten- or eleven-hour day, for white males and females under twenty-one working in textile mills and machine shops. White workers may have participated in the movement that put the law on the books, but the Georgia Mechanics' Association, a group dominated by masters and manufacturers, took the credit. Whoever led the change, it was the only fruitful one in the entire region: no other Southern state passed a similar law before the Civil War.

One of the more remarkable features of labor evangelicalism was its toleration of religious difference. The Lowell Female Labor Reform Association may have been perceived as a Protestant force by Irish immigrants then coming into the factories but it did not bait Catholics despite their indifference to the cause. Such magnanimity stemmed from the fact that Yankee textile operatives had no skills to protect and were less likely to look upon the Irish as economic competitors. Alternatively, in places like Lowell, Irish religious and social institutions were still primitive and political aspirations modest, or at least not daring enough as yet to upset Yankees.

Far different indeed was the Irish community in the city. The Irish who arrived after 1846 were refugees from the Great Famine that blighted the potato crops and wheat fields of Northwestern Europe during the second half of the 1840s. Former peasants without craft skills or industrial backgrounds, the Famine Generation would in time become strong unionists in America once they settled into their new surroundings and learned the rules of the industrial game. For the greater part of the antebellum period, however, they were more concerned with finding work than struggling to better conditions. The newcomers took more easily to community organizations and ethnic politics than to unionism. From Boston's Fifth Ward to Pittsburgh's riverfront and New Orleans's "Old Third," early Irish settlements had spun a tangle of organizations and institutions, both secular and religious, in the opening years of the 1840s before their impoverished countrymen arrived. Street gangs and fire companies included teenagers and young males proud of things Celtic and quick to defend neighborhoods and egos from the intrusions of outsiders. For the nascent Irish middle class there was the Ancient Order of Hibernians, the leading fraternal lodge, which dispensed welfare payments, and Irish ritual and ceremony. The American Catholic Church responded to inchoate Irish-Catholic self-consciousness and the early roar of nativism with a network of parochial institutions. Urban archdioceses headed by "brick and mortar" prelates built hospitals and dispensaries to care for their own people as well as parish churches and schools to enrich spiritual life and insulate the flock from Protestant influence.

The Democratic party was the political choice of the Irish and of their colorful leaders. None was more memorable than Mike Walsh of New York. The son of a Cork woodworker and veteran of the 1798 United

Irishmen rebellion, Walsh pressed the radicalism learned from his father and from New York City's dissenting artisans in the columns of his own newspaper, the *Subterranean,* and in the streets through the Spartan Association. The Association was comprised of a disciplined band of Irish workers who joined the antics of street toughs with Walsh's politics. Elected to the state assembly in 1846 on the strength of Spartan votes, the flamboyant Irishman cut quite a figure in Albany; Walsh was shabbily dressed but never without his diamond ring and silver-tipped cane. He attacked Yankee entrepreneurs and advocated laws that would put government on the side of the poor; Walsh later degenerated into a drunkard and outspoken supporter of slavery. More typical were the Irish clubhouse politicians and ward heelers. No less sympathetic to the Southern wing of their party, Irish politicos disregarded the abuses of the marketplace and vigorously denied the ameliorative powers of the state. To them, active government was the instrument of overwrought Protestantism that would deprive the workman of his dram of beer and subject his children to the humiliations of the public schools.

The public schools had long been centers of Protestantism. Teachers opened the school day by reading passages from the King James Bible, and drilled students with textbooks that depicted the Catholic Church as an antirepublican conspiracy and the Irish as uncivilized people. In the 1830s German-speaking immigrants in the Midwest were granted bilingual schools without causing much opposition. In the midst of the revivals, in the early 1840s, Irish requests for public funding of parochial schools and demands for excusing Catholic children from opening school exercises caused an uproar. Outraged orthodox and Arminian ministers drew together in the American Protestant Association in 1842 to sound the alarm against "papist" ambition in hysterical sermons and broadsides. They energized American Republican Associations, political companions of the APA, which reaped the nativist whirlwind. American Republican office seekers, an array of former Whigs and Democrats as well as political newcomers, campaigned against the Irish with great vigor. As if to incite adversaries to violence, they descended on Irish neighborhoods to stump for extending the naturalization period to twenty-one years in order to prevent foreigners from voting. Philadelphia's hand-loom weaver districts, stirred up by the strikes of 1842–43, were shaken by still another work stoppage punctuated by fights between strikers and scabs. In spring 1844 when nativist demagogues mounted a platform at a market in the heart of Irish Kensington, a shouting match erupted into a three-day riot between the nativist invaders and besieged

Irish that left dozens of buildings in rubble and the streets strewn with sixteen dead men and boys, most of them Irish. The city that had seen native-born artisan and immigrant worker stand shoulder to shoulder in the General Trades' Union a scant seven years earlier flared with sectarian hatred worthy of modern-day Belfast. Quaker City nativists and their co-religionists as far west as Pittsburgh parlayed the disorder into landslide victories in the 1844 elections. American Republicans, however, were political amateurs unable to cement voter loyalty or counteract the nativist appeals of Whigs who undercut their support. Within a few years nativist majorities dwindled and many local parties were absorbed by the Whigs.

While the organizations of popular temperance and political nativism proved equally ephemeral, nativist fraternal orders spread like wildfire. The Mechanics' Mutual Protective Association, started by the Scottish dyer Robert MacFarlane in upstate New York in 1841, raged through the upper Midwest and extended into some Eastern cities after 1845. The Order of United American Mechanics, a direct outgrowth of the Philadelphia riots in 1844, shot up in the North and even reached into the South. Leaders of the OUAM were veterans of the Washingtonians, American Republicans, or both, and the order reflected this background. Lodges had a minority of small entrepreneurs and master craftsmen and a majority of journeymen from the better callings, even though all trades were represented. Journeymen usually elected employers to leadership posts and both groups collaborated in upholding the morality of evangelicalism. Members drew sick, unemployment, and death benefits only if they abstained from drink and foul language and avoided brothel and gaming room. Brothers were duty-bound to report violations, and the guilty were not only denied benefits but were also liable to fines, suspension, or expulsion. They also boycotted immigrant-owned businesses, which were thought to undermine "honest" American proprietors, and blacklisted foreign labor.

Temperance and nativism were aspects of a broader social outlook not entirely unfamiliar to Northern artisans. Labor nativism was a hybrid of free laborism, a fusion of the evangelical spirit and the labor theory of value. Artisans dominated the OUAM because official policy restricted membership to mechanics, men who worked with their hands. Merchants and lawyers, it is true, were sometimes admitted, but they had to bear criticism as nonproducers and pay homage to productive labor. On the Fourth of July and other patriotic holidays, American Republican devotees and nativist lodge men turned out to honor themselves as the foundation of the republic, the source of real wealth and incorruptible government. The resemblance to the artisan spectacles of the past, and the Grand Federal Processions of 1788, is hardly accidental. Nativist mechanics cast a nostalgic look back to a simpler era when masters and journeymen broke bread together and commingled in trade societies for mutual benefit. But theirs was not what one historian calls the "politics of nostalgia," for at the same time nativists had the Whiggish penchant for glorifying the genius of the American mechanic and the Protestant aptitude for technological innovation and economic progress. They delighted in comparing the nation's economic achievements with those of European powers and Latin American colonies in the orbit of the Church of Rome. It was no coincidence to them that Catholic nations were synonymous with feudal social orders and backward economies. The Church was not only an antidemocratic conspiracy but also a drag on progress, a reactionary force that kept productive labor in the thrall of dependence.

This specter of dependence, as much as fears of Irish-Catholic political demands, impelled native-born masters and journeymen in the North to embrace nativist free laborism. Nativism would exorcise that ghost with a comprehensive program suffused with nationalism and premised on a community of interest between employer and employee. Anti-immigrant orators declared unions to be divisive and unnecessary, impotent agents of reform compared with nativist politics and fraternalism. Nativists also held up successful mechanics who paid "fair wages" as proof of the honor of the small employer and living examples of the possibility of getting ahead. As the printer-turned-publisher H. H. K. Elliot told an assembly of OUAM members, every American community had onetime journeymen who achieved "high places, great wealth, and much respect." The individual who observed the order's motto, "Honesty, Industry, Sobriety," bettered himself on his own merits and had no need for unionism.

· · ·

All native-born workmen did not succumb to nativism. Some veterans of the 1830s uprising swam against the divisive cultural crosscurrents of the second half of the 1840s. No old radical loomed larger in this effort than George Henry Evans, the former New York Working Man and trade unionist, who left the city for a New Jersey farm in the mid-1830s in order to regain his health and collect his thoughts. During his convalescence Evans developed a land reform program cleansed of the stain of

Skidmore's "General Division." Evans's scheme of National Reform, as it was christened, would have the federal government carve up the public domain into 160-acre farms for distribution to any family on demand. These holdings would form parts of planned townships with parks, public meeting houses, and warehouses where yeoman and mechanic exchanged goods and services without merchant or jobber playing any part in the transaction. National Reform was to this generation of labor radicals what cooperation had been a decade before.

Evans attracted an instant following upon unveiling his plan to former GTU stalwarts in New York in 1844. John Commerford, John Windt, and Thomas Devyr, the most noteworthy erstwhile radicals, comprised the inner circle of the National Reform Association. Commerford likened the NRA to the labor movement of the 1830s, but there were notable differences. National Reformers had more in common with labor reformers than trade union militants, even though the line between the two was always hazy and for some radicals it was not a line at all. For Evans and his partisans, however, that distinction between reformers and militants obtained. While they appreciated the imperative to strike, they considered work stoppages to be distractions and dead ends. They nonetheless put together the only major labor movement culture between the mid-1840s and the Civil War. National Reform headquarters in New York published a newspaper, *Young America,* held yearly meetings known as Industrial Congresses, and dispatched lecturers to preach the gospel. Local NRA clubs charged initiation fees and monthly dues and sponsored rallies and debates. At election time the clubs doubled as ward committees working for candidates of any party that endorsed the slogan "Vote Yourself a Farm," rallying cry of National Reform. Evansism resonated deeply within the upper Midwest, presumably among marginal farmers and farm-bred workmen. It then established a wider following in the city, once the agitation took hold and Evans endorsed cooperation and the ten-hour day, the burning issue for factory hands and growing numbers of shop workers.

Resurgent unionism also helped National Reform. This rebirth, which lasted from the late 1840s into the early 1850s, can be traced to two separate groups. One consisted of German immigrants, many of them refugees from the revolutions of 1848 who settled in American communities with second- and third-generation countrymen. "Forty-eighters," as these newcomers were called, toted heavy cultural baggage: their nation's legendary fondness for beer and song along with a radical mentality that recalled William Heighton and stood in sharp contrast to the insularity and parochialism of previous German immigrants. German-American communities, heretofore preoccupied with preserving their native tongue and beer gardens, were never quite the same. Forty-eighters created boisterous free thought societies and a forceful press. The turnverein, a paramilitary group formed in the wake of Napoleon's conquest to drill young men for a war of national liberation, also fell under forty-eighter influence. The group raised funds for European revolutionaries and purchased steamship tickets for immigrant radicals eager to return home to fight against monarchy.

Foreign causes did not consume radical Germans. They attacked slavery from the vantage point of free-soilism or abolitionism but did not slight grievances at the workplace. The typical German immigrant, after all, was a trained craftsman, the graduate of a rigorous apprenticeship lured to America partly by hopes of retaining artisanal traditions and honing skills destined to become of little use in the industrializing homeland. Service tradesmen and luxury craftsmen found their manual expertise in demand. A competency based on wage labor or a small business was possible for the neighborhood butcher or local cabinetmaker crafting bespoke work for the rich. But seasoned artisans, already an elite corps, were few compared with the mass of Germans who worked in the garrets and sweatshops of the shoe, clothing, and woodworking trades that made a mockery of artisanship and paid only slightly better than unskilled work. Never ones to forbear, many German shoemakers and tailors and then printers and others organized craft unions that merged into confederations similar to the city centrals of the 1830s.

The other and more unlikely group of trade unionists consisted of nativist artisans. Wages were not uppermost in their minds; the earnings of such better-paid tradesmen began to rise at the end of the 1840s. But working conditions continued to deteriorate, so much so that nativist journeymen reassessed the ideal of community interest that had brought them together with employers in the American Republican party and the Order of United American Mechanics. Disillusioned bricklayers spoke for them when in 1850 they reaffirmed their admiration for "legitimate" masters, traditional mechanics who compensated labor fairly and respected the conventions of the "craft"; they assailed the "butchers and tinkers who never learned the trade" and besmirched the reputation of journeymen by taking on "hordes of unfinished workmen piling together brick, unsightly to the eye and disgraceful to the trade—driving men like slaves that they may enrich themselves from the blood and sweat of those whose necessity knows no law." Probably some of these workmen

cursed and condemned immigrants rather than their employers. On the
other hand, more and more workers in Eastern metropolises and then in
trans-Allegheny cities turned against entrepreneurs in self-defense by
organizing unions from the ground up; others deserted fraternal orders
controlled by employers for unions restricted to workers. Printers did
both. Compositors and pressmen from Washington to Cincinnati evalu-
ated their craft at the end of the 1840s and published reports that
confirmed what they suspected. Conditions of work were degenerating,
and earnings, they claimed, were just enough to hold life and limb
together. Militants waved the sobering reports under the noses of
complacent fellow tradesmen on the rolls of the Order of United
American Mechanics and the Franklin Typographical Association, one of
the oldest beneficial societies. And it worked. Journeymen left the
Franklin in droves for local unions that in 1852 coalesced into the
National Typographical, the nation's first national trade union. Building
tradesmen and others formed unions in 1851–52 confined to single cities
that drew together under the aegis of Industrial Congresses.

These Industrial Congresses arose independently of Evans's bodies but
were clearly inspired by National Reform. They confederated male
craftsmen—women, blacks, and the unskilled were excluded—but even
so had a broader ethnic representation than the central unions of the
1830s, with large contingents of English and German tradesmen. The
Irish, who worked chiefly as casual laborers, were ineligible. The
Congresses proposed to advance labor's collective interest, a goal more
easily defined fifteen years before when rank-and-filers were more
ethnically homogeneous and more responsive to radical leadership. Labor
chieftains of the 1830s, after all, had moved deftly from trade unionism
to cooperation, and had brought followers along without much resistance.
By the early 1850s agreement was more elusive, for the Congresses
housed workmen with different outlooks. One was trade unionist and it
had two aspects, a "bread and butter" tendency that centered on wages
and a control tendency that focused on procedures in the workplace. New
York tailors hewed to the first. In 1850 nearly one thousand staged a
strike for a rate increase that caused the Industrial Congress to swing into
action. Congress spokesmen headed overflow rallies in support of the
embattled tailors, and several affiliates prepared to strike in sympathy in
what appeared to be a reenactment of 1835. The difference lay in the
ethnic composition of the tailoring trade changed by the influx of
immigrants. Some German as well as most Irish were either too needy to
sacrifice wages or disinterested in unionism. Repeated skirmishes be-

tween striker and strikebreaker brought in the police to bridle groups of tailors on the prowl for scabs and subcontractors said to be giving out work. On August 4 a contingent of police put tailor picketers to flight at the corner of Ninth Avenue and Twenty-eighth Street and in the fracas two workmen were killed, the first such fatalities in an American labor dispute. Widespread scabbing and the police broke the strike.

Control strikes were the stock-in-trade of skilled journeymen with something other than wage scales to protect. Some set limits on output and enforced laboring traditions through informal work groups or shop committees. Others, including the printers of Cincinnati, began to rely upon contractual provisions. These craftsmen proposed to "regulate all things appertaining to the printing business" and by 1851, hardly a year after the birth of their union, seem to have had the run of their workplaces. They already controlled access to their ranks and craft training by dint of a "Plan of Apprenticeship," which spelled out the rates and responsibilities of student printers in minute detail.

Industrial Congresses also heard from cooperationists and land reformers. Each group endorsed the other's program, but both lost patience with the trade unionists and in 1850–51 voted down their requests for strike support. Some union men walked out in disgust, leaving Congresses to bickering factions of cooperationists and land reformers. Evans's men held the upper hand and used Congress meetings as nominating conventions to endorse Free-Soil Democrats and office seekers from mainstream parties who would commit themselves to support homestead laws of one kind or another. They got their way at the expense of the movement, for the cooperationists and what remained of the trade unionists drifted away. By 1851 Congress after Congress had lost its popular base.

· · ·

Unionism ran in fits and starts through the rest of the 1850s. Some national organizations and city centrals arose but were buffeted about and weakened further by the depressions of 1854 and 1857. More debilitating still were the related forces of immigration and political realignment. Indeed the tide of immigration, which deposited over 2 million foreigners on American shores in the 1850s, brought a fundamental reconstitution of the working class. Highly skilled callings alone withstood the onslaught, and they were rare given the use of machines and the reorganization of handwork in the crafts. Depending upon the trade, the simplification of tasks sent either trickles or torrents of foreign-born workers into the handicrafts. In every major Northern city by 1860 just about a third of the printers, almost half of the building tradesmen, and nearly three-fourths of the shoemakers, tailors, and cabinetmakers were foreign-born. Even the Irish, heretofore stuck in unskilled work and hand-loom weaving, established a foothold in the trades, usually as semiskilled tailors and shoemakers. The labor market was overwhelmed with inexperienced hands less conscious of their class than their ethnic origin.

The immigration bulge also stirred up the latent anti-Catholic feelings of native-born workmen. Secret nativist groupings, called "Know-Nothings" by a political wag, proliferated furtively across the nation and chalked up landslide victories in the elections of 1854. Midwestern cities that had returned few American Republican votes in the first nativist upsurge of the mid-1840s installed Know-Nothing mayors and city councils. Massachusetts nativists not only elected the governor but also won every seat in the senate and all but a few of the 390 seats in the assembly! Once in office, Bay State Know-Nothings, as expected, worked to curtail foreign influence by purging the state payroll of immigrant workers, disbanding Irish militia units, and passing a constitutional amendment that established a literacy test for voters. As if to flaunt the popular base of nativism, however, Know-Nothing lawmakers showed themselves to be as critical of inequality and class privilege as they were of Catholics. They put the finishing touches on the blueprint drafted by the Working Men in the early 1830s by abolishing imprisonment for debt, closing loopholes in the mechanics' lien law, expanding the public school system, and prohibiting manufacturers from employing children under fifteen years of age who did not attend school for eleven weeks a year. Yet in the end Know-Nothingism proved a way station for Northern native-born workers before they joined the antislavery crusade of the Republican party.

Indeed, antiforeignism and antislavery derived from the common source of the ideology of free labor. For nearly ten years free labor ideologues had vented their spleen against Catholicism. By the mid-1850s it appeared that expansionist ambitions of the planter aristocracy, a social order as feudal and backward as any in Europe and located on American soil, posed an even greater menace to the liberties and opportunities of the independent mechanic. The imminence of the "Slave Power" appeared more palpable in 1854 when Illinois Democrat Stephen Douglas, out to win Southern support for a try at the White House, proposed repeal of the Missouri Compromise, which had kept slavery bottled up in the South. Douglas unwittingly provoked nativists into directing their animosities from the immigrants to the haughty planter.

Nativists and Free-Soil Democrats, most of them Northern farmers and workingmen, began to move into the newly formed Republican party, weakening the Know-Nothings and Democrats and destroying the Whigs.

Most Republican wheelhorses were former Whigs rather than Know-Nothings. More politically adept than the nativists, they were better at holding followers in line. In electoral districts with large concentrations of English and German workingmen, they shrewdly downplayed nativism and temperance. Stripped of xenophobia, this version of free laborism underwent additional changes in emphasis from its American Republican incarnation to Republican. When Republican orators spoke of labor, they had something more in mind than wage earners or even master mechanics. In the words of Horace Greeley, publisher of the influential New York *Daily Tribune,* anyone in ''any useful doing in any capacity or vocation'' fell under the rubric of labor, one great family of productive peoples free to rise out of manual work in what Abraham Lincoln was fond of calling ''the race for life.'' Republicans would preserve such opportunities by standing fast against Southern expansionism and promising a new start through the Homestead Act. This act, borrowed though it was from the NRA, was not to be the brake on capitalism that Evans had intended. ''It does not bring down the rich,'' said a leading Republican, ''but . . . raises the low,'' by providing an escape from wage labor. But distinctions between radicalism and the received culture of Republicanism mattered less and less during the deepening sectional crisis. It was no time to quibble over who belonged in the house of labor and who did not, or whether its occupants had much to gain from Republican tariffs and internal improvements. Free men of the North, it was believed, would wind up in chains if the lords of the Cotton Kingdom had their way. ''There was such a thing as the Slave Power,'' wrote an agitated Midwestern columnist in the aftershock of the Dred Scott decision, the Supreme Court ruling that effectively gave slavery the force of law. For this Republican regular, and for labor radicals, that horror was reason enough to close ranks behind the free laborism of the Republican party.

The nativist tremors of the mid-1850s also shook the South. The Order of United American Mechanics, the Benevolent Order of Bereans, and other nativist brotherhoods prospered during the late 1840s and early 1850s, and by 1854 the region's urban centers raged with ''election riots,'' in which nativists sought to prevent immigrants from exercising their right to vote. In Louisville in August 1855 over twenty lives were lost on ''Bloody Monday,'' and in New Orleans unknown numbers of rioters were killed in five disturbances between 1854 and 1858, the second of which ran ten days. Southern nativists also flexed their muscles at the polls. Millard Fillmore, presidential candidate of the American party in 1856, collected half his popular vote in the South, while urban office seekers simultaneously carried every city in the region.

Southern nativism still awaits its historians. Its outlook, social composition, and legislative achievements are unknown, but fragmentary evidence suggests some similarities with its Northern variant. The urban concentration of the party vote suggests a large working-class following. Native white workers were no more eager to share labor markets with immigrants than were Northern journeymen. After the 1856 landslide, "the labouring men of our city," U.S. Senator John Pearce from Baltimore presumed, "sustain the Know Nothings because they wish to banish the competition of foreign labourers." While observers in the Deep South agreed, nativism was not simply the expression of workers in fear for their jobs. It also expressed slaveholder fears of an emergent working class.

Many defenders of slavery in the South, of course, welcomed immigrants as political allies. "No native can *even* exceed, in idolatry of slavery, the mass of ignorant foreign-born laborers," said a confident South Carolinian to the Northern observer Frederick Law Olmsted in the early 1850s. If Olmsted's informant had the Irish in mind, he surely had a point. Irish workers abhorred abolitionists as much as free blacks. But some planters and many industrialists were not so sure of Irish loyalty to the "peculiar institution." They stressed the dangers of a "mass of foreigners coming into this country . . . feeling utterly hostile to . . . slave[ry]." It was they who probably coined the phrase an "Irishman was a nigger turned inside out," but as the historian Fred Siegel reminds us, "Paddy" was "a nigger with a vote," a Trojan horse. Far more worrisome were the German radicals in East Texas and Baltimore who made no secret of their opposition to slavery. The San Antonio newspaper publisher Adolph Douai editorialized against slavery in *Die Zeitung,* and in Baltimore *Der Wecker* called for universal suffrage and an end to Sunday closing laws along with freedom for people of color. If Southern nativists were more consistently anti-immigrant than anti-Catholic, it was precisely because of the antislavery force of German radicalism, a force potent enough to ease tensions between employee and employer.

While the efflorescence of nativism helped restore some social harmony in the South, its decline set the stage for sharper class antagonism. Once it became clear that nativism failed to eliminate the immigrant as a political factor, Southern industrialists had to tap different reservoirs of tractable labor. After 1857 they followed two courses which revealed their distrust of free labor, as well as white labor's distrust of them. They first joined the revived campaign to reopen the African slave trade, which had been outlawed in 1808. Originally proposed by secessionists in the early 1850s, this campaign picked up at the close of the decade. Even William Gregg and Charles DeBow, leading proponents of Southern free laborism, were among its adherents. But the very idea of hordes of slaves fresh from Africa caused a commotion in several quarters of Southern society for any number of reasons apart from general apprehensions of further distorting the racial imbalance. Up-country yeomen feared it would make the powerful planter elite stronger, and planters in the upper South argued it would undermine their monopoly of the internal slave traffic. Even normally quiescent workers spoke out. A Georgian explained that his "opposition springs from interest. . . . If we are to have negro labor in abundance, where will my support come from? . . . the poor will grow poorer and the rich . . . richer."

The loss of this battle over reopening the international slave trade was deeply upsetting to Southern manufacturers. It left them dependent on free workers they did not trust. As a South Carolinian noted, "If we [slaveholders] cannot supply the demand for slave labor then we must expect to be supplied with a species of labor we do not want, and which from the very nature of things is antagonistic to our institutions." To some manufacturers, this meant immigrants; to others, white workers in general. "All sources," says Southern historian William Barney, "were suspect." Indeed some manufacturers in Virginia and Georgia, the region's leading industrial states, were so disturbed that they proposed the unthinkable. They would make do with free white workers as long as they were deprived of the suffrage. Industrialists talked of disenfranchising all white labor on the eve of the secession crisis, and even after Virginia had left the Union, Alexander Stuart of Richmond brought such a proposal before the secession convention. "Despotism of King Numbers would ensue and the outcome would be agrarianism," he warned fellow Confederates, unless the state's white workers were denied the right to vote. But this measure proved just as controversial as reopening the slave trade and even more poorly timed. Few convention delegates were prepared to alienate workers needed to fight the impending war against the North.

What are we to make of such desperate measures? That both revealed the pervasive and mounting fear of a working class hardly needs elaboration. Both initiatives also tell us something about the changing tactics and strategies of at least some Southern manufacturers. If we can assume that the champions of reopening the African trade intended to use slave labor in abundance, it is clear that they broke the tacit social contract with white labor with regard to limiting the use of slaves. Such employers also repudiated the ideology of free labor. Their idea of free labor, after all, had been premised on restricted employment of bonded labor so as to spare white labor the "nigger work" and thereby inflate their status. For these onetime free laborists, it was only a short step to arguing for disenfranchisement once the option of additional slave labor was closed off.

Some Southern industrialists, however, continued to speak of free labor and enjoy the support of white workers even while they used slaves. Nowhere was this clearer than in Charleston, the last bastion of free black artisans and slaves hiring their own time. Racism welled up in the late 1850s as the depression of 1857 hit and whites became the majority for the first time. In 1858 and 1859 white mechanics lobbied state lawmakers without success to ban the self-hiring of slaves, but a year later convinced the mayor to enforce regulatory laws, long honored in the breach, requiring slaves to wear badges purchased by owners. That summer police patrols harassed free blacks and not only rounded up bondmen without the badges but had them resold into slavery as provided by law. As the "reenslavement crisis" struck terror in black Charleston, white journeymen joined the electoral campaigns for state representative of James Eason and Henry Peake. We still know very little about Eason and Peake apart from the fact that both operated machine shops and owned about thirty slaves between them. Nativism may have been their political baptism. Whether it was or not, both men had the popular touch, a knack for stirring up voters with the rhetoric of Southern free labor spiced with racism and class antagonism. *"Free* negroes—negroes free in *fact,"* read a broadside, "but held by trustees, and slaves hiring their own time—plague spots in the community, affecting pecuniarily and socially, only working men," since blacks were already barred by law from the professions and mercantile positions. A supporter of Eason and Peake continued in this vein with a direct attack on the idle rich and an oblique one on large planters. "Professional men who have never done a day's work," he sneered, "may talk of *dignity of labor,* and deem their listeners fools; but has any *white mechanic* ever felt this indignity of labor when unsuccessful in estimating for a job, he finds that it is awarded to one of our *very respectable free persons of color?''* Swept into office by working-class voters, Eason and Peake drafted bills that would have barred all free blacks from mechanical pursuits and provided for their gradual reenslavement.

While both bills were overwhelmed by the secession crisis, they disclose another pattern of class relations in the South. In contrast to Gregg and other large industrialists who came down against white workmen, smaller manufacturers like Eason and Peake used the rhetoric of white egalitarianism and free labor to propitiate free white labor. Only additional research will determine which group proved more influential. In the end, however, both employers and workers pulled together in defense of their region and a system of slave labor that white workingmen found difficult to live with and impossible to live without.

In the North neither the blandishments of free labor ideologues nor the ambitions of the slavocracy completely diverted workers from the encroachments of the market at the close of the 1850s. The swings of the economy and the steady advance of the factory system churned up pockets of acrimony. The sharp downturn of 1857 set off demonstrations of the unemployed that rebuffed Republican counsel. Irritated workers brushed off the homilies of the evangelical clergy and took umbrage at paternalists for recommending private giving. "Would it not be better," asked a Lynn, Massachusetts, critic of upper-class benevolence, "for the manufacturers to give the full price? Let the rich come forward," he fumed, "and say we will give you half the profits we made." The unemployed in other places demanded public works, the first such proposals from labor. And when hard times ended, strike committees and more permanent unions, some of them national in scope, took hold in trade after trade.

Militancy exposed fissures in the coalition of free labor. No bourgeois free laborite endorsed public building projects and very few supported private charity in the depression winter of 1857. Leading Republicans viewed both measures as unwarranted interventions in free labor markets that would sap the will to work. Some party journalists pronounced a short spell of adversity to be just the thing to sober up profligate workmen who spent families into penury in good times and who had the nerve to demand public assistance in bad ones. Such columnists were just as disdainful of workers who rushed from unemployment demonstrations to union halls during the upturn of 1858. One of their number looked in vain for the "oppressed wage slaves" and "cruel and heartless . . . capital-

ists" described by the Lynn Mechanics' Association. "That is all
moonshine and flummery," he shot back. "The laboring class," he
knew, was "in the main, a free, happy, and independent class."

One would not have gleaned so much from the unrest pulsing through
New England shoe towns. Grievances centered on inadequate pay along
with speedups brought on by partial mechanization of the production
process. The deployment of sewing machines in the mid-1850s concentrated more labor into factories by displacing slower if cheaper handworkers employed at home. Mechanized stitching also increased the
work load of bottomers and other specialized workers who had to keep up
with machine-driven output. The male shoemakers responded by resur-
recting unions dormant since the 1840s and then demanded extra pay.
When turned down, they walked off their jobs in a strike that began in
good republican fashion on Washington's Birthday in 1860 and involved
as many as 10,000 workers in eastern Massachusetts. Lynn was its
center. Ethnic hostilities, rife in a town that had returned a resounding
nativist vote, were submerged by the rising class feeling. Though still a
minority, the Irish overlooked the sins of workmates and marched in the
parades and processions that maintained morale throughout the cold
winter. The chink in labor's armor lay in male chauvinism and the uneven
development of the shoe industry. Male workers traditionally excluded
women from their unions and flatly refused to support the factory
stitchers who put forth wage demands of their own. On top of this, the
factory women unwittingly eroded the wage economy of outworker
families by displacing the female hand stitchers, many of whom were the
wives of the workmen on strike. It is still not clear if the women
outworkers lined up with the stitchers in an act of sisterhood or agreed to
hold down their own rates for fear of encouraging even faster displacement. What is clear is that outworkers beyond the circle of the Lynn
Mechanics' Association and neighboring unions strengthened the owners'
hand by taking on work and allowing a war of attrition against labor. As
the winter snows melted in April, the strikers trooped back to work.

Lynn evoked the past and anticipated the future. The placards of
parading strikers and the oratory of the shoemakers' leaders suggested the
persistence of the radical creed that had inspired the labor movement
thirty years earlier. A banner with the slogan "American Ladies Will Not
Be Slaves" waved above a crowd addressed by a speaker who thundered
that it was unnecessary to go to "Bleeding Kansas" to seek out "labor's
oppressors." They were right there in Lynn, insidiously "drawing the
chains of slavery and riveting them closer and closer around the limbs of

free laboring men.'' At the same time, the Lynn strike was not a strike of shop workers or domestic employees like the struggles of the past. Instead, it was a struggle waged by factory hands, possibly the first major work stoppage on the part of artisans-turned-workers. Such wage earners faced off not only against manufacturers but also against the militia, which was mustered within the first week to escort wagoners delivering stock to scabbing outworkers. Not a shot was fired or a single life lost—this time. The military presence, however, was a harbinger of ruder things to come for Gilded Age workers involved in mass strikes.

A new struggle soon commanded national attention. Workers enlisted in the Union Army in droves, usually with the blessing of their employers, as alarmed as they by slavery. For most native-born workers and many Germans, if not the Irish, the war against slavery was enormously popular. The Civil War had begun. It is difficult to sort out the motivations of the men in the Union Army. Those who felt for the slave were probably outnumbered by those who thought the slave system a threat to free labor. But fight they did. It is hard to understand why without appreciating the power of evangelical Protestantism and the ideology of free labor. The same religious and ideological currents that diluted radicalism ironically propelled Northern labor into one of its most honorable campaigns.

''The obstacles that confronted labor at mid-century,'' writes Sean Wilentz of New York City workers, ''were as formidable as they had been in the days of the Working Men.'' This insight may be applied to American workers as a whole. Union men were no closer to resolving any number of dilemmas on the eve of the Civil War than they had been when Andrew Jackson was first elected President. They were still wary of women's labor, the unskilled, and in the South, at least, even more hostile to blacks. Nor had they settled on a strategy for operating as an independent political force within the received culture of the two-party system. Following the debacle of the Working Men most labor activists turned away from independent politics and many turned to the Democratic party. Some would bolt to the Free-Soil party in 1848, an ephemeral party without formal ties to organized labor. During the 1850s when the memory of the Working Men had worn off, some workers warmed to political insurgency in response to crises originating within workshops. Few had much to show for their efforts, and those who did elect their favorites to public office campaigned on thin platforms and achieved very little. In Lynn a Workingmen's ticket rode the crest of militancy generated in the Great Strike to a resounding victory, but the single achievement of the new regime was ousting the old city marshal. The republican legacy of limited government continued to stifle labor's political effectiveness both on the hustings and in office.

On the other hand, there were also noteworthy discontinuities, changes of some significance between the 1830s and the late antebellum years. In the heyday of unionism, radicals had been of different minds as to the causes of oppression. Some pointed to landlords, others to bankers, and still others to employers. Not a few rank-and-filers drawn into unions in the heat of the ten-hour movement, moreover, held demon rum to blame. Nonetheless after 1835 a consensus began to emerge that saw exploitation in the production process and prescribed cooperation as a way out. The persuasive powers of talented leaders help account for this transformation. So does demography. This working class, after all, consisted largely of native-born Americans brought up in the city or reared on the farm. Such workers had grown up with the tenets of popular republicanism and were receptive to leaders who spoke its language, understood its customs, and were skilled at channeling economic resentment into a movement for worker ownership.

If the depression of 1837 destroyed the labor movement, European immigration in the second half of the 1840s shattered the ethnic unity of the working class in both the North and the South. Hard times also invigorated the evangelical crusade that fueled the fires of discord in both regions. In the North radicals preached to a fractious working class more receptive to the politics of ethnicity. They also spoke of radicalism with different emphases. There was an evangelized radicalism best expressed by William Young and a secular version espoused by George Henry Evans. The first cherished self-reform and social reconciliation; the second offered retreat to the land as well as cooperative production, not in the city as in the 1830s, but in rural utopias. Each had a romantic, even escapist quality, and both, along with labor's nativism, were ultimately subsumed by the politics of free labor. Indeed it is doubtful that the ideology of mature free labor would have enjoyed such popularity in the North had it not been for the mounting sectional crisis. Slavery became the cause of the hour, even as labor unrest grew in the North and class strife grew in the South. Sectional and class conflict coexisted, but the former carried the day.

4.

Coming Apart

Post-Civil War Americans left behind a society transformed and an unfinished economic revolution. Prewar America was studded with economically parochial "island communities" with slow and inefficient means of transportation, local labor, capital, and commodity markets, and individually owned businesses with rudimentary technology. The three decades following the Civil War hastened the market, transportation, and industrial revolutions that overwhelmed these island communities and shattered customary patterns of everyday life. Recognizably modern words and economic institutions replaced older ones. No one spoke of artisans, mechanics, or even master craftsmen by the closing decades of the nineteenth century: these terms went the way of the wooden plow, the keelboat, and the journeyman shoemaker's lap stone. Indeed wage workers did not refer to themselves as journeymen any longer. Distinctions of skill endured and even sharpened, but manual employees thought of themselves as workers, just as employers became manufacturers or businessmen. Workplaces grew larger, machines replaced hand tools, and standardized products spilled out of factories corporately owned and hierarchically structured. Prometheus was finally unbound.

. . .

Three years of recession and twelve hours of drenching rain could not deter the crowds converging on Philadelphia for the grand opening of the Centennial Exposition on the morning of May 10, 1876. Over 100,000 early risers drenched to the bone jostled at the gates hours before opening time. One hundred thousand more would pass through the turnstiles on that day and nearly 8 million more fairgoers from every state in the Union and corner of the globe would visit the grounds over the next six months, tramping the miles of streets and walkways etched into the sprawling

450-acre site with planned gardens and pavilions housing such exotic delights as French porcelains, Siamese ivory, and Russian sable. Folk arts and crafts fashioned by amateur artists could be seen in halls erected by the states. The nation's pride and the talk of the fair was Machinery Hall, a fourteen-acre edifice with a display of 8,000 machines and mechanical devices. This museum to American ingenuity exhibited power looms and ring spinners, steam presses, and sewing machines of antebellum vintage along with such Gilded Age inventions as molding and iron rolling machines and upright drills—as well as something called a typewriter. A maze of belts and pulleys linked the equipment to George Corliss's double-acting duplex steam engine, a metal behemoth forty feet high and capable of generating 2,500 horsepower. Indeed the festivities did not officially begin that morning until President Grant himself pulled the lever that tripped the mighty Corliss.

The battery of technology in Machinery Hall offered a glimpse of the broadened sweep of economic change following the Civil War. As sightseers gawked at Thomas Edison's multiplex telegraph and Alexander Graham Bell's telephone, both on view for the first time, acrobatic linemen were already at work stringing the wire of a communications system that would knit together the nation. By the mid-1890s over 300,000 telephones and thousands of telegraph offices made for instantaneous communication between distant points. While the overhead telegraphic wires buzzed, knots of laborers pounded spikes into the T rails of a railway network that expanded from just under 40,000 miles at the first transcontinental hookup in 1869 to 240,000 a short two decades later. Ownership was gradually concentrated in a few corporations that by the 1890s controlled half the mileage and an even larger share of the traffic. Corporate ownership facilitated the standardization of track and of numerous aspects of quotidian life for ordinary Americans. Nearly everyone was brought within the reach of the market. Yeomen farmers in the South saw trunk lines penetrate the up-country, ending generations of economic isolation. Freight trains supplied local retailers with interchangeable parts for household technology along with national name brand foods prepared to appeal to the majority of consumers. Railwaymen even abolished "local mean time," a preindustrial tradition in which each community set its clocks according to the sun. In 1883, without legislative sanction, railway executives divided the continent into the four time zones that obtain to this day. Americans would thereafter gear their lives to industrial time.

Machinery Hall symbolized technological advance in another way.

Situated on a bluff overlooking the waters of the Schuylkill, it signaled an end to the time when factories were confined to riverbanks in order to take advantage of water power. Proximity to rushing streams, after all, was the reason for the existence of Lowell, Paterson, and other early manufacturing towns. Water power was cheap but fickle, for waterwheels slowed to a crawl in late summer and came to a halt in the North in the dead of winter. In the late 1860s design improvements and lower costs made steam engines more reliable and affordable than water power, and two decades later Thomas Edison unveiled the miracle of electric power. Both new power sources unleashed the centripetal force that pulled factories into metropolitan centers and medium-sized cities, reversing the antebellum tendency of industrial dispersal.

The industrialization of the city, in turn, spurred urbanization. Between 1860 and 1890 the proportion of Americans living in municipalities with more than 2,500 residents nearly doubled to 30 percent. The rate of population growth in cities, closely attuned to economic rhythms, peaked in the prosperous 1860s and 1880s and fell off in the depressions of the 1870s and 1890s. Urbanization was as uneven as it was cyclical, heaviest in the industrializing Northeast and upper Midwest, which in 1890 together had thirty-nine of the fifty largest cities. No region was without its expanding commercial centers, not even the South. Border state cities grew smartly, the new industrial towns of Birmingham and Chattanooga appeared, and medium-sized communities sprinkled the landscape. Indeed the number of towns with more than 10,000 residents increased from about 100 in 1860 to over 200 in 1890, even though under 10 percent of Southerners lived in urban places in 1890.

Above all, Machinery Hall underlined the transition from the labor-intensive methods of the sweating system to the capital-intensive, machine-paced processes of the factory. Accelerated industrialism was not comprehensive. No less an authority than Samuel Gompers, a young cigar maker fresh from an East London ghetto, recalled in the 1870s casually rolling quality smokes by hand in New York City factories during that decade. Gompers's trade, women's clothing, and a few other backwater industries, it is true, were dragged into the industrial flow by bunching machinery, improved sewing machines, and other devices. Such attenuated technological change, however, brought about the proliferation of sweatshops and outwork and thereby reinforced industrial decentralization. Nor did all innovations deplete skills. Linotype machines and mechanized steel rollers, in fact, required highly trained workers.

The dominant trend lay in concentration. Average shop size jumped from six to over twenty workers between 1860 and 1890, and in both years firms in the most technologically advanced sectors were several times larger than the average. Factories with forty to seventy workers were common in older industries and they were dwarfed by the huge textile and steel plants with several hundred employees.

The largest establishments in 1890, moreover, were not mere magnifications of entrepreneurial shops geared for production alone. They were incorporated businesses with main offices in metropolitan centers and branch plants that integrated nonproductive with productive functions. Meat packers, biscuit bakers, cigarette manufacturers, and producers of other consumer goods marketed and promoted brand names with advertising personnel and legions of salesmen. Manufacturers of metals and heavy equipment sought control of raw materials and transport by buying up quarries and mines as well as shipping fleets and railways. In each case a few giant firms already dominated select consumer and producer markets before the merger wave at the end of the century.

As if anyone at the time did not know, meat-packing magnate Philip Armour told Senate investigators in 1889, "We are here to make money. I wish I could make more. . . . I know I couldn't in the old-fashioned way." By "old-fashioned" Armour meant the artisanal system in which a single workman slaughtered and dressed livestock one at a time with hand tools. This traditional method suited the picky individual consumer but not the anonymous multitude Armour aimed to supply. So the inventive industrialist pioneered what the historian Siegfried Giedion called the "mechanization of death" in ten short years following the development of the refrigerated railway car in the late 1870s. Rapid-fire rifles felled livestock that were stripped of hides by machine and then lifted onto overhead motorized conveyors circulating sides of beef to butchers stationed at benches paring away fat and waste. In one Chicago plant in the late 1870s a gang of fifty-seven hands performed eighty-seven operations at breakneck speed; by the mid-1880s a splitting team of five dressed eighty cattle in an hour. Ten years later more machines and faster conveyors reduced the team to four and nearly doubled the hourly output.

Even before the sides of beef tumbled off Chicago disassembly lines, segments of production in other handicrafts had already been harnessed to machines. This resulted in a mix of manual and machine methods, an uneven productive process with slower handworkers interspersed among faster machine operatives. A surge of capital investment in the wake of the depression of 1873 further eliminated pockets of manual work, though technological lag and worker resistance kept the advance spotty. Shoe lasters could rightfully boast of being the only handworkers in footwear and even they were being displaced by machine operators in the 1890s. Iron molders stubbornly held out against mechanization as well. Molders at International Harvester, emboldened by a successful strike in 1885, presented Cyrus McCormick II with an awesome list of demands the following spring that included a rate increase for all workers, preferential hiring of "old molders," immediate dismissal of nonunion men—and unlimited time in the water closet. McCormick's refusal to accept the closed shop caused another work stoppage that would reach a tragic end. It failed miserably, not because of the tumult over the bombing at Haymarket Square on May 4, but because of a preemptive decision by management. McCormick had installed pneumatic machines that made it possible to run the plant with semiskilled labor even as hand molders picketed outside.

It was not simply a matter of replacing skilled handworkers with machine tenders. Mule spinners and lathe operators head a long list of autonomous and fiercely independent machine workers. Owners took care of such troublesome operatives by substituting simpler equipment for complex machines. Fall River textile owners got the better of contentious mule spinners in a day. One Saturday afternoon after the hands had left, cotton boss Colonel Richard Borden bragged, "we started right in and smashed a room full of mules with sledge hammers. On Monday morning [the spinners] were astonished to find there was no work for them. The room is now full of ring frames run by girls." Women were less of a concern to skilled machinists than the division of labor and standardization of parts. Indeed, by the early 1880s standardization had progressed to such an extent in the manufacture of sewing machines that it took no fewer than "300 men to make the different parts. You simply go in and learn whatever branch you are put at," said a disgruntled machinist, "and you stay at that unless you are changed to another."

The vertically integrated firm spewing forth high-volume goods for national markets was not unknown to the South. The North Carolina tobacco entrepreneur James B. Duke was the first to exploit the market for cigarettes, a relatively new product made by skilled handworkers whose total output stood at about 3,000 units a day in the late 1870s. In the early 1880s, James Bonsack patented a continuous-process machine that made 70,000 cigarettes in a ten-hour day. In 1884 Duke purchased two Bonsacks and within a few short years his Durham factory saturated the market. He then literally manufactured demand through a national and international marketing system that used such advertising techniques as distributing free samples and getting endorsements from celebrities and star athletes. In 1890 his American Tobacco Company, a merger of several small firms that controlled over 90 percent of the market, sold over 100 million cigarettes a year for gross sales of over $5 million.

American Tobacco typified Southern industrialism only insofar as it processed agricultural goods grown in the region. The area's five leading industries in 1890—lumber milling, tobacco processing, cotton textiles, iron and steel production, and turpentine distilling—were likewise tied to staple crops or natural resources close at hand. Firms were small, centered in towns or dispersed through the countryside, and technologically primitive by comparison to Northern businesses. Factories continued to rely on the hand methods or simple technologies of the sweating system and usually featured cheap goods, such as textiles or products not manufactured in the North, such as turpentine.

Scarcities continued to plague Southern industrialism in spite of and indeed because of the abolition of slavery. The war ruined a fair number of wealthy men with disposable capital and devastated credit because slaves, valued at $1.5 billion in 1860, had been the preferred form of collateral. With or without credit, industrialists were hobbled by chronic shortages of capital and labor. Skilled labor continued to be in short supply, and semiskilled and unskilled labor, which in theory should have been abundant because of emancipation, was not readily available. As the economic historian Gavin Wright tells us, the South was a "low-wage economy in a high-wage country," with a wage structure that had a dual effect. Low wages discouraged immigrant workers, who either bypassed the region or were lured away by higher pay scales in the North and West. Poor pay also provided a weak incentive for native-born whites and newly freed blacks, not trapped in debt, to leave farm for city.

· · ·

The last third of the nineteenth century also marked a major transition from old to new management methods. In this respect it is helpful to recognize two distinct systems of the social relations of production: industrial craft systems and paternalistic systems. As David Montgomery observes, craft systems rested in part on the "superior knowledge" of skilled workers, "self-directing at their tasks." Glass blowers, coal miners, typographers, and others set their own stints, sometimes determined the quality of output, and almost always hired their own help.

After the 1840s a variant of craft control took shape with "inside contracting" in armament and machine manufacture. Inside contractors made agreements with owners to furnish parts of a product, say gun barrels or engine castings, for a given price by a set deadline, and then recruited, directed, and paid crews of skilled hands using materials and equipment supplied by owners. Such boss contractors were as functionally versatile as preindustrial master mechanics. Part worker, part foreman, and part employer, they both worked and supervised manual labor and earned daily wages as well as "job payments," personal profit based on the difference between sales to the company minus labor costs. Some contractors at the Whitin Machine Works in Whitinsville, Massachusetts, reaped princely sums from job payments, sometimes earning up to $10,000 and $15,000 a year by the mid-1870s. In such instances inside contracting probably degenerated into a sweating system even though wages far outdistanced scales in light industry. For a time at least, contractors shared the "shop culture" of their men and refrained from imposing the worst features of wage labor. Indeed, as Dan Clawson argues, inside contracting proved the industrial tradesman's way of exercising "control over the craft system from the inside."

Paternalism also came in several varieties. Philip Scranton has identified three distinct types of paternalism: corporate, familiar, and fraternal. The corporate paternalism in Lowell faded away by the 1850s. Familiar paternalism originated with the proprietary textile firms of Rhode Island, eastern Pennsylvania, and the southern Piedmont, and following the Civil War blossomed in the mill villages of the South, where, as Dwight Billings comments, "the paternalistic ethos of the plantation was extended . . ." into the factory. The textile patriarchs of the "New South" ruled over self-sufficient industrial enclaves with housing, churches, company stores, and social institutions that produced dependence on the family economy and on the benefactions of the "better people." They rummaged through the backlands "personally soliciting the services" of dirt farmers willing to have a try at industrial work, and also recruited help through families already in their employ. Yeoman and tenant-turned-factory worker experienced paternalism at its most pathetic. The Southern textile millhand was at the total mercy of the mill-village overlord and his retinue of preachers, foremen, and retailers. Vestiges of familiar paternalism could be found in Northern firms whose size seemed to preclude personalized treatment. The Vandalia Railroad had a payroll of 1,200 at its Terre Haute yards and repair shops in the 1870s, but that did not stay the familiarity of Charles Peddle, chief engineer, supervisor,

and founding member of the firm in 1852. Twenty years later Peddle
collected recommendations for vacancies from current employees and
personally interviewed each one. When the Peddles of industrializing
America referred to their companies as "our family" they were not being
disingenuous. Son and nephew worked along with father and uncle at the
Vandalia and other large enterprises.

Fraternal paternalism, perhaps the least well understood, likewise
involved kin hiring and management with the personal touch. All
resemblance to other kinds of paternalism stopped there. According to
Scranton, it thrived in the textile industry of Philadelphia (but may have
spilled over into other trades). The workplaces were small spinning,
weaving, or other single-process shops staffed by skilled labor making
quality goods on "flexible equipment" adaptable to new designs and
products. Owner and worker were British and Irish immigrants who lived
in the same neighborhoods and met in taverns and fraternal societies. The
felicity hinged partly on neighborliness, common ethnic heritage, and
"reciprocal respect" for craftsmanship. In addition, there were comparatively open avenues to ownership because fathers passed on firms to
sons and proprietors helped ambitious employees start their own businesses. Far from being the oppressive workplaces of the mill village with
asymmetrical social relations and limited scope for individual improvement, these workshops were hothouses of entrepreneurship.

Neither of these social systems of production worked well in the
economic instability of the Gilded Age. No employer, no matter how
craft-minded or paternalistic, could withstand the frenetic competition
and recurrent recessions without trimming costs and exercising more
control of the labor process, either by deploying new machines, by
fortifying chains of command, or by using some combination of these
possibilities. Producers of machines and armaments wearied of inside
subcontractors, who diverted revenues and ruled over what became
principalities of production. Beginning in the 1870s they phased in
reforms that began with paying workers directly, proceeded through
striking harder bargains over salaries, and ended with replacing internal
contractors with foremen. Waltham Watch completed this transition by
the end of the 1870s, Singer Sewing Machine a decade later, and
Whitinsville Machine Works by the 1890s. The substitution of foremen
for contractors was part of a larger managerial change that followed the
increase in plant size and mechanization of production which together
complicated the challenge of integrating an increasingly fragmented labor
process. It should be stressed, however, that the growth of industrial

bureaucracy did not snuff out worker autonomy any more than did power-driven equipment. As David Montgomery cautions, worker control "was not a condition or state of affairs which existed at any one point in time, but a chronic battle of industrial life which assumed a variety of forms." Nor did all managers wield absolute power. Overseers in small-batch production had wider discretion than overseers in high-volume industries who were accountable to supervisory personnel. They would soon establish that infamous "foreman's empire," which incurred the wrath of a generation of engineers and management reformers that came of age in the 1880s. The young Frederick Winslow Taylor and his acolytes fumed at the "rule-of-thumb methods" and subversive collusion between foreman and worker, the "soldiering" and shirking that held down output. The more typical foreman tyrannized over labor through a blend of "authoritarian rule" and "physical compulsion." At one mill foremen were "variously charged with impurity and profanity, with driving, overbearing, unsympathetic administration of their power, with discriminating unfairly against the best help because of jealousy." At another they also resorted to the obscenities of "Rolling Mill English" and snapped at those who took offense: "If you don't like it, get out."

The rigors of the market economy were no less fatal to the varieties of paternalism that survived the Civil War. Familiar paternalists traded off personal management for private welfarism and conspicuous investment in civic institutions. They gave senior employees watches and medallions in appreciation of loyal service, honored retirees at company dinners, and footed bills for plant excursions to amusement parks and seaside resorts. Few were wealthy enough to match the bequests of Andrew Carnegie and other captains of industry, but some did bestow modest gifts in compensation for a firmer hand within the factory and in hopes of currying favor in the wider community. Endowments included libraries, concert halls, perhaps even donations of land for parks as well as benches and water fountains for public squares. Philadelphia textile manufacturer William Baird left his community a social center with meeting rooms, offices for fraternal lodges, and a twelve-hundred-seat theater. This legacy came in the midst of a prolonged crisis. As Baird prepared to retire in the early 1870s, area manufacturers shifted from specialty goods to staple cottons and woolens, which necessitated changes in technology and labor. They installed simpler machines and replaced skilled males with women, only to find themselves in cutthroat markets and badly overstocked. Prices slipped in the financial collapse of 1873 and then fluctuated downward for thirteen long years. Incessant wage cuts and impersonal management triggered two outbursts of strikes during the mid-1870s and mid-1880s. The second of these turned into an organizing drive that left textile districts teeming with unions and the reciprocity of fraternal paternalism in a shambles.

A fair number of the Quaker City's textile manufacturers were poor men who had made good. So were many industrialists in Gilded Age America. The representative iron, tool, and machinery maker in Paterson, New Jersey, studied by Herbert Gutman, "arrived in the city as a skilled iron worker or a skilled craftsman as a young man who learned his skill by apprenticing in a . . . machinery works. Individual proprietorship or copartnership allowed him to escape from dependence and start his own firm." William Watson, born in 1819 to a Lancashire textile hand, drew his first wage at the early age of ten working alongside his father in a Belleville, New Jersey, factory. He apprenticed to a Paterson machinist and went to work as a journeyman before rising to foreman in a New York City shop. The mid-1840s found him back in Paterson at the head of an ironworks, which grew from a mere ten employees to over a thousand within thirty years. For Watson and myriad other sons of the working class, social advancement was no fiction.

The fact remains, however, that the Carnegies and the Watsons were obviously atypical. Frances W. Gregory and Irene D. Neu, the most thorough investigators of Gilded Age business elites, found that very few textile, railway, and iron and steel executives climbed out of society's mudsills. Fewer than one in ten were the offspring of skilled workers and just one in four born to farmers. About two-thirds came from business and professional backgrounds; nearly all were native-born Protestants; and the vast majority refrained from gainful employment of any kind until they were graduated from high school. Over a third attended college or had professional training. "Only at about eighteen," they conclude, did their representative industrialist "take his first regular job," and he rose "from it . . . not by a rigorous apprenticeship . . . but by an academic education well above average for the times."

· · ·

Far different indeed was the demographic profile of the men and women who worked for such manufacturers. The great immigration during the 1850s had given the industrial work force of urban America a foreign complexion. By the eve of the Civil War, between a third and a half of large cities, and even larger shares of the labor force, consisted of German, Irish, and British immigrants. Over the next thirty years the proportion of immigrants in such urban places fell to under a third as the war-torn 1860s and lean 1870s reduced the influx. The return of prosperity in the late 1870s prepared the way for the deluge of the 1880s in which over 4 million more foreigners landed, equaling the number of arrivals over the previous twenty-five years. What replenished the stock of native-born Americans was the fecundity of first-generation immigrants. In Massachusetts immigrant parents in the 1870s had nearly two more children each than American parents of native birth. By the 1880s fully three-fourths of the largest cities consisted of first- and second-generation immigrants. Foreigners and their children made up 87 percent of Chicago, 84 percent of Milwaukee and Detroit, 80 percent of New York and Cleveland, and 78 percent of St. Louis and San Francisco. Given the relatively low levels of immigration and high birth rates of settled foreigners, it is clear that the second generation outnumbered the first. Put another way, the foreign-born and their offspring were not recent arrivals unfamiliar with wage labor, but a combination of older and younger men and women with a growing store of industrial experience. Irish immigrants in cities with tight labor markets broke away from unskilled labor. By the 1880s the Irish dominated machine molding in Troy, New York, and made their way into the construction trades everywhere. Their sons made even deeper inroads into the trades and semiskilled jobs in industry. Clearly, we must look beyond the bustling immigrant enclaves of the city for the source of new workers.

The largest untapped source of labor came from the Northern farm, where natural disaster and economic change forced rural hands to leave for the cities and industry. Brutal winters and periodic infestations of insects caused hardship on the Great Plains. An epidemic of grasshoppers in 1872 followed by devastating blizzards in the winter of 1873 strained public relief and private charity to the breaking point and forced the federal government to take the extraordinary step of ordering the Army back from the Indian frontier to distribute food and clothing on the Plains. Those still employed on the Northern farms had to contend with new market pressures. Between 1860 and 1890 the number of farms tripled to nearly 6 million and the acreage brought under cultivation surpassed the total opened to production between 1607 and 1870. New farmers were not self-sufficient yeomen tilling fields of every imaginable crop for their own use. The enormous expansion of railroads, coupled with the interventions of middlemen, turned farmers away from generalized agriculture to cash crops. Outside the South, where new land-tenure systems developed and cultivation remained labor-intensive, market farmers adopted modern techniques. A study of start-up costs placed the value of farm equipment at $750 in the 1890s, several times the average in 1860. The reapers and combines in the grain fields of the Midwest sharply cut the need for manual labor while churning out surpluses that wreaked havoc on commodity prices and brought on indebtedness. Some farm families were bankrupted and forced into tenancy, which increased throughout the North after the Civil War. Many more headed cityward in a stream of rural-urban migrants that widened with the addition of the sons and daughters of prosperous farmers able to choose new vocations. No one knows precisely how many men and women in the North left farm for city from 1860 to 1890. Estimates range from a low of 5 million to a high of 8 million. Whatever the actual figure, it is clear that these "buckwheats," as they were called, preferred small and medium-sized towns to the metropolises and distributed themselves widely among occupations. Women made up the majority. A few took jobs in clerical work; many more turned to domestic service and manufacturing. The men were employed on the lower rungs of nonmanual work and semiskilled and unskilled factory jobs.

Market forces had a different impact on Southern agriculture. Nearly everyone, from the previously self-sufficient white yeoman to the newly freed black, got pulled into cotton growing. The burgeoning railway network was partly responsible, but far more important was the power of those who controlled land and credit and pulled the levers of politics. Landowners and merchants shaped two tenure systems, one for whites and one for blacks: tenancy, on the one hand, and wage labor and sharecropping, on the other. For poor whites in need of cash or credit, the reality was that cotton was needed for both immediately after the Civil War. They looked to "furnishing merchants" in market towns who advanced money or supplies on the condition that borrowers raise cotton. By the mid-1870s, read a Department of Agriculture report, debt-ridden Southerners "must raise cotton till they break." Many did fail when the bottom fell out of the cotton market in the 1870s and 1880s. Some farmers remained independent proprietors, but growing numbers became tenants working land that had passed into the hands of creditors.

Black workers in the rural South wound up in different but even more dire straits. In 1865–66 planters strapped for farm labor relied on two devices to return blacks to the cotton fields under conditions reminiscent of slavery. They tried to negotiate contracts that required the newly freed blacks to work in gangs and submit to close supervision at work and in their living quarters. Blacks Codes enacted in every Southern state during

1865 and 1866 accorded freedmen some legal rights—to sue and be sued, own property, and have marriage legalized—but also strengthened the planters' hand by ordering blacks to sign contracts by a deadline, usually the first of the year, or face fines or imprisonment. The codes, however, were invalidated by the Fourteenth Amendment and the Civil Rights Act of 1866 and were abrogated at the local level by the agents of the Freedmen's Bureau, the federal agency set up in 1865 to care for the former slaves. For their part, blacks were determined to exercise their newly found freedom and declined not only to make contracts but to work under conditions that smacked of slavery. They refused to do chores outside the fields, quit work before sundown, and resisted gang labor. Early freedmen had won an important skirmish for autonomy.

Political and economic developments, however, quickly thwarted black resistance to subordination. The black worker's dream of acquiring land faded when in 1865 President Andrew Johnson rescinded the historic Circular 13 promulgated in July by Oliver O. Howard, which had instructed Freedmen's Bureau agents to divide land confiscated during the war into forty-acre farms for black families. As the land was restored to its former owners, Freedmen's Bureau workers, motivated by the ideology of free labor, encouraged blacks to sign the contracts in the naïve and mistaken belief that they would eventually improve their status. Many blacks continued to resist but in 1866 they were more compliant with the first of two successive crop failures. Driven to desperation, larger numbers reluctantly became contract laborers either as individuals or as part of a group. Two distinct labor systems developed. Young and single men contracted as individuals for wages and became migratory hands moving among the plantations. Groups of families worked for "share wages," a portion of the crop that was sold by the workers, who then paid themselves. The groups soon became synonymous with families, as black resistance to gang labor persisted, and families became synonymous with sharecropping, a new system that evolved out of the "share wages" system. Sharecroppers who supplied tools and a mule were entitled to three-fourths of the yield; those who offered manual labor alone got half. These arrangements looked advantageous to the laborer but worked to the benefit of planter and merchant. In the 1870s state laws gave landlords privileged rights to the crops and court decisions defined sharecroppers as laborers with no rights to their product. Blacks were also victimized by unscrupulous creditors who charged usurious interest rates. Fewer wage laborers and sharecroppers may have been caught in the trap of debt peonage than historians once believed. As Gavin Wright insists, what tied blacks to the land and to a single community was their need for credit and "need to be known" by lenders. Only those blacks who stayed in one place and established reputations as good risks were allowed to borrow. In addition, they were immobilized by the absence of other employment opportunities in the region. With few exceptions manufacturers simply refused to hire blacks, who were inexorably transformed into a rural proletariat.

These tenure systems shed further light on the retardation of Southern manufacturing after the Civil War. The economic and social relations of credit and debt held down the rural-urban migration that supplied much of the industrial work force elsewhere. The conditions of farm labor, moreover, explain why the South continued to be a "low-wage region in a high-wage country." According to Wright, black farm laborers who were compensated in cash earned a minimum wage that became the standard for their race in other sectors, a kind of universal black wage. The freedman Floyd Thornhill left his master in 1866 to work in a Lynchburg tobacco mill. He put in twelve years and was promoted to a "boss." "I have done more than anybody else in that business," said Thornhill with obvious pride to Senate investigators in 1883. Yet even with over a decade of seniority and a management post he commanded a wage only marginally better than a common field laborer. Floyd Thornhill was unique in two respects: he left the land and enjoyed some job mobility, if not much wage improvement. Given the uniform wage structure for blacks, there was nothing to be gained by working in a factory. The few who did seek out industrial work were put in rigidly segregated jobs with slim chances for better ones. A study of Birmingham, Alabama, the "Pittsburgh of the South" in the late nineteenth century, shows that while nearly half the white workers who stayed in the city a decade or more moved into better jobs, only 8 to 17 percent of the blacks did. "Black workers, in fact," concludes Paul Worthman, "were constantly pushed out of various occupations toward the bottom of the occupational ladder."

Southern industrialists also used the artificially low wages for blacks to depress the wages of whites. The black wage set the general wage for unskilled and semiskilled factory workers, whose earnings were a third to a half of their Northern counterparts. It comes as no surprise that promoters of Southern industrialism overcame their aversion to immigrant workers. In 1865 a North Carolinian confessed that "immigration would, doubtless, be a blessing to us." But, as we have already seen, efforts to attract immigrants ended in failure. Few foreigners were prepared to work for such paltry sums and those who did go south either left or were fired because they were too fractious. New York immigrants brought in to run James B. Duke's Bonsack machines in the mid-1880s were sacked for complaining about "tyrannous shop rules" and heavy-handed foremen. Native-born whites, the only other labor source, were deterred by the same economic conditions that kept blacks on the land. If the textile industry is any indication, they entered the factory at a glacial pace. In 1890, when cloth was the third largest industrial sector, there were only 30,000 operatives, just 20,000 more than in 1860. Ten years later, in 1900, this work force tripled to 90,000, far surpassing its nearest competitor. This would suggest that it took the devastating depression of the 1890s to uproot rural labor in appreciable numbers.

• • •

Industrialization in the Gilded Age seems to have further skewed the maldistribution of wealth that had taken place in the first six decades of the century. An analysis of probate records for 1859–61 and 1889–91 conducted by the Massachusetts Bureau of Labor Statistics strongly indicates as much. At the beginning of this thirty-year span, Bay Staters with real and personal property valued at under $1,000 owned 20 percent of the total; at its end, their share had shrunk to a mere 2 percent. Wealthier people with holdings in excess of $100,000, less than 3 percent of all property owners in both periods, increased their share from 40 to 50 percent. This redistribution toward the top was even more pronounced in the industrial counties of Essex, Bristol, and Middlesex, in which no one was worth $500,000 or more on the eve of the Civil War. Thirty years later a few super-rich individuals with more than $500,000 in each county controlled between 12 and 15 percent of the wealth.

Findings on the distribution of income tell an unexpectedly different story. Daily wages and annual earnings of all workers in the North and South actually rose by nearly 50 percent between 1860 and 1890, easily the greatest percentage increase in the century. Real daily wages went from $1.00 a day to $1.50, and real cash annual earnings from under $300 to over $425. The gain in real income, however, was not the result of wage increases alone. The redistribution of labor from low-wage consumer industries to flourishing and better-paying producer goods industries also led to higher earnings. Perhaps even more important, following the inflationary spiral of the immediate post-Civil War years, the consumer price index fell from a high of 100 in 1873 to a low of 71 in the early 1890s.

This rising standard of living was not uniform. Indeed the 1850s witnessed the beginnings of a gap in worker incomes that widened in time. In the 1850s, when skilled males in the North averaged $300 a year, only $100 separated the best-paid workers from the worst. By the 1880s there was a spread of $250 between the top and the bottom, and it was not unusual for the highly skilled to earn up to three times more than the unskilled. The privileged stratum of 10 to 20 percent of the working class, depending upon the industrial configuration of a given locale, came from all trades but centered on metals, printing, and building construction. Often referred to as the "aristocracy of labor," these workmen earned in excess of $700 a year during the 1880s and sometimes reached $1,000 at a time when semiskilled male shoe and textile hands were lucky to bring home $550. Such families lived well on the income of male heads of families alone. Wives rarely worked outside the home and children postponed gainful employment until formal schooling ended at age sixteen. Families of semiskilled workers, in contrast, depended upon multiple incomes derived from boarders and the wages of children sent out to work in their early teens. According to surveys conducted by state bureaus of labor statistics in the 1870s and 1880s, youthful workers contributed up to $250 a year to household incomes, lifting most families above the recognized poverty line of $600 and closer to the earnings of labor aristocrats.

Even with two or three breadwinners, differences in the living standard of the less privileged and the labor aristocracy persisted. Relatively few industrial workers were homeowners. Only those who stayed in a single community over several decades and were extremely frugal saved the $1,000 or so for the purchase of a small house. Most wage earners rented, and as the Cincinnati printer William H. Foster told a Senate committee in 1883, labor aristocrats, or "first class mechanics" in his parlance, enjoyed better quarters than "second class" and "lower class" workmen. Massachusetts labor aristocrats lived in unattached houses or relatively spacious tenements described by observers as neat, clean, and situated in pleasant neighborhoods on the outskirts of cities or in new working-class suburbs. They worked in their backyard gardens and had enough disposable income to acquire sewing machines and primitive washers. They also furnished their homes with the amenities of middle-class respectability. Several rooms were carpeted, and the parlor, the household showcase used for entertaining, was filled with overstuffed furniture, bric-a-brac, and a piano or an organ. Some semiskilled and even unskilled workers of three- and four-income families approached this standard of living. Most, though, had to rent three- and four-room tenements with the barest of furnishings and none of the desired comforts. In the best of circumstances, apartments were tidy and neighborhoods agreeable; in the worst, especially in the squalid city slums, lodgings were damp and filthy cellars scarcely fit for human habitation, local streets were strewn with rubbish, and the sewers were open and noxious moats. Fortunately, falling prices for food and the labor of children kept outright starvation from the poorest households.

No working-class household, however, knew much security. In the opinion of one worker, machine-driven production created shorter employment cycles. "The manufacturers," he explained, "equip themselves to turn out their product in a shorter time, and the seasons of employment are shorter and more uncertain." Unemployment data are too patchy to allow firm comparisons. A recent analysis of joblessness in Massachusetts between 1875 and the 1920s, however, paints a grim picture for the Gilded Age workman. It distinguishes between the "rate" and "frequency" of unemployment. The first refers to the percentage of the work force idle at "any one time," the second to the percentage of employees out of work "at some point during the year." The unemployment rate hovered between 7 and 10 percent in the depression years of the mid-1870s and 1890s; the unemployment frequency, which is a more telling measure, stood at a shocking 30 percent. Even in prosperous times fully one in five workers was unemployed at some point in the year, and likely to be idled for three to four months. Depressions, of course, were socially blind: hard times hammered labor aristocrats as heavily as machine operatives and ditchdiggers. Labor aristocrats had a bit more to fall back on, but much more to lose. They were the most vulnerable of all workmen since their status depended upon skills continuously under assault. They were not much of an aristocracy at all if by that one means automatic transfer of rank from one generation to the next. For many, privilege was often fleeting.

For their part, leading businessmen and conservative economists were resigned to wild oscillations in the economy. The booms and busts, they assured themselves and the public at large, ensued naturally from the immutable laws of political economics which no amount of government meddling could amend. Price deflation, however, was another matter entirely. The same industrialists who revered individualism and who had complete faith in laissez-faire found nothing wrong with collusion in the cause of reversing the downward price spiral. In the early 1870s railwaymen worked out agreements for sharing traffic and dispensing rebates to cooperative shippers. This firmed up schedules to some degree but rebates were so generous, sometimes reaching 50 percent, that gross earnings and operating revenues fell to perilous levels. Pools and price-fixing accords with provisions for kickbacks to participants replaced rebates among railroaders and were later adopted by manufacturers. The National Butchers' Protective Association, a group of Eastern meat packers and handlers formed to boycott Midwestern beef, became a trade association to fix prices. Steel producers dealt with the superior market power of corporate buyers by creating a pool that stabilized rail prices, but not until the late 1880s. John D. Rockefeller, no stranger to market manipulation, was unimpressed and scoffed at consortiums as "ropes of sand." As the wily oil magnate implied, pools dissipated in hard times and in good times mavericks dropped out in order to get the competitive edge. Not a few of those who persevered could resist the temptation to submit phony vouchers and falsify accounts. The cupidity did not ruffle railroad promoter John Murray Forbes, who confessed, "We can stand a good deal of cheating better than competition."

While it is difficult to assess the impact of corporate collusion in fixing commodity prices, it is clear that for all the economic instability and grumbling over deflation, industrialists managed to accumulate fortunes that dwarfed the holdings of antebellum businessmen. Edward Pessen's investigation of the Jacksonian elites turns up hardly any truly wealthy manufacturers and only a few millionaires, nearly all of them merchants and financiers. The portfolios of the wealthiest manufacturers seldom approached $500,000 and commonly were trivial compared with the millions of such merchant princes as the Girards and Astors. Civil War inflation and generous wartime contracts, to be sure, spawned a small class of millionaire industrialists. Marcellus Hartley, the armaments merchant and manufacturer who made a fortune selling defective equipment at exorbitant rates to the Northern government, was only one of a number of mushroom aristocrats nurtured by the war. Not until the postwar period, however, did manufacturers approach financial and social parity with the mercantile elite. Few were the equal of Andrew Carnegie, several times a millionaire long before being bought out by J. P. Morgan for one and a half billion dollars in 1900, but many blended imperceptibly into the nation's upper class. It is only in the Gilded Age that one can speak of a class of wealthy manufacturers, or indeed of a bona fide industrial bourgeoisie.

Rich Americans had a long history of high living and lavish entertaining. The diary of antebellum socialite Philip Hone betrays a frenetic social calendar of lunches, teas, and dinner parties with the first families of New York, who were served gourmet meals and vintage wines at tables and place settings fit for royalty. If the names of manufacturers did not appear on Hone's lengthy guest lists, it was not solely for want of social cachet or resources to reciprocate in kind. Evangelical morality and republican sentiment frowned on ostentation of any kind and took special offense at conduct that smacked of self-indulgence. But the older taboos melted away under the fantastic capital accumulation of the period. Even parsimonious New Englanders, paradigms of Protestant asceticism, submitted to what the historian Ray Ginger aptly called the "Age of Excess." The founding fathers of Fall River textiles, who had spent half their lives in wood-frame homes within earshot of the clatter of the mills, after midcentury moved to more distant and prestigious turf. Colonel Richard Borden, paterfamilias of a tight-knit kinship group of textile owners, set the pace by building a palatial home maintained by a cortege of servants on "The Hill," a gentle slope far from the bustle below. Sons and nephews settled down in opulent mansions of cut stone and carved wood, and played host to one another at soirees that would have won the envy of Hone himself.

Provincial Fall River was a distant second to grand big-city people when it came to social excess. The industrialists of New York were first among such exclusive equals. The dowager Mary Mason Jones shocked the cocktail circuit when in 1871 she deserted her lower Manhattan brownstone for a mansion in the Parisian style on Fifth Avenue between Fifty-seventh and Fifty-eighth streets. Delmonico's restaurant, the dining spot of the rich in Hone's day, took a shorter step uptown a few years later, moving from Fourteenth Street to Fifth Avenue and Twenty-sixth Street. The uptown migration continued during the depression of the 1870s as wealthy New York filled in the mile or so of prime real estate north of Twenty-sixth Street with French châteaus and Renaissance-style mansions that made upper Fifth Avenue into one of the most elegant addresses in the nation. William H. Vanderbilt, grandson of the legendary Commodore and son of William K., finally gained the social acceptance that had evaded his family for two generations. His Fifty-second Street palace of stone and stained-glass windows imported from France was the scene of the ball of the age in March 1883, a costume party and housewarming which gave vent to the wildest fantasies of the urban rich. Even the William Astors, titular heads of the city's "Four Hundred," who had snubbed parvenu industrialists, found the tables turned and paid a humiliating visit to Alva Vanderbilt in order to snatch a last-minute invitation. Vanderbilt greeted his guests dressed as the Duc de Guise; his brother, Cornelius II, appeared as Louis XVI in a *"habit de coeur* and breeches of fawn-colored brocade, trimmed with silver point d'Espagne"; Mrs. Pierre Lorillard came as a phoenix in a gown of gray silk bordered in flame-colored satin. "The shifting gleams of gorgeous color and quaint and curious outlines flittering through the rooms— themselves a study for an artist," wrote the New York *Herald,* "made up a scene never rivalled in Republican America."

Republican America? Private life in Fifth Avenue mansions reveals just how far Gilded Age financiers and manufacturers had strayed from the course of republican simplicity. It took an eccentric like John D. Rockefeller to acknowledge the austerity of earlier days, for as business historian E. C. Kirkland observed, the captains of industry "believed that economic activity stood apart from moral and personal considerations." Few felt pangs of conscience or much compulsion to defend the new hedonism, and most honored a tacit code of silence. When asked, "How do you feel this morning, Governor," the railroad baron and former California chief executive Leland Stanford snorted, "Wouldn't you like to know." Public endeavor, however, would not bear such arrogance. Hounded by nagging journalists and probing public officials, businessmen had to speak up for themselves and the new order. Much like Charles Elliott Perkins, president of the Chicago, Burlington, and Quincy Railroad, they spouted the aphorisms of thrift and industriousness, perseverance and sobriety. "If a man by hard work and intelligence, honestly acquires property and takes care of it," said the self-educated railwayman, "while his neighbor, equally honest and intelligent, acquires property and fails to take care of it, are the products of the industry of both of them unjustly distributed?"

Increasingly, idioms of economic law embellished this language of free laborism. Industrialists spoke more fervently of laws of supply and demand, liberty of contract, and other axioms of the free market, not so much in behalf of private accumulation as against government intervention. The specter of an energetic state loomed larger with the passage of the Thirteenth, Fourteenth, and Fifteenth amendments, worker movements for a legal ten- or eight-hour day, and Radical Republican talk of stamping forty-acre homesteads out of plantation land. At the same time, farmer insurgencies in the Midwest resulted in public regulation of the railroads. Such ominous extensions of state power invested Smithian economics with renewed relevance in business circles, and by the last quarter of the century, in the estimation of historian Sidney Fine, "laissez

faire was championed . . . as it never was before." E. L. Godkin, editor
of *The Nation*, joined the outcry against state activism along with the
former free-soiler Rev. Henry Ward Beecher. Sermonizing during the
carnage of the railroad strikes of 1877, Beecher amused his middle-class
parishioners with an exegesis on the "elementary principles of political
economy." He reprimanded workers for laboring under the misconcep-
tion that strikes overturned wage cuts because there "must be continual
shrinkage until things come back to the gold standard, and wages, as well
as greenbacks, provisions and property must share in it. It was true," he
went on, "that $1 a day was not enough to support a man and five
children, if a man would insist upon smoking and drinking beer." But $1
a day was more than enough for water, which "costs nothing. (Laughter.)
Men cannot live by bread . . . but the man who cannot live on bread and
water is not fit to live. (Laughter.)" He conceded there "might be special
cases of hardship, but the great laws of political economy cannot be set
at defiance."

Beecher's callous conservatism owed as much to the new Social
Darwinism of Herbert Spencer as to classical economics and post-Civil
War Protestantism. Indeed Spencer proved to be the intellectual darling
of conservatives, a ubiquitous presence from the Fifth Avenues to the
back porches of Middle America. Carnegie befriended the Englishman
and fellow industrialists wined and dined him at Delmonico's; Edward
Livingston Youmans dedicated his *Popular Science Monthly* to the new
creed; and John R. Commons described his Indiana upbringing as the
fusion of "Hoosierism, Republicanism, Presbyterianism, and Spencer-
ism." Beecher, never at a loss for culinary imagery, called Spencer his
"meat and bread." Spencer's followers disputed the fine details of his
Darwinian universe. Yale sociologist William Graham Sumner, perhaps
his most prolific protégé, doubted both the inevitability of progress and
the sanctity of natural rights. "Before the tribunal of nature," he once
said with characteristic acridity, "a man has no more right to life than a
rattlesnake." The heart of the matter was to pursue self-interest in a
marketplace unfettered by man-made law and guided only by the force of
natural selection, which sorted out the weak from the strong in an
evolution toward higher economic and social forms embodied by the
wealthy businessman and the modern corporation.

As Herbert Gutman cautioned, however, Andrew Carnegie's admiration of Herbert Spencer does not mean that "jungle ethics reigned
supreme" in industrializing America. Quite the contrary, Gilded Age
businessmen failed to establish ideological hegemony or wield unlimited

power. Working-class spokesmen steeped in the older values—whether radicalism, evangelicalism, or indeed popular communitarianism—poked fun at the political platitudes mouthed by leading industrialists and rebuked apologists for elite philanthropy. When in 1894 Carnegie predicted that "individualism will continue, but the millionaire will be the trustee of the poor" in his vaunted "Gospel of Wealth," the *Locomotive Firemen's Magazine* sneered: "flopdoddle" and "slush." The moderate *National Labor Tribune* was even harsher, ridiculing the "Gospel" in a mock prayer that began: "Oh, Almighty Andrew Philanthropist, who are in Europe spending the money of your slaves and serfs," went on to thank him for grinding the faces of his charges, and ended: "So we commend ourselves to thy mercy and for evermore sing thy praise. Amen!" Several years earlier an amateur poet and Knights of Labor activist captured in verse a "world turned . . . completely over," in which Jay Gould appeared as a brass-band musician, Commodore Vanderbilt a doctor, and President Grover Cleveland a streetcar conductor sharing the added disgrace of earning $1.00 a day each.

Workmen were not content to mock the power brokers of the new industrial order. They challenged corporate America in workshops and at the polls in what Gutman called an earnest "search for power" that did not go unrewarded. Village workmen in communities shaken by economic change, and urban colleagues to a lesser extent, could count on the assistance of local shopkeepers and entrepreneurs in battles with national corporations over wages and working conditions. Local support stemmed from the intimacy of village life, shopkeeper dependence on worker patronage, and popular perceptions of railways and branches of national corporations as outsiders, alien forces that disrupted traditional ways of life. Gutman went on to argue that labor activists directed this anti-elite feeling into reform legislation that belies the traditional picture of a political culture under capitalist domination.

Again and again workers and their allies acted out the script that Gutman described. In the winter of 1873–74, shopmen and linemen and then trainmen in the employ of the Pennsylvania Railroad walked off their jobs in protest against wage reductions, irregular pay intervals, and excessive hiring of helpers and apprentices. The work stoppage engulfed seventeen lines whose centers were in the yards and depots of rural towns across the East and Midwest. Defiant workers took possession of repair shops, uncoupled cars, tore up track, and for good measure cut telegraph wires in a dress rehearsal of the general strike on the rails in the summer of 1877. Such bold strokes against corporate property did not unnerve the larger community. Indeed local unions gave generously to the Erie workers' strike funds; shopkeepers contributed food and extended credit to the families of strikers; newspaper editors assailed the "absolutism of the Napoleons" of the railways. At Susquehanna Depot, Pennsylvania, home of a major Erie installation, management moved swiftly to sack strikers and enlist the police power of the state, demanding protection of company property. Sheriff H. B. Helme marched a posse to the terminal where a cordon of workmen forced the police to lay down their arms before proceeding. Scenes of disarmed policemen fraternizing with strikers on Erie ground so angered company officials that they raised a private army. Helme's men then rearmed to the cheers of strikers, marched the soldiers to the town limits, and sent them on their way. Strikes in other locales during the depression-blighted winter of 1873–74 and in the immediate future ran a similar course. Militiamen declined either to muster or to exert much force against workers; local merchants refused to provision company police or outside military units; and editors assailed railway owners. The Scranton *Times* found the Susquehanna strike easily understandable: the "Erie has wronged its labor grossly and got its blow."

   Labor's political activism also produced results. Urban and small-town workers alike often defeated uncooperative public officials and elected partisans from their own ranks and the middle class to city halls and state legislatures. Lobbyists did their part as well, few as effectively as J. P. McDonnell, the Dublin-born Irish nationalist and socialist who landed in New York in 1868 but, distressed by the city's unruly left, settled down in quieter Paterson, New Jersey. There he divided his time between publishing the *Labor Standard,* a leading workers' sheet, and serving as chief lobbyist for the Legislative Committee of the state affiliate of the Federation of Organized Trades and Labor Unions and later the American Federation of Labor. The intrepid labor advocate assembled a bloc of legislators from each side of the aisle that enacted a long list of reforms in the 1880s and early 1890s. He succeeded in abolishing the hated prison labor system, reducing the use of child labor, establishing a factory inspection commission, and repealing the state's archaic conspiracy laws. Labor lobbyists in Ohio, Pennsylvania, and other industrial states had legislators outlaw private armies and scrip payments, the bane of miners and ironworkers, and after 1870 establish bureaus of labor statistics following the lead of Massachusetts. Coalitions of workers and agrarian radicals, sometimes in league with small businessmen and with patrician devotees of paternalistic government in rural states, regulated railway rates and grain elevator charges. Gilded Age workers did enjoy some political leverage, as Gutman pointed out.

Worker power was not a fixed and immutable quantity but involved a constant, even daily, struggle with a shifting balance that ultimately tilted toward capital. Recession and technological innovation created reserve contingents of the unemployed in need of work and the underemployed eager to better themselves. Both groups were routinely brought in as strikebreakers. Owners who were refused police protection for "black-legs" by local officials usually got a friendlier hearing from higher authorities in governors' mansions as well as the White House. For every militiaman who declined to support the established order, scores more rose to do their duty with enthusiasm and went about their work with great efficiency. A government study showed that state troops were called out to calm labor unrest nearly 500 times between 1875 and 1910. Most of these interventions occurred in the last quarter of the nineteenth century, and by the 1890s, as we shall see, federal troops were being used to supplement state forces. A more subtle if seldom used but equally powerful weapon for employers, then as now, stemmed from their ability to pull out of a community. As the resolution of the tumult on the Erie line at Susquehanna Depot suggests, the mere threat of leaving was usually enough to bring labor back to work and discourage middle-class supporters. The village of 8,000 became an armed camp when in March 1874 Sheriff Helme eventually buckled under Erie pressure and agreed to call out the militia. By the end of the month 1,800 citizen soldiers, moved in on special trains supplied by the railroad, sealed off company property. The militia patrols, backed by a declaration of martial law, however, did not dishearten labor and/or diminish the anti-Erie resolve of the local middle class. But when the company announced plans to move to Elmira, New York, workers began to reapply for their berths and local business-men turned against them in fear for their own livelihoods. A solid citizen who had opposed the military intervention went so far as to supply the railroad with the names of strike leaders for blacklisting and prosecution. A decade later some boss stove molders of Troy, New York, dogged by militant iron molders, sought a favorable labor climate elsewhere. They moved to Cincinnati and other cities, leaving scores of jobless and embittered molders, helpers, and unskilled hands on street corners. Labor simply had no answer to capital flight.

While historians of the Gutman School have noted the limits of worker power within communities, they have slighted the restrictions on worker influence in politics. Their contribution to the politics of this stormy period stops at rectifying the conventional wisdom of an impotent working class rendered weaker in an arena made rotten by the corruption of the elite. A closer look at the balance of political forces indicates, however, that industrialists gradually eroded social reform and effectively rolled back some of labor's major achievements. The quiet lobbying of labor activists and noisier insurgencies of farmers set off a backlash. Business leaders firmed up their trade associations, redoubled their lobbying efforts, and lectured lawmakers on the dangers of active government. Corporate leaders also bought political influence with munificent contributions to politicians in both parties. ''In a Republican district I was a Republican; in a Democratic district I was a Democrat,'' Jay Gould confessed to a legislative committee. He then added that ''in a doubtful district I was doubtful; but I will always be Erie.'' Leading businessmen placed far more faith in the efficacy of rule by nonelective officials insulated from the misguided fancies of an ignorant and petulant public. The Interstate Commerce Act of 1887, which set up the Interstate Commerce Commission, marked a step in this direction by transferring the burning question of regulation from the jurisdiction of popularly elected officials to presidential appointees. Federal government by commission, however, was still experimental and to the businessman not wholly reliable. The judiciary, much like federal troops and militias originating outside the flash points of strikes, seemed more trustworthy. ''There are so many jackasses about nowadays who think property has no rights,'' said an irritated Charles Elliott Perkins, ''that the filling of Supreme Court vacancies is the most important function of the Presidential office.'' Perkins and his colleagues looked to the courts for relief, not just in Washington but in state capitals as well, and they were not disappointed.

The scores of cases heard in state and federal courts are too many to review here in detail. It is enough to repeat Sidney Fine's view that jurists gradually became the ''special guardians of the negative [inactive] state.'' State courts began the assault on reform in a series of cases in the mid-1880s that widened entrepreneurial liberties and restricted worker freedoms. In 1885 New York Superior Court Judge Robert Earl wrote his infamous ''freedom of sweatshop'' opinion that found an 1884 law prohibiting cigar making in certain tenements to be an unreasonable abridgment of property rights. In 1886 and 1893 the supreme courts of Pennsylvania and Missouri, respectively, invoked ''freedom of contract'' to nullify statutes prohibiting wage payment in anything except legal tender. In 1891 the state supreme court of Massachusetts struck down a law enacted earlier in the year outlawing fines imposed by employers, and in 1895 the Illinois court declared unconstitutional a clause in an antisweatshop law passed in 1893 that legalized the eight-hour day for women and children. State jurists also began to issue injunctions sought by employers against strikes and demonstrations. In repudiation of the historic *Commonwealth* v. *Hunt* (Massachusetts, 1840), which had held that unions were per se lawful organizations and collective action in and of itself was not evidence of conspiracy, several state courts enjoined workers from striking for closed shops in the mid-1880s. At the end of the decade the Supreme Judicial Court of Massachusetts proscribed informational picketing because the "marching up and down with intimidating placards" disturbed the peace. In 1893 New Orleans dockers, locked in a struggle against British shippers, were ordered to desist from interfering with strikebreakers. Later that year the city's teamsters were hit with sweeping injunctions that anticipated the crippling court orders against the American Railway Union in 1894. In issuing the first injunction on the grounds of the Sherman Antitrust Act, Louisiana District Court Judge E. C. Billings allowed that the "congressional debates show the statute had its origins in the evils of massed capital," but proceeded to argue that when "Congress came to formulating the prohibition . . . the subject had so broadened in the minds of legislators that . . . they made the interdiction to include combinations of labor, as well as of capital." One could go on endlessly citing cases in a similar vein and still only suggest the extent of conservative judicial rulings.

United States Supreme Court decisions were also very much in this same spirit. Justices appointed after the mid-1880s replaced the foundations of regulatory law with an impregnable wall that insulated corporations from legislative action. Led by archconservative Justice Stephen J. Field, the Court eventually accepted the proposition that the due process clause of the Fourteenth Amendment, originally intended in part to guarantee the procedural rights of freedmen, also covered "substantive rights" and thereby ensured the liberty to pursue business and accumulate profit unfettered. It then declared corporations to be "persons" in the eyes of the law, conferring on business enterprise the same privileges and immunities as individual citizens. These novel rulings rendered government powerless in the face of the corporation and opened up a never-never land of business freedom. Not even the seemingly unambiguous language of the Sherman Antitrust Act withstood the onslaught of reaction. In *United States* v. *E. C. Knight,* the first case brought under Sherman in 1895, Chief Justice Melville W. Fuller drew a distinction between manufacture and commerce and affirmed that federal jurisdiction extended only to the latter sphere. Since Knight, which controlled over 90 percent of sugar refining, engaged in manufacture, it was safely outside the purview of the law.

Fuller's legalistic hairsplitting did not convince Associate Justice John M. Harlan, the lone dissenter in *Knight*. Harlan disputed the idea that the Constitution obliged government to "fold its arms and remain inactive" while aggregated capital "distorted the prices of necessities." His was not the only discordant voice, but to find others one had to venture beyond the chambers of the Supreme Court and the drawing rooms of bourgeois America. John D. Rockefeller may have been correct in confidently asserting that "the combination is here to stay." But those who worked in the nation's fields and factories saw it differently. They staged massive strikes in the late 1870s and early 1890s and between these convulsions organized a national federation of craft unions and formed the Knights of Labor, the most broadly based "movement culture" in the nineteenth century.

The timing of the mass strikes during the 1870s and 1890s is instructive. Previous economic collapses in the 1830s and 1840s had chilled collective action at workplaces, brought down popular movements, and fired religious revivals, with the cumulative effect of weakening radicalism and infusing workers with the spirit of the received culture. No longer. The protracted recessions of the 1870s and 1890s activated a clergy with diminished influence. For the first time workers ignored sermons and fought back in ways that were as insolent as they were unique. What had happened? The emergence of the new social and technical systems of the factory, of a strange conservative idiom, and of an aloof and arrogant class of manufacturers swept away the received cultures of the workplace that once cushioned the impact of industrialization. Workers were herded into impersonal and authoritarian factories whose machines cheapened their manual skills and made their livelihoods more uncertain. The growth of the plant, writes Robert Ozanne of the McCormick and International Harvester works at Chicago in the 1870s, "destroyed the personal contact which had formerly characterized the Works. The size of the plant now made it inevitable that the workmen would henceforth deal only with hired managers" adverse to the intimacy of paternalism and the fraternity of handicraft production. The huge profit reaped from such businesses, moreover, catapulted owners from modest homes in close proximity to the workshop to elite neighborhoods remote from the centers of production. The men of industry were no longer sympathetic masters who earlier in the century were familiar faces on the block. They now moved in exclusive social circles, flaunted their wealth, and spoke a lusty materialism far different from the shared belief in evangelical Protestantism and free laborism. They also relied on force and coercion to enforce their will. The social and ideological connective tissue between employer and employee had been fatally wounded.

5.

The Rise and Fall of the Knights of Labor

"In ordinary times a collision would have been inevitable," said the iron molder William Sylvis of relations between labor and capital during the Civil War. "Nothing but the patient patriotism of the people and the desire in no way to embarrass the [Union] government" prevented widespread unrest. The nationalism that maintained class peace behind the Union lines, however, had worn thin by the midpoint of the Civil War. The popular slogan "rich man's war and poor man's fight" took on new meaning in spring 1863 following the first draft call for troops. The provision that allowed a draftee to designate a stand-in or buy his way out for $300, the rough equivalent of an unskilled worker's yearly income, inflamed the antiwar passions of Irish immigrants everywhere. On July 11, Irish longshoremen in New York City, fresh from a major strike marred by battles with black strikebreakers and angered by publication of the conscription lists, vented their frustrations in a four-day rampage. Roving gangs sacked conscription offices, plundered the homes of the wealthy, and laid into blacks with special fury. Over one hundred New Yorkers, most of them black, lost their lives before troops ordered in from the battlefield of Gettysburg restored order. Unjust conscription policies and wartime hardship also aroused Southerners. Confederate soldiers deserted in droves and in 1863 urban women reacted to runaway inflation and food shortages with uncommon rage. In Mobile women bearing a banner that read "Bread or Peace" raided food stores, and in Richmond they marched into the business district and helped themselves to provisions.

As food riots subsided in the South trade unionism grew in the North in response to continued inflation. In 1864 union locals in the region multiplied fourfold to 270 and came together in trade assemblies. The union revival, predictably followed by a flurry of strikes, drove Northern employers to seek the assistance of government. They first called on U.S.

consuls in Europe to stoke up immigration in order to ease the wartime labor shortage and thus gain the upper hand in dealing with employees. When that failed, they brought pressure to bear on state lawmakers for antilabor measures. Several states tried to thwart picketers by making it a criminal offense to prevent anyone from going to work. "More successful" than laws, writes David Montgomery, "was the use of force to break strikes." On three occasions in 1864 federal troops, sometimes operating under martial law, forced machinery workers back to their jobs. Such interventions, Montgomery adds, "stimulated the political awareness of the working classes."

This rising class awareness carried over into peacetime. Two labor organizations—the National Labor Union (NLU) and the Noble and Holy Order of the Knights of Labor (K of L)—emerged within five years of Appomattox. The NLU was a congress of trade unionists and sympathetic reformers that met ten times from 1866 to 1870 and 1873 to 1875. It gave labor advocates a forum for publicizing cooperation, land and monetary reform, and trade unionism, as well as the eight-hour day. In 1866 and 1867 the NLU supported workers who went on strike for shorter hours and pressured lawmakers in state legislatures and in Washington to place legal limits on the workday. Unionism fell off in 1868 and the NLU was taken over by middle-class radicals who spent the next four years organizing a labor party that never got off the ground.

The Knights of Labor were more durable. "The Order," as the Knights were popularly known, evolved from an obscure brotherhood in 1869 and concentrated in Pennsylvania for most of the 1870s into a national organization of gigantic proportions by the mid-1880s. Two to three million people passed through its portals between the early 1870s and mid-1890s, and nearly every county in the nation had at least one Knight lodge at some point during this period. Membership skyrocketed by over 600,000 between summer 1885 and spring 1886. It peaked at nearly 750,000 in summer 1886 but fell just as precipitously. By the early 1890s membership cards were collectors' items and lodge halls gathered dust. However, no other movement had such an impact on the American working class.

• • •

As the Knights discussed plans for their first national convention in 1877, miners and railway workers grabbed national headlines. Twenty Irish mine laborers convicted of murdering eastern Pennsylvania colliery officials in the notorious Molly Maguire trials nervously paced jail cells in anticipation of a hangman's noose. The trials had been highly irregular. The star witness for the prosecution was James McParlan, a Pinkerton detective who claimed to have infiltrated a cabal of Molly Maguires within the Ancient Order of Hibernians that allegedly committed terror and murder in the mine fields. One of the prosecutors was Franklin Gowen, a mine owner who had hired McParlan to spy on the Mollies. Nonetheless on June 21 militiamen marched four of the condemned two by two to a gallows in Mauch Chunk. Six more Mollies, John Boyle and Hugh McGehen among them, trekked to the scaffold in nearby Pottsville bearing large red roses, symbol of eternal Ireland. "Justice at last," screamed the Philadelphia *Times,* forgetting perhaps that the final chapter in the nation's first execution of labor militants would not be written until December 1878, when John Keefe, the last of the twenty, plunged through the trap.

The hangings of the Molly Maguires did not distract the nation's railwaymen from their balance sheets. Indeed, on the day of the executions in Mauch Chunk, a railway manager gloated that wage reductions "had been successfully carried out" by all the railroads that have "tried it of late." "I have no fear of any trouble," he added, "if it is done with a proper show of firmness . . . and . . . [workers] see they must accept it cheerfully or leave." News of the wage cut, however, brought turmoil to the railway brotherhoods, independent unions restricted to skilled and better-paid hands. Brotherhood leaders urged caution on restive members, just as they had done during the first round of wage cuts three years earlier, but wound up discrediting themselves. Rank-and-file militants bolted to the Trainmen's Union, the first industrial union on the railways, which had called a regional meeting to plan its course of action. But the Allegheny City gathering ended in chaos over a strike resolution and the Trainmen's Union disintegrated on the spot. It looked to the railroads as if "trouble" would be avoided. The apparent disarray, however, encouraged the Baltimore and Ohio, which had not participated in the June reductions, to take its turn. In early July the board of directors approved two resolutions before adjourning for the summer. One ordered a 10 percent dividend, the other a concomitant wage cut to take effect on the sixteenth of the month. It was a fateful decision.

The shock waves first rocked the quiet village of Martinsburg, West Virginia, a B&O relay center west of Baltimore. On July 16, a cattle train pulled in, but Martinsburg trainmen, instead of replacing the crew, uncoupled the cars, drove the engine into the yard, and announced that no rolling stock would leave until the wage cut was rescinded. In early evening a crowd converged on the depot and prevented the mayor and police from arresting the strike leaders. Dawn found railway workers and townsfolk disrupting freight traffic and railway managers beseeching Governor Henry M. Matthews to clear the track. Matthews ordered out the Berkeley Light Guard but to no avail. As a train guarded by the Berkeleys pulled out of the yard, a melee ensued in which shots rang out and hit a striker and a soldier. The horrified militiamen not only threw down their arms but went over to the strikers. More militia units tried desperately to keep the peace as strikes and mayhem broke out at other B&O depots east of Martinsburg. By the end of the week federal troops were required to restore order in riot-torn Baltimore, home office of the B&O.

Pittsburgh was to the Pennsylvania Railroad what Baltimore was to the B&O. Martinsburg was the talk of the city when on July 19 the Pennsylvania, widely despised as "the Monopoly," foolishly ordered a change in work rules that amounted to a speedup. By midday the city was awash with gangs at railway junctions coaxing crews from trains and tearing up track. Railroad leaders pleaded with the sheriff for help, but as at Martinsburg, very few militiamen suited up and those that did openly mixed with the crowd. "The sympathy of the people, the sympathy of the troops, and my own sympathy," confessed a public official, "was with the strikers." Troops mustered in Philadelphia and brought in by train braved the fury of small-town Pennsylvanians along the way and arrived to an even rougher reception in the Steel City. On the morning of July 21 state militiamen strategically positioned at railway crossings shot down twenty civilians and brought down the wrath of the city. Enraged Pittsburghers chased the militia into a roundhouse located in a small valley. "We'll have them out if we have to roast them out," came the cry from a crowd on the high ground which peppered its quarry with rocks and then pushed railways cars aflame with coal and oil down the tracks to the roundhouse below. The burning cars flushed out the militia, but that was the least of the railway's problem. By the time plebeian Pittsburgh completed its work on Monday morning, railway buildings were in ruins and over 100 engines and 500 freight cars immobilized.

As Pittsburgh smoldered, labor violence gripped cities and railway centers as far south as Galveston, Texas, and as far west as Chicago. Even the most unlikely places teetered on the edge of rebellion. Omaha prevented certain turbulence only when the superintendent of the Union Pacific, fearful of the "lawless mob," canceled a wage reduction. Over

3,000 federal troops and several times that number of militiamen from different states patrolled elsewhere. No one knows the extent of property damage, but authorities agreed that the uprisings claimed over 100 lives.

Local protests varied in particulars but conformed to a larger pattern. Spontaneous work stoppages on the railroads brought on general strikes with the active or tacit approval of segments of the middle class; job actions were usually peaceful if impassioned until the intervention of "outside" forces of law and order; and except at St. Louis, strikers vied for economic and not political power. St. Louis came close to insurrection thanks to the Workingmen's party of the United States, the coordinator of the work stoppage, which fleetingly exercised de facto civil authority. Party cadre had displaced the constabulary and had seen to it that suppliers of such basic needs as bread stayed on the job but then fell back on orders from party leaders. Even in the Gateway to the Midwest, however, workers and their partisans thought of their struggle not so much as an act of class warfare as a blow against "monopoly" and "alien authority."

This was not the first instance, nor would it be the last, of antimonopoly outrage. The wage cuts and unilateral changes in work rules imposed by mine and railway owners in 1873–74 had aroused populist tendencies in the "island communities" of the nation's heartland. The same Susquehanna, Pennsylvania, journalist who had denounced the Erie chastised the governor for using the militia against honest workingmen "who ask nothing but their hard-earned wages." Residents boarded passengers who had been marooned by the strike and shopkeepers refused to provision militiamen. Nor was village America more hospitable to Pinkertons or other private police in the pay of corporations. The mayor of Braidwood, Illinois, scene of a miners' strike against a pit owned by the Chicago, Wilmington, and Vermillion Company in summer 1874, laughed off company demands to vest Pinkertons with the power of arrest: for good measure, the mayor deputized miners and their friends, who then cleared the streets of the despised Pinkertons. Asked to account for his actions, the mayor allowed that he objected to "strangers dragooning a quiet town with deadly weapons"; he feared citizen miners "a good deal less than . . . the Chicago watchmen."

The Susquehanna and Braidwood disturbances did not remotely approach the intensity of Baltimore or Pittsburgh four years later. Lives were not lost and no tipples or terminals were put to the torch, even though some were occupied by vengeful strikers. Nor did these labor brushfires stir the backlash of 1877. Conservative columnists and

politicians likened the strikes to the Paris Commune and cried out for
retribution, lest, as journalist E. L. Godkin put it, the nation "surrender
to a body of day laborers of the lowest grade of power." The dispatch of
militiamen and federal troops was the most visible aspect of official
repression. Strike leaders were also hauled before state and federal courts
for conspiracy, inciting to riot, and other offenses. Juries were reluctant
to convict, but some workingmen were found guilty and sent to prison.
State governments punished insubordinate militiamen and moved deci-
sively to restore discipline and beef up forces. Militia units were
consolidated and brought under centralized control. Budgets were increased, training mandated, equipment improved, and armories con-
structed around expected trouble spots in urban centers. Railway
management responded with both carrot and stick. Some established
regular pay periods and graduated wage scales based on seniority; others
set up welfare funds and doled out cash bonuses to loyal hands who
worked through the strikes. Most major carriers also fired suspected
leaders and shared blacklists.

· · ·

Terence V. Powderly seized upon the immediate significance of
employer recrimination. The firings and blacklists made "victims of
hundreds of Knights of Labor, who left . . . [Pennsylvania] in all
directions" with the gospel of Knighthood. The young machinist was in
a good position to know. Powderly had spent the Long Depression out of
work and on the move, finally getting a job in a Scranton railway shop
near his place of birth on the eve of the 1877 riots. Within a year he
would be elected Grand Master Workman of the Noble and Holy Order
of the Knights of Labor.

Powderly was a bundle of contradictions. A wiry man of medium
height with a walruslike mustache and deep-set eyes that squinted
through a pince-nez, he cut a stately figure in his customary black
broadcloth coat and starched white collar. The labor journalist John
Swinton wrote that "English novelists take men of Powderly's look for
poets, gondoliers, scullers, philosophers, and heroes crossed in love, but
no one ever drew such a looking man as the leader of a million
horny-fisted sons of toil." But a labor leader he was in spite of
administrative skills and a social personality more suited to a small
pulpit. Self-righteous and maddeningly thin-skinned, Powderly made
enemies easily and turned against his best friends but was revered by
those who knew him from afar. Some Knights named their sons after

him, but he mistook such reverence for foolishness and wrote insulting letters to those who would even consider such a thing. He avoided the saloon and rough centers of working-class sociability. He was most at ease when he was alone, writing, gardening, and poring over his collection of rocks and geological specimens. The son of a Catholic, he spoke in evangelical idiom and abstained from liquor until he was forty-five. He served three terms (1878–84) as Greenback-Labor mayor of Scranton while leading a movement whose manifesto read like a political platform, but he loathed politics and clamped down hard on third-party talk within the Knights. "Our Order," he once said, "is above politics." He also believed the Order was above the class struggle. In his second autobiography his boast was: "Not once did I, during my fourteen years in the office of Grand Master Workman, order a strike." No one ever thought him or his organization easy to fathom.

Powderly spent his formative years in small-town America. He was the eleventh of twelve children born to Irish immigrants Terence and Margery Powderly, who arrived in the United States in 1826 and settled briefly in Ogdensburg, New York, where Terence toiled as a day laborer for local miners and farmers. Three years later in the midst of the coal boom in eastern Pennsylvania, Terence moved his family to Carbondale and took a job at a colliery. Fifteen years with pick and shovel paid off; in 1845 he opened a mine of his own. By the time his son Terence was born in 1849, the family had achieved a stake in society, and judging from his father's election to the town council two years later, some prominence as well. The Powderlys were secure enough to keep their son at school until age thirteen, and sufficiently connected to arrange a job for him with a local railroad. Young Powderly rose quickly from switch tender to brakeman and might have made engineer, the pinnacle of railway work, had his father not convinced James Dickson, master mechanic at the Delaware and Hudson shop, to take him on as a machinist's apprentice. Young Powderly spent an enjoyable three years learning the craft and developing a deep respect for his teacher. Family connections again opened the way upward when in 1869 Powderly's father importuned William Scranton, paternalistic owner of the Delaware, Lackawanna, and Western, to hire his son. The wealthy railwayman and the budding machinist got on famously. Scranton dropped by the shop floor for friendly chats and probably fancied arranging a romance with his daughter. He also shielded Powderly from the wrath of foreman James Dawson, who once and possibly twice wanted to fire him. Powderly never quite forgot the patronage of Scranton or Dickson. He remembered both men as model bosses whose benefactions gave the lie to those who believed in the inevitability of class strife.

Dawson made an 1873 firing stick, possibly because of the onset of hard times, and Powderly found himself in a fruitless search for work in upstate New York and as far afield as the Mississippi Valley. "Only the man who stands utterly alone, friendless, moneyless, ill-clad, shirtless, and hungry," he would later recall, "can know what it is to be a real tramp. The experience was mine, through no fault of my own." He came close to being hired on no fewer than four occasions but was turned down at the last minute because of a blacklist circulated among repair shops by the vindictive Dawson. The want and isolation of these years reinforced a growing conviction of the need for some form of organization, something that offered fellowship and security. Powderly had taken a step in that direction in 1871 or 1872 upon joining the Machinists' and Blacksmiths' International Union, if only because it offered a life insurance plan and other benefits. Within a year he was elected president of his union lodge and in 1874 was its delegate at an antimonopoly convention in Philadelphia, hometown of the Knights of Labor. There he met William Fennimore, an early member of the Knights, who inducted him into the Order.

The Knights were still in their infancy when Powderly became a member. Founded five years earlier by a group of Philadelphia garment cutters, the Order had only a few assemblies in 1872, all of them in the Quaker City. "It was difficult," wrote the labor reformer George McNeill, "to find earnest and active members" willing to risk the infamy of the blacklist. Widespread fears of detection by employers, paired with the fact that charter members belonged to fraternal orders with clandestine traditions, led to a policy of secrecy. The Order was not referred to by name in public before 1882. Members learned of meetings by word of mouth or symbolic announcements scribbled on sidewalks or published in the labor press. The notation

$$8\frac{329}{14}$$

meant that Local Assembly 14 would meet on March 29 at 8 p.m. The meaning of these signs was soon clear to greater numbers of workers in and around Philadelphia. The Knights were part of the great expansion of unionism that accompanied the eight-hour movement beginning in the summer of 1872. Over the next eighteen months scores of local assemblies emerged in Philadelphia and some were established in the coalfields north and east of the city. At least forty assemblies met in Philadephia by late 1873, but the growth was short-lived. The panic brought down about half the lodges and those that survived probably lost as many members as they gained, a pattern that would plague the Knights for years in good times and bad. Few new lodges were founded in Philadelphia during the depression but hundreds took root elsewhere, so that by 1877 there were some 500 assemblies with about 6,000 members. The economic recovery of 1877 through 1880 saw the membership rise to just under 30,000 and the number of assemblies increase to over 1,600.

The Knights had no national officers until the Reading convention of 1878. Before that the Order relied on a foundation of local assemblies and district assemblies. Local assemblies had at least ten members and covered wards or neighborhoods in urban places and counties in rural areas. The locals elected delegates to district assemblies, which typically represented entire cities or larger political units. There were equal proportions of urban and rural assemblies before the precipitous membership decline after 1886, but in that year, since urban locals were larger, two-thirds of the members were from the cities. Lodges with a plurality of workers from a single craft were known as trade assemblies, while those with members representing several different occupations were called mixed assemblies. Mixed assemblies were established by the Knights and favored by Powderly and his supporters to lessen the divisiveness of craft unionism. In their view, mixed assemblies promoted brotherhood and broader social identity. There were two deviations from this structural pattern. State assemblies were authorized in sparsely settled regions in 1883, and workers in the same trade were occasionally permitted to form district and national trade assemblies. The historic Reading convention had also established the General Assembly, a yearly congress of delegates elected at the local level, and a panel of national officers, headed by the Grand Master Workman, who formed the General Executive Board, which carried out policy made by the General Assembly and managed daily affairs.

Membership in the Knights was open to all manual workers. Bankers, stockbrokers, and lawyers—individuals historically associated with idleness and parasitism—were barred, along with liquor dealers, gamblers, and others thought to abet vice and corruption; merchants and manufacturers could join, if just, morally upright, and sympathetic to Knighthood; indeed some did hold Knight cards. Middle-class Knights usually hailed from what Norman Ware called the "last frontier of semi-itinerant craftsmen and small shopkeepers." Local Assembly 3184 in Onekama, Michigan, said a local observer, included "a number of our best citizens," as did numerous backwoods assemblies. But the middle classes of urban America, where social lines were more sharply drawn, did not join and left the Knights to wage earners.

Even before the runaway expansion of the mid-1880s, the Order cast a wide net. Its magic lay in a comprehensive program that offered a little something for just about everyone. West Coast workers, enraged by the presence of Chinese labor, responded enthusiastically to Knight organizers promising to end importation of the hated "coolies." Powderly's ethnic lineage and work for the Land League appealed to Irish workmen. Socialists found the Knights an attractive alternative to craft unions. Unskilled workers, long scorned by the labor movement, finally found a place to hang their hats.

The broad sweep of Knighthood was manifested in its platform and preamble adopted at Reading. Though amended from time to time, the Reading platform reflected the guiding values of the brotherhood. It included such essentials of bread-and-butter unionism as the eight-hour day, abolition of contract and convict labor, and the establishment of government bureaus of labor statistics along with loftier demands for social reform in the name of the "producing masses." The reference to producers, labor's traditional self-description, was the thread that tied the Knights to the revivalistic radicalism of the 1840s. "The recent alarming development and aggression of aggregated wealth," the preamble read, "will inevitably lead to the pauperization and hopeless degradation of the toiling masses" unless checked by a counterforce that honored the "divine injunction, 'In the sweat of thy brow shalt thou eat bread.' " It comes as no surprise, therefore, that Knighthood evoked such venerable pieties as the repeal of "all laws that do not bear equally upon capital and labor" and the establishment of "co-operative institutions, productive and distributive." Trade unionism remained strongly identified with social reform.

But it is inaccurate to insist, as some writers have, that the Reading platform represented old wine in new bottles. For just as time improves the vintage, so did it transform the radical tradition. Several Reading planks suggest that the Knights looked forward as well as backward and adapted radicalism to the contingencies of the new industrial order. The Knights reflected the latest thinking on monetary reform by endorsing Greenbackism, a scheme that would have government-owned banks issue paper money convertible into interest-bearing bonds. They also demanded government regulation of the "health and safety of those engaged in mining, manufacturing, and building pursuits," and by the 1880s called for public ownership of the railways and telegraphs. Insofar as Green-backism and health and safety regulations vested government with powers never contemplated by antebellum radicals, the Knights assumed the mantle of latter-day pioneers extending the frontiers of radicalism. Such demands not only pushed the Knights beyond early radicalism but also outside the political consensus of the Gilded Age. Neither mainstream political party, in lockstep retreat from the active government of the Civil War years, was likely to nationalize the banks and railways or redistribute the plantation lands of the old Confederacy. Yet the Knights never did formally endorse a labor party or establish their own political organization. National leaders demurred and steadfastly refused to draw the Order into the political fray, even though many were Greenbackers. There were decided limits to the politics of Gilded Age radicals.

Late radicalism also put forth contradictory proposals calculated to ease labor's travail in the routine relations between employee and employer. Its goal, enshrined in the Reading platform and reiterated in print and oratory, was the "abolition of wage slavery" through cooperative production and land reform. While both measures would erase the invidious distinction between labor and capital, in the short run workers could expect a continuation of the naked social combat prevalent in postwar America. That troubling prospect lay behind the Reading plank calling for the "substitution of arbitration for strikes." This was not unique to the Knights or entirely naïve. During Reconstruction and the Gilded Age labor leaders in the United States, and in England for that matter, first turned to arbitration, which was understood to mean negotiations and not third-party interventions. The National Labor Union considered work stoppages to be a "last resort," and beginning in the late 1870s several national craft unions adopted constitutional provisions that greatly restricted the ability of local unions to declare strikes. The founding fathers of the Knights continued to believe in the policy of the NLU while applying it in a flexible way. Uriah Stephens and James L. Wright, founding members of the Order in Philadelphia, preached social pacification but that did not stop them from sharing rostrums with Marxists in the Eight Hour League during the early 1870s or condoning work stoppages when all else failed. Nor did the Reading men believe arbitration would come easily. Their own plank recommended it "wherever and whenever employers and employees are willing to meet on equitable grounds." Problems arose not because of the no-strike policy but because some leaders and members of the rank and file alike would raise it to a dogma, refusing to believe it would take more than professions of good faith or unilateral declaration of peaceful intentions to call off the class war.

In ideological terms, Knighthood may be seen as a middle ground between the individualistic libertarianism of bourgeois America and the collectivism of working-class socialists. Like the former, Knights affirmed the sanctity of private property even as they reviled its excessive accumulation and decried acquisitive individualism. Theirs was an older ethic rooted in the perfectionism of the evangelical church, a popular position that defamed corporate capital as the "anti-Christ" and imagined a "new Pentecost" in which "every man shall have according to his needs." They tied this moral outlook to the well-being of the work group, proclaiming "an injury to one is the concern of all." But they were not socialists despite their collectivist language and the recognition of the need for more forceful government—the demands for public ownership of financial and transportation institutions—reflected in the Reading platform. Knights repudiated the public control of modern socialism along with its doctrine of irreconcilable conflict between labor and capital. "I curse the word class," said Powderly. To him, as to most early Knights, wage earners were "producers," capitalists were "accumulators" and "monopolists," and his movement aimed to abolish "wage slavery," not overthrow capitalism. Here was a language and outlook any antebellum radical would have easily understood.

How do we explain the endurance of this ideology? Radicalism, after all, remained the language of North American labor long after European workmen learned more modern social vocabularies. Part of this American peculiarity lies in the fact that radicalism went unrivaled longer in the United States than in Europe, where theories such as Marxism had more exposure after 1850. American workers were hardly aware of Marx as late as 1870, but even if revolutionary socialism had had wider currency, it is doubtful that it would have gained a wider following. Gilded Age Marxists lectured to a working class weaned on a creed that denied the basic proposition of revolutionary socialism regarding the seizure and exercise of state power. The old republican axiom that reliance on government corrupted the body politic flew in the face of Marxism. At the same time, the Civil War invigorated the language of radicalism. The war had been fought squarely on radical terms for the preservation of "free labor" against an odious "slave power." To Northern workingmen it was a heroic time, to be sure, but it also postponed the struggle against "wage slavery." Long after Appomattox they continued to respond to labor journalists and politicians who spoke of taking the war to the "Vicksburgs of Labor's enemies." This would suggest yet another answer to the old question first asked by the German sociologist Werner Sombart: "Why is there no socialism in the United States?" Socialism, it would seem, was so weak because radicalism was so strong.

Demographic factors and occupational mobility also replenished radicalism. As Herbert Gutman observed, "many persons new to the urban-industrial world would not settle easily into a factory-centered civilization." A good portion of newcomers were not only immigrants but former farmers and villagers reared on radicalism. The traditional antimonopolistic instincts of rural America that fueled the Granger and Alliance movements also found an outlet in Knighthood. On the other hand, opportunities for social advancement in the city were still available for rural-urban migrant and longtime urban dweller alike. Workers who did set up on their own did not always turn their backs on those they had left behind. Uriah Stephens and fellow Knight founder Robert McCloskey ran a garment store in Philadelphia; Arsene Sauva, the militant New York Knight, owned a tailor shop that was also a meeting place for neighborhood radicals; and the New Haven publisher Alexander Troup was one of numerous small printers in the Order. Much like the Fall River job printer John Keogh, small employers did not think of themselves as capitalists. Asked by a Senate investigator if he ran his "own business" as he "please[d]," Keogh answered, "Yes, but I do not consider myself a capitalist." Neither did scores of other former workers who continued to identify with their class of origin and its radical sensibility.

Life on the job could also soften ruder aspects of work and restore faith in radicalism's belief that differences between employer and employee could be resolved. The trade unionist, labor politician, and amateur writer Martin Foran captured as much in his 1886 novel *The Other Side*. Richard Arbyght, its protagonist, is a farm-bred lad who, like Foran himself, completes a cooper's apprenticeship but faces tragedy when his father is robbed and murdered by a rogue who later becomes Richard's employer. A better future is possible when Richard recovers the stolen money, marries well, and goes into business for himself to produce an unnamed but "useful commodity." He is a humane and considerate employer, a radical's dream, who welcomes unionism and on top of this offers his hands a profit-sharing plan. Real life sometimes imitated this bit of popular art even in the bare-fisted labor relations of the Gilded Age. Terre Haute railway promoter Riley McKeon struck the pose of the fraternal paternalistic, the fair boss loyal to workman and community, and for a time, he was accepted in just this way. His admirers included the youthful Eugene Debs, a member of the local lodge of the Brotherhood of Locomotive Firemen in the mid-1870s. In the aftermath of the 1877 railway strikes, which Debs loudly condemned as fellow lodgemen walked picket lines, McKeon lent him $1,000 to rebuild BLF headquarters and consorted with other business leaders to guarantee Debs's bond as treasurer of the brotherhood. McKeon would later back Debs's first bid for elective office. That Debs had a more generous patron in McKeon than Powderly had in William Scranton matters less than the larger implications of such relationships. Any employer who willingly shared profits with workers or lent a hand to those in need could surely be persuaded to go a step further by enlisting in the crusade to terminate "wage slavery."

Radicalism became the touchstone of Knighthood's movement culture. Soon after the first local assembly appeared in 1869, and fully a decade before the advent of paid organizers, recruiters appeared in the guise of "sojourners." Later joined by workers fired after the railway strikes in 1877, sojourners took to the field with the zeal of missionaries, albeit clandestine ones with a slightly different scripture. Their initiates went through a lengthy ceremony packed with rite and ritual of the Order meticulously spelled out in the *Adelphon Kruptos*. Each inductee signed his name to a card, or had to learn to do so, before being escorted into a room to clasp hands with brothers in a symbolic circle of unity and pledge himself to "heaven ordained labor" and to "defend the life, interest, and reputation, and family of all true members." Other publications used symbols to convey a more explicit political message. The traditional symbol of the Order was a triangle whose corners symbolized "Secrecy, Obedience, and Mutual Assistance." A Knight journalist reinterpreted the "full pyramid" to represent what "labor earns." A heavy black line drawn through its center stood for the "unholy part taken by the fiend's hired men, the usurers, the bloodsuckers, who don't work—who live by the sweat of other men's brows." Stump speakers hammered home similar themes. Larger local assemblies published their own organs to supplement the *Journal of United Labor,* official voice of the Order. Fellow lodgers organized poetry clubs and theater groups along with singing societies and brass bands that performed after meetings were adjourned and provided entertainment at official functions. Picnics and dinners were especially popular. Years after Henry Ward Beecher's vulgar sermon on the railway strikers in 1877, lodges continued to hold "Bread and Water Beecher Banquets" and guest speakers still attacked the arrogant cleric. A Michigan Knight chided the "pot-bellied millionaires who eat Porterhouse steaks, drink champagne, smoke 15 cent cigars, who will ride out with their wives, or more likely other people's wives," a reference to Beecher's scandalous love affair with Elizabeth Tilton, the wife of a prominent reform editor.

Much like antebellum radicals, Knights promoted total abstinence. The drinker was seen as a social dependent, a servile and irresponsible soul who brought disrepute to his class and poverty to his family. But he was not to be scorned or punished, or indeed used as an excuse to outlaw liquor sales. Powderly deplored prohibitionists who "patronized labor" and would "regulate our appetite for liquor . . . [and] everything else." Knights, like the antebellum Washingtonians, practiced voluntarism and used the moral suasion of the group to rehabilitate the problem drinker. Lecturers and columnists stressed the baleful effects of drink and lodges barred spirits from official functions, meetings, and even picnics. Members helped brothers overcome their habit and were duty-bound to report cases of backsliding. Unreconstructed drinkers and wayward members charged with "conduct unbecoming a Knight" answered to courts of lodgemen. One-time offenders usually got off lightly; recidivists were fined or dismissed.

This spirit of mutuality also gained expression in cooperative stores and workshops. Ambitious plans for producer and consumer cooperatives funded and coordinated by the Executive Board never panned out. Indecisive leadership, a mark of Powderly's rule, produced only a single cooperative of much importance, a mine that soon failed. Equally damaging was Powderly's appointment of John Samuel to head the Co-operative Board. Samuel resisted using funds in the national coffers for local projects, which threw assemblies back on their own resources. Lean budgets hampered progress, for as Powderly noted in 1884, "to be successful . . . *capital* is required. The workingmen who have a little capital cling to it, and hold aloof from co-operation, those who have no capital cannot embark in it." Local assemblies still persisted and by the early 1880s many ran cooperatives that turned out light consumer goods and supplied fuel and groceries to their members at a discount.

No movement culture, however, remains static. None was more variable than Knighthood, if only because it had a longer history, more time to change, than any predecessor. The Order underwent a transition of sorts in 1882 following the hotly disputed decision to abandon secrecy and reform the ritual in response to criticism by the Catholic Church. Meetings lost much of their mystical aura and induction ceremonies became a bit bland. Loyalty and cohesion may have suffered some, but reformed Knighthood also brought compensations. Partly as a result of operating in the open, interest picked up and membership in the Knights climbed to nearly 100,000 by 1884 from about 40,000 in 1882. Larger lodges erected spacious meeting halls, established newspapers, and printed their own propaganda. Rallies and demonstrations grew larger and members grew more aggressive at the workplace, which exacerbated inherent tensions with national officers; differences, however, were usually settled without much ill will. Through the early stirrings of militancy, the Order maintained a balance between the practical concerns of unionism and the ideals of labor reform. It was the mounting class conflict from 1884 through 1886, commonly known as the Great Upheaval, that would upset this delicate balance.

STRIKE TRENDS, 1881–96

Year	No. of strikes	Workers involved (in thousands)	% of wage strikes	% ordered by unions	% sympathy strikes
1881	474	101	79.8	47.3	0.8
1882	454	121	75.4	48.5	0.9
1883	478	122	77.2	56.7	0.6
1884	443	117	74.1	54.2	0.2
1885	645	159	72.9	55.3	3.1
1886	1,432	407	63.0	53.3	2.9
1887	1,436	273	54.8	66.3	4.7
1888	906	103	55.2	68.1	3.8
1889	1,075	205	59.0	67.3	6.1
1890	1,833	286	50.9	71.3	9.9
1891	1,717	245	48.9	74.8	11.5
1892	1,298	164	50.4	70.7	8.9
1893	1,305	195	58.8	69.4	4.5
1894	1,349	505	63.7	62.8	8.8
1895	1,215	286	69.6	54.2	0.6
1896	1,026	184	57.6	64.6	0.6

From David Montgomery, *Workers' Control in America: Studies in the History of Work, Technology, and Labor Struggles* (New York: Cambridge University Press, 1979), p. 20.

Between 1880 and 1884, as the table shows, the number of work stoppages fluctuated around 450 a year, rose to 645 in 1885, and soared to over 1,400 in 1886–87. Nearly half the strikes in 1880–82 were the spontaneous actions of nonunion workers. By 1883 and increasingly thereafter more and more were called by unions, so that by 1888 two-thirds enjoyed official sanction. For the Knights' part, the most significant of these centered on the railways of the Southwest. Twice in 1884, in May and August, local assemblies along Jay Gould's Union Pacific fought off wage cuts and firings. The following spring brought two more victories against Gould lines, first the Wabash and then the Missouri, Kansas, and Texas. The Wabash strike was supported by a boycott of Gould rolling stock that was ordered by the General Executive Board. The disdainful "robber baron" who was said to have bragged that he "could hire one half of the working class to kill the other half" had been humiliated. "No such victory," wrote the St. Louis *Chronicle* in amazement, "has ever been secured in this nation or any other."

The rash of strikes brought great numbers of new members into the Order. From July 1, 1885, to June 30, 1886, alone, the number of district assemblies jumped from 4,800 to over 11,000, and the 6,200 added in this short time surpassed the growth in the previous sixteen years. Membership swelled from a respectable 110,000 in July 1885 to an all-time high of nearly 750,000 a year later. "Never in history," exulted John Swinton, "has there been such a spectacle as the march . . . of the Knights of Labor at the present time." That national and some district leaders did not share Swinton's enthusiasm is easily understood. Many officials were unnerved by the deluge of raw recruits ignorant of Knighthood. They especially feared expansion triggered by strikes that swept in militants with no higher objective than improving wages and conditions. As early as 1880 Powderly had been deeply concerned about the appeal of work stoppages, warning the General Assembly that "the remedy . . . lie [sic] not in the suicidal strike, but . . . in thorough, effective organization." He became alarmed when in 1882 rosters lengthened in the midst of a slight upturn in strike activity. "The tidal wave of strikes," said the jittery Powderly, flowed directly from "exaggerated reports of the strength of the Order." "Such a course," he believed, "may lead men into the Order . . . but by a path that leads them out again . . . as soon as they become deceived and lose confidence." Alarm turned into panic when in the flood tide of March 1886 Powderly ordered a forty-day moratorium on admissions. "The majority of the newcomers," he would later explain, were not of the "quality the Order had sought in the past."

Who were these newcomers? A fair number were skilled workers, labor aristocrats from the old handicrafts and newer industrial sectors

who had different union backgrounds. Most were either first-time
unionists or dual unionists who held membership in existing craft unions.
Others had been expelled from craft unions for scabbing, working under
scale, or other infractions. Most of the new members, however, were
semiskilled and unskilled workers customarily excluded from craft
unions and heretofore a minority within the Knights. As May Day 1886
approached, membership in the Knights resembled a pyramid: skilled
workers of American birth at the peak and an expanding base of
semiskilled and unskilled workers largely Irish, German, and English in
origin. Even Polish immigrants, a small but growing group of "new
immigrants," rushed into the Knights.

* * *

The extraordinary growth of 1885–86 also breached the barricades of
race and gender. Blacks had undergone mixed experiences in the wake of
emancipation. Victimized by racist violence during Reconstruction,
freedmen continued to exercise the rights of citizenship conferred by the
Fourteenth and Fifteenth amendments and were not yet shackled by Jim
Crow legislation; disenfranchisement and *legal* segregation would come
in the 1890s. Their economic condition was gradually deteriorating in the
late 1860s but their expectations ran high. Blacks believed they were
entitled to compensation for their years in bondage, if not in cash as some
preferred, then in land. Blacks "have the idea," said a surprised official
of the Freedmen's Bureau, "that they had a certain right to the property
of their former masters, that they had earned it."

The broken promise of "forty acres and a mule," slogan of radical
Republicanism during Reconstruction, did not diminish black hopes for
independent livelihoods and social improvement through education. Nor
did the development of sharecropping and then debt peonage or the paltry
wages of the few that did leave farm for factory. Their strong resolve for
independence told in small ways. Blacks on the land, Roger Ransom and
Richard Sutch tell us, "duplicated (and perhaps emulated) the work-
leisure patterns of other free Americans. Adolescents in their early teens,
women and children, elderly men and women worked significantly fewer
hours per day and fewer days per year than had been the standard under
the oppression of slavery." No black had the slightest intention of
slipping back into slavery under another name. As an Alabama black man
told Whitelaw Reid, "I's want to be a free man, cum when I please, and
nobody say nuffin to me, nor order me roun'."

"Can white workingmen afford to ignore colored ones?" asked the

Boston *Evening Voice* shortly after the Civil War. White labor's first response was a qualified "no." In its 1867 "Address . . . to the Workingmen of the United States," the National Labor Union invited the "colored race" to "cooperate with us," but then reconsidered its commitment at its annual convention later in the year. A committee formed to investigate the black question reported that the problem was "involved in so much mystery" and opinion was so divided that it was best to defer the matter until the next congress. It, too, refused to act despite the urging of William Sylvis, who predicted unorganized blacks would be used as strikebreakers by employers and political pawns by Republican politicians, thus foiling his plans for an independent labor party. National Labor Union leaders renewed their invitation in 1869, by which point blacks themselves began to stir under the leadership of Baltimore ship caulker Isaac Myers, who with the assistance of white benefactors had formed a cooperative dry dock for black artisans driven from jobs by returning Confederate soldiers. Myers headed a black delegation to the National Labor Congress and, accorded the courtesy of the podium, told the biracial audience that his people were prepared to "let the dead past bury its dead" and cooperate with white brothers under certain conditions. Blacks would demand access to the trades and would not stand for criticism of the Republican party, the party of liberation.

Within the year Myers started the Colored National Labor Congress. The CNLC, an amalgam of labor leaders, preachers, and politicians, promoted public education, apprentice training for blacks, black unionism as well as mutual understanding between labor and capital, and support for the Republican party. Its second gathering in 1870, however, was its last. Black unions that had sent delegates to the CNLC either folded or were repressed by white authorities. Others were taken over by Republican politicians, both black and white, who diverted attention from unionism. In South Carolina, Republican politicians had got themselves elected to the CNLC by the Longshoremen's Protective Union of Charleston, a fledgling black union movement that had conducted several strikes between 1867 and 1869. In 1870, when Myers went to Charleston to address a labor meeting, only a few blacks showed up to hear him emphasize the importance of unionism over party politics. The LPU regrouped a few years later and went on strike for a wage increase that mobilized blacks in factories and workshops but failed as white workers refused to participate, employers hired strikebreakers, and the Democratic regime sent in police to obstruct picket lines. The first experiment in multiracial unionism had foundered.

The Knights offered another opportunity to bring the races together. As local assemblies met furtively in the industrial belt of the North during the 1870s, Southern blacks turned to self-help through clandestine fraternal lodges and secret societies. Closely tied to Methodist and Baptist churches and headed by a new generation of leaders raised in freedom and with more class and race consciousness than their forebears, the Good Samaritans, the Golden Rule Society, and the Rising Sons of America flourished in the black ghettos of the urban South and reached into the countryside. These societies became staging grounds for blacks to become Knights during the mid-1880s, and not simply because of the stimulus of the Great Upheaval. The rites, rituals, and evangelical ethos of Knighthood meshed neatly with popular black culture; its structure suited a population of casual labor; and its program of land reform attracted a people determined to claim what was due them. Open-minded leadership also helped: belief in white supremacy was not one of Terence Powderly's many shortcomings. Powderly genuinely believed in racial brotherhood and, unlike the chieftains of the NLU who had headed a loose federation of trades, he could get compliance with his orders. He was also aware of the force of a symbolic gesture, a show of goodwill. His organizers had met disappointment in the Black Belt before 1885. One wrote in frustration that the "continued cry of nigger! nigger!" and the "abuse and social ostracism" blunted any progress. That same year, however, Powderly paid a visit to Richmond and made a point of personally organizing a local assembly of black cigarette makers. Local Assembly 3564 inspired several more black lodges that spring, and later in the year, at the Hamilton, Ontario, meeting of the General Assembly, Powderly shrewdly invited Richmond's Joseph Brown Johnson, the lone black delegate, to the rostrum and, grasping his hand, "pledged . . . the services of the Order for his race." In much the same spirit Powderly opened the 1886 assembly at Richmond by introducing Frank Farrell, a black Knight from Brooklyn. It was not a casual choice. Farrell had been at the center of a storm the previous day when he and several white colleagues, denied rooms at a Jim Crow hotel, went to black boarding-houses. The following night Foster and friends again defied the region's racial etiquette by conspicuously seating themselves in the "white only" section of the Academy of Music for a performance of *Hamlet*. White Richmond responded with race-baiting and forced Powderly to disclaim publicly any wish to foster social equality. "Every man has the right to say who shall enter under his roof," his letter to the local press read, "and I have no wish to interfere with this right." But he refused to renounce organizing blacks or promoting "uplift [of the] race from a bondage worse than that which held them in chains twenty-five years ago." "In the field of labor and American citizenship," he told a mortified white Richmond, "we recognize no line of race, creed, politics, or color."

Powderly's encouraging words reverberated throughout the black South. The Knights suddenly became the fascination of churchmen and fraternalists, their best hope since the heyday of radical Republicanism. Black labor beat a stampede to local assemblies or organized scores of new ones in an astonishing endorsement of Knighthood. Estimates of black membership vary, but it is likely that nearly 60,000, just under 10 percent of the Order, signed up by summer 1886. No labor movement had ever claimed such a prominent black presence, and none would until the coming of the Congress of Industrial Organizations (CIO) in the 1930s.

Simultaneously women flowed into the Knights and also reached about 10 percent of the membership. They, too, formed their own assemblies, typically along ethnic, racial, and occupational lines. Nearly half were located in the shoe and textile centers of the Northeast, which suggests why there were women's lodges at all. More than any other groups of female wage earners, shoe stitchers and textile operatives had a long if checkered history of collective action. The Great Upheaval rekindled this spirit, but the climate of the moment carries us no further for women than it does for blacks. The National Labor Union, after all, had taken only tentative steps toward extending a welcome to female labor. Indeed the few women admitted to the 1868 congress were not workers at all but middle-class suffragists looking for new allies in the aftermath of the split within abolitionism over the Fifteenth Amendment. Some returned to the 1869 gathering, but Susan B. Anthony bore the disgrace of expulsion when it was disclosed that members of her Working Women's Association had helped break a strike of New York printers. The Knights proved considerably more hospitable to female labor. The accent on solidarity made room for women otherwise banned from craft unions. Homemakers also found a place, according to Susan Levine, because male and female Knights reinterpreted the tradition of separate spheres. Women's special moral consciousness, it was believed, infused public life with a moral and cooperative imperative compatible with Knighthood. Their domestic role of shopper and consumer, moreover, made them strategically important in supporting boycotts, the Order's most effective weapon against unfair employers.

It would be foolish to suggest that all male Knights shared this sentiment. Beyond question, however, national leaders did, and as in the case of blacks, the men were not shy about upbraiding recalcitrants. Powderly once told a doubtful brother who didn't want his wife leaving home to attend lodge meetings, "I regret that you entertain so poor an opinion of your wife, as to say of her that you would not allow her to mix among a lot of men who are sworn to defend her life interest and reputation." "If the assembly is a bad place for a woman to go," he added, "it is a bad place for a man to go." In addition, centralization of authority made it easier for enlightened leaders to find a place for women. After 1881 Powderly chartered women's assemblies directly and in 1886 proposed the Department of Women's Work, which was approved by the Richmond General Assembly. Headed by Leonora Barry, a tenacious agitator who delivered over 500 speeches in the next three years, the department issued yearly reports on the status of women workers, encouraged women's membership, and as we shall see, constituted an important force for labor reform. No labor organization had gone so far in behalf of working women.

Race and gender relations, however, varied considerably. The liberal position was held primarily by the union's national leaders. Local assemblies evinced grudging acceptance and flashes of sympathy but usually showed indifference and often hostility. Peter Rachleff's conclusion that "the movement culture pushed against but rarely penetrated . . . the color line" summarizes the nature of race relations not just in Richmond but throughout the nation. White and black Knights honored one another's pickets and boycotts but rarely paraded together or met at picnic grounds. Lady Knights in urban centers also received a more favorable hearing at General Assemblies than in their own hometowns. The Garfield Assembly, a large local of shoe stitchers in Philadelphia, was at loggerheads with bosses and union brothers alike through the early 1880s. Male leaders twice called off strikes in 1882 and 1883 and grew so frustrated with the militant women that in 1884 they tried without much success to organize a renegade assembly of stitchers to divide their ranks.

While tensions over race and gender persisted into the Great Upheaval, black and women Knights did not disrupt the movement culture. We need to know more about women and blacks, but the smattering of evidence indicates that each group built an organization that paralleled the movement culture. The lady Knights of Olneyville, Rhode Island, used the ethic of cooperation to suit their needs by investing funds raised from fancy fairs in a child-care center and community kitchen. Less is known of black Knighthood, but it is clear that local and district assemblies in the South assumed social and beneficial functions traditionally performed by fraternal lodges. District Assembly 92 in Richmond commemorated Emancipation Day, and in a rare show of biracialism, some members joined the cooperative building and loan society of white District Assembly 84. Blacks and women may be seen as constituents, not opponents, of the movement culture.

. . .

Women and Afro-Americans, of course, were a small part of the torrential flow of members into the Knights during the Great Upheaval. The mainstream, or over three-fourths of the 600,000 new followers, were white males who brought different cultural and political orientations. Socialists and craft unionists joined in great numbers. The craft unionists were business unionists in the making, men who accepted class conflict as an inevitable fact of industrial life, who excluded blacks, women, the unskilled, and nonworkers from their unions, and who favored trade autonomy rather than the centralization of the Knights. In politics they were pragmatists and trenchant critics of radical reform and third parties who pursued limited legislative objectives through nonpartisan lobbying. This strategic and tactical perspective arrayed business unionists against Lassallean socialists, the leading socialist group following the collapse of the Marxist International Workingmen's Association in the mid-1870s. Lassalleans agreed that antagonistic class relations was the natural state of affairs under capitalism, but worked to bring about a socialist society that would establish cooperative factories and workshops subsidized by government but owned and operated by workers. They lambasted business unionists for accepting capitalism, for working with established political parties, and for restricting their unions to skilled workers. They formed separate unions, in theory, at least, open to all wage earners, but they treated unions more like political groups than collective bargaining agents. Their unions were adjuncts of the Socialist Labor party, the most important socialist group during the 1880s.

Socialists and trade unionists were no strangers to Knighthood. Veterans of Marx's International Workingmen's Association and leading lights in the Socialist Labor party had organized local assemblies of the Order in leading industrial centers throughout the nation. Socialist activists Joseph Labadie, Albert Parsons, and Frank Roney founded the first assemblies in Detroit, Chicago, and San Francisco, respectively, and

164

such craft union leaders as Samuel Gompers of the Cigar Makers' International and John Davis of the Amalgamated Association of Iron, Steel, and Tin Workers dated their initiation into the Knights to the early 1870s. This pattern of multiple affiliations grew more complex with the revival of trade unionism following recovery from the Long Depression of the 1870s. Craft unionists came together in the Federation of Organized Trades and Labor Unions (FOTLU), a loose body of local and national trade unions founded in 1881 that prefigured the American Federation of Labor (AF of L), founded in 1886. Urban federations of craft unions, known as Trades Councils or Labor Assemblies, simultaneously took shape in every major industrial city. Socialists banded together on their own in separate Central Labor Unions, so that by the eve of the Great Upheaval three labor movements operated in most Northern urban centers. If Chicago was typical, and there is every reason to believe it was, trade unionism closely followed ethnic lines. The Knights and Labor Assemblies shared Anglo- and Irish-American constituencies. Central Labor Unions, as a rule, were confined to German immigrants, many of them refugees from Bismarckian repression and some on the road from socialism to anarchism. Occupational configurations also conformed to a pattern of a sort. Labor Assemblies represented more skilled workmen; Central Labor Unions, sweated tradesmen and the unskilled. The Knights included all kinds of labor: women, blacks, and workers who belonged to Labor Assemblies and Central Labor Unions.

The wild expansion in membership during the Great Upheaval was not an unalloyed blessing. The Knights were larger and more militant but also less cohesive; members held strong and competing views momentarily kept in check by the heightened class awareness. As Richard Oestreicher puts it, the Great Upheaval set free the contradictory forces of "solidarity and fragmentation," each of which registered at the polls and on the job.

Knights' politics, Leon Fink tells us, went through the discrete but occasionally overlapping stages of nonpartisan lobbying (1884–86), grass-roots insurgencies (1885–87), and active courtship of third-party movements (1890–94). The first stage, which actually began in the early 1880s as a reaction to disappointment with Greenbackism, witnessed a tacit alliance with craft unionists first in Washington and then in the legislatures of industrial states. This partnership was responsible for such national laws as the Chinese Exclusion Act of 1882 and the Foran Anti-Contract Labor Law of 1885 as well as a flood of state laws. In 1885 Powderly was impressed enough with the Order's success to propose stronger lobbying efforts in state houses and appoint Ralph Beaumont chief of the newly formed National Legislative Committee in Washington. Pressure-group politics picked up but was eclipsed by mass political insurgencies unleashed by the Great Upheaval. Between 1885 and 1887 labor parties campaigned in over two hundred communities in thirty states and many made impressive showings. In 1886 third parties nearly installed mayors in New York and Chicago and elected hundreds of lesser urban officials in other cities. Within a year, however, external and internal forces combined to defeat labor politics. In some cities reformers stole labor's thunder by legalizing the eight-hour day or making gestures to contain corporate power. In addition, a ruthless anti-union offensive by employers that stretched into 1887 demolished Knight assemblies and thus smashed the popular base of insurgent politics. On the other hand, district and national leaders of the Knights enforced Powderly's directive to "let politics alone" by withholding official sanction or resolutely fighting third-partyism. Their actions dampened support at the grass roots and deprived the movement of sorely needed national coordination.

Factional discord was also disruptive. Some craft unionists, to be sure, took part in the insurgency. Even Samuel Gompers, leading business unionist and future president of the American Federation of Labor, took to the hustings in behalf of Henry George, who was running for mayor of New York on a social welfare platform. Gompers worked for George less out of conviction perhaps than because he realized the utter futility of standing still against the tide; most craft unionists seem to have stood aloof, content to vote Democratic or Republican. Elsewhere German Lassalleans and radicals participated but not always together. Detroit socialists left the Independent Labor party when the party endorsed bourgeois politicians in the established parties. Within a year the party that had been the political voice of Detroit labor since 1882 was in ruins. Similar disputes sank labor parties in Milwaukee and Cincinnati. Racial antagonism weakened the Citizens' party in Kansas City and ripped apart the Workingmen's Reform party in Richmond.

Factionalism took an even greater toll on Knights' unions. Samuel Gompers mused in 1891 that the "Knights never intended to be other than an educational organization" and deserved "no legitimate place in the field occupied by trade unions." This verdict influenced early labor historians, who considered the Knights confused utopians poaching on the terrain of realistic trade unionists like Gompers. Some modern-day historians, including the "new labor historians," accept this dualism. An otherwise illuminating study of Chicago labor concludes that "if the trade unions challenged the capital but not the capitalist system, the Knights challenged capitalist order but not capital.'' There is a grain of truth in this, quite apart from Powderly's fulsome disapproval of strikes and craft assemblies. The occupational diversity of its members proved an endless source of frustration within local and district assemblies. Small-town workers sometimes complained that the inclusion of employers inhibited discussion at lodge meetings. Fellow tradesmen in places with mixed economies had to contend with district assemblies with officials from different occupations who failed to appreciate the problems peculiar to specific callings. Detroit iron molders spoke for such workers in charging that district leaders "do not take enough interest" in the "technical . . . matters" of their craft.

Other evidence indicates, however, that the Knights were creative trade unionists. In the years immediately preceding the Great Upheaval, lodges not only evolved from instruments of agitation into agencies of struggle but also developed new systems of trade union coordination and labor-capital relations. These innovations were especially helpful in urban industries where work was splintered into specialized jobs. The jurisdictions of local assemblies followed lines fixed by job fragmentation, so that different lodges represented workers in the same industry but employed in scattered settings. Locals could not operate effectively without joining forces, and by the early 1880s collaborative efforts were under way. Lodges first worked out common dates for presenting bargaining demands and then formally merged into city- and region-wide trade districts both to coordinate negotiations and to circumvent the authority of district assemblies. They also formed shop committees composed of representatives from all lodges in a single mill or factory, which enforced contractual provisions, adapted industry-wide agreements to local conditions, and served as the first step in a graduated process of dispute settlement. Grievances not resolved by shop committees or laden with trade-wide implications were handled by the executive board of the trade assembly or the district assembly. Around mid-decade executive boards and employer associations referred stalemated disputes to third parties in what may have been the first examples of modern arbitration. The development of this very early but sophisticated system of industrial relations convinced the historian Judith Goldberg that the Knights stood for "modernization" and "formality," not utopian reaction or insensitivity to trade unionism.

Arbitration also reflected the Order's goal of harmonizing the social relations of production. Powderly lieutenant John W. Hayes called it bringing "the employer and employee closer together." Powderly himself thought this possible ever since he had benefited from the paternal benevolence of William Scranton. Arbitration worked reasonably well as long as goodwill prevailed and the players acknowledged the rules. It was put to a severe test, however, in the aftermath of the sharp economic downturn in 1883. Strike activity went up in 1884–85 as workers sought to recoup wages lost in the slump, protest firings of fellow unionists, or resist technological innovations. As we have seen, it soared to new heights in the spring of 1886 during the national strike for the eight-hour day. The tumult brought on a crisis described by most historians as a widening rift between an explosive rank and file and a cautious national leadership.

There is much to this interpretation. Ever since he became Grand Master Workman in 1878, Powderly had used his office as a platform for urging conciliation. As the 1880s progressed, he not only became a more outspoken leader but a more active one as well. This shift happened to coincide with the expiration of his tenure as mayor of Scranton in 1884. For the first time in six years, the Knights had a full-time chief executive no longer driven to distraction by the responsibilities of public office and determined to roll back the strike wave no matter what the price. His constant interventions into local union affairs crystallized the conflicting tendencies of militancy and moderation and forced members at all levels to choose between defiance and accommodation. The operative phrase here is "at all levels," for the lines of fissure followed vertical as well as horizontal axes thanks in part to the dramatic growth in membership from 1885 to 1886. Powderlyism prospered as the Order deepened its urban base and spread through the countryside. The Knights of the village, organized largely in mixed assemblies, brought a parochial perspective more in the tradition of antimonopolism than trade unionism and closely akin to Powderly's outlook. Their urban counterparts remain mysterious. Recent historians of the Order in Philadelphia and Detroit describe them as "new men," latecomers to trade unionism and critics of strikes who nonetheless got elected to district assemblies even as their cities were rocked by general strikes. These moderates did not always vote as a bloc either in district assemblies or at the General Assembly, nor were they consistently arrayed against the growing factions of socialists, trade unionists, and increasingly vocal militant radicals. But they did pull together behind the national leadership on the questions of trade unionism and strikes.

Local bodies of national craft unions were never pleased with the

Knights. Leaders of locals of iron molders, granite cutters, carpenters, and other trades repeatedly scolded the Knights for inducting members ejected from their unions for violating their rules. At one time or another, moreover, nearly every craft union engaged in the production of consumer goods complained of being penalized by Knights' boycotts. Given the inherent perils of dual unionism, these frictions come as no surprise. What is surprising is the extent to which squabbles remained localized and subject to resolution. Both sides, it seems, were determined to coexist, if only because each was weak and feared a confrontation in which both would lose. The forbearance came to an inglorious end, however, over a festering internal quarrel between cigar makers.

The irony is that the origins of the cigar-maker debacle had nothing to do with the Knights or Powderly. It originated in a tactical schism within Cigar Makers' International Union Local 144 of New York between pure and simple unionists and Lassallean socialists over eliminating tenement house work. Both sides settled on seeking a legislative ban, but the socialists cried "bourgeois collaborator" when, in 1882, the English-speaking leadership endorsed the candidacy of a Democrat friendly to labor, and then bolted the CMIU for the Progressive Cigar Makers. The rival unions first aired their differences in a fervent and sincere war of words, but in 1884–85 stooped to scabbing on one another. The Knights were drawn in by virtue of having agreed to boycott a firm being struck by the Progressives of New York in 1885. The dispute was inevitably magnified. To begin with, the Progressives forged a link with the Knights through the Home Club, the shadowy inner ring of District Assembly 49 in Brooklyn and center of urban anti-craft union sentiment. When the Home Club made the Progressives' cause their own, they picked a fight with the likes of Samuel Gompers, member of Local 144, architect of FOTLU, and foremost spokesman for craft unionism. A brilliant tactician with a superb sense of timing, Gompers had been biding his time, awaiting the moment to take on the Knights. The recrudescence of craft unionism in the upturn of 1885, paired with Knights' meddling in the affairs of his own union, brought the moment closer; Powderly's behavior in the eight-hour strikes of 1886 precipitated it.

American workers had never failed to answer the clarion call for a shorter workday. Struggles in 1835 and 1872 had raged into general strikes, but few could have predicted the enormity of 1886. Gabriel Edmonston, leading trade unionist in Washington, D.C., but hardly a household name, sounded the first note in a resolution at the 1884 FOTLU convention stating that "eight hours shall constitute a legal day's work after May 1, 1886,'' and soliciting the support of the Knights of Labor. The resolution scarcely commanded notice from craft locals, and as if to show his contempt, Powderly circulated a secret letter within the Order recommending that members "write short essays on the eight-hour question." The rousing Southwest strikes of 1885, however, infused the hours question with new urgency. By fall of that year Knights and trade unionists across the nation staged eight-hour rallies that grew more boisterous as winter turned into spring. Even Chicago's anarchists, who had dismissed the cause as "soothing syrup for babies," changed their tune and took command of podiums festooned with eight-hours bunting and the black flags of the Anarchist International.

Enthusiasm ran so high that thousands of workers jumped the gun and in mid-April petitioned employers for eight hours. Nearly thirty thousand achieved their goal before the deadline and well over ten times that number around the nation packed thoroughfares and public squares in vast demonstrations on May 1. The fervor spilled over metropolitan centers into such single-industry towns as Troy, New York, and backwoods depots like Grand Rapids, Michigan. One observer proclaimed "it was the workingman's hour." In Chicago "no smoke curled up from the tall chimneys of factories and mills," wrote a journalist, adding that the city had a "sabbath-like appearance."

The industrial hub of the Midwest was not so quiet. Forty thousand Chicagoans put down their tools on Saturday, May 1, to march with an equal number of sympathizers in a mammoth procession down Michigan Avenue. Paraders and picketers took a break on Sunday but swung into action on Monday in behalf of striking shingle shavers near the McCormick works. As anarchist orator August Spies rose to speak, a fight broke out between his listeners and strikebreakers leaving the McCormick plant. A police contingent stationed nearby moved in and indiscriminately fired into the crowd, killing two and scattering many more. Spies and his fellows dashed to their headquarters to consider their answer.

Anarchists in Chicago spent the evening printing and distributing flyers announcing a meeting to be held at Haymarket Square the next evening to protest police violence. A disappointing crowd of 2,000 or so showed up and dwindled to a few hundred as the rains came. Undaunted, Spies, Albert Parsons, and other anarchists who took their turn on a makeshift platform on the back of a truck denounced the police and proselytized for the cooperative commonwealth while cautioning against precipitous action that would invite even more carnage. Samuel Fielden, the last speaker, was interrupted by Police Captain Bonfield, a bitter foe of the Black International, which sponsored the event. Bonfield strode to the platform and ordered the crowd to disperse. To this day, no one knows who was responsible for the ensuing calamity. But no sooner had Fielden uttered, "All right, we'll go," than a bomb sailed through the air and exploded in front of the police. One policeman fell instantly and seven more sustained injuries that later proved fatal. The rest fired in panic, wounding at least sixty fellow officers and killing seven or eight in the crowd. Thirty or forty more onlookers lay bleeding from the "wild carnage."

"The city went insane," said miner organizer "Mother" Mary Jones, "and the newspapers did everything to keep it like a madhouse." Press and pulpit immediately accused the anarchists, and the verdict took on a life of its own in an outburst of popular hysteria. "The only good anarchist," read a typical editorial in the Cincinnati press, "is a dead anarchist." A police dragnet in Chicago yielded hundreds of arrests and the eventual conviction of eight Black Internationalists on circumstantial evidence. Within a year and a half four would die on the gallows, and a fifth would take his own life in a prison cell. The others would eventually be pardoned by Governor John Peter Altgeld in 1893. "The bad news from Chicago," wrote the socialist cabinetmaker Oscar Ameringer, "fell like an exceedingly wet blanket on us strikers." In Ameringer's Cincinnati and other centers fighting for an eight-hour workday labor returned to work in the face of police and militia. The general strike came to a halt within a week. "A single bomb," wrote a shaken Samuel Gompers, "had demolished the eight-hour movement." It was a lesson he would not soon forget.

May Day 1886 also sharpened the factionalism within the Knights over strike policy and relations with craft unionists which over the next two years would culminate in wholesale desertions and some defections to the craft unions. Powderly must take much of the blame for the damage—for his ham-handed rule during the strikes and for deliberately antagonizing the craft unionists. To hold him solely responsible for the disastrous decisions of 1886, however, is to make too much of the influence of one man. The fact is that Powderly enjoyed the support of one faction or another depending upon the issue at hand, and as it turned out, enough of it to remain in control, even as his ship took on more and more water. It is perhaps testimony to the strength of his convictions and the depth of his following that Powderly plunged headlong into defiance of the militancy that brought the Knights from obscurity to being front-page news in

1886. Even as eight-hour fervor rose, on March 13 he reiterated his position in yet another secret circular that warned that "we have never fixed upon the first of May for a strike of any kind . . . and will not do so. No assembly of the Knights must strike . . . on May 1st under the impression they are obeying orders from headquarters." Less than two weeks later the General Executive Board agreed to end a strike of five district assemblies, unrelated to the eight-hour movement, against the Southwest Lines, in return for an understanding that arbitration would begin once the trains started moving. When the railway owners broke their promise at the end of March, the Board reversed itself and ordered the strike to resume. In early April the Gould men were again on strike. A month later, in early May, a committee of citizens in St. Louis that had been working behind the scene for weeks asked the General Executive Board to call off the strike in "the public interest"; on May 4, the day of the Haymarket tragedy, the Board suddenly ordered the men back to work again, this time for good. "It was," according to the historian Norman Ware, "a complete capitulation and the severest blow the Order had suffered."

As betrayed Southwest men tore up their Knight cards and the nation reeled from Haymarket, Powderly scheduled a special session of the General Assembly at Cleveland to consider measures for bridling an unruly membership. Given his bungling of the Southwest strike and unpopular stand on the eight-hour movement, one would have expected a roasting from craftsmen, socialists, and militant radicals, with every right to expect more responsive leadership. There were searing attacks from the floor and acrimonious words among the delegates, but debate ended in triumph for moderation and Powderlyism with the approval of a change in the bylaws which, as one historian put it, "would have made a strike an impossibility." All assemblies were forbidden to announce work stoppages without first taking secret ballots that passed by a two-thirds vote; the General Executive Board was authorized to demand polls on the advisability of continuing strikes; and if the Board was not asked to settle a dispute, it could withhold financial aid. Powderly carried the day easily.

The Cleveland convention also did nothing to improve deteriorating relations with the craft unions. Earlier in the year the Progressive Cigar Makers of New York, backed by District Assembly 49, made a separate peace with manufacturers that left the Cigar Makers' International Union in the lurch. Though national CMIU leaders complained, local officials thought better of confrontation and proposed a joint conference to discuss a merger of all cigar makers into the CMIU, which would then affiliate with the Knights and abide by its policies. Had the Executive Board agreed to consider this overture, wrote Norman Ware, "the whole course of the labor movement in America might have been changed." But the Board flatly rejected negotiations. The rebuff returned the initiative to Gompers and his allies, who drafted yet another proposal, both broader in scope and more severe than the first. Known as the "Trade Union Treaty," it listed six provisions that would have prevented the Knights from organizing workers or issuing union labels in trades without "the consent of the local union of the national or international union affected." For such hard-bitten enemies of Powderly like Gompers, the "Treaty" was an ultimatum aimed at precipitating a break; for moderates like Peter J. McGuire, it was probably a proposal for negotiation. It is hard to know precisely what McGuire had in mind, but in light of the narrow base of trade unionism, he may have imagined an accord that left the highly skilled to the crafts and the semiskilled and unskilled to the Knights. Anti-unionist forces within the Knights, however, saw to it that no agreement was reached at all, not at the special convention in Cleveland or at the regular General Assembly in Richmond later that fall.

Anti-unionism at the top was strengthened at Cleveland. A decision to expand the General Executive Board to six auxiliary members resulted in the election of four Home Club candidates, anti-union socialists all, displeased with Powderly's antics during the eight-hour movement but in agreement with his union views. Rural moderates and the "new men" of the city completed a growing anti-union alliance that still failed to defeat a resolution calling for a committee to pursue talks with the crafts. An obdurate Executive Board quietly closed the door on negotiations by ignoring the resolution. The showdown came later in the fall of 1886 at Richmond, where, as militant radical Joseph Buchanan would observe, "the seal of approval was placed upon the acts of those members who had been bending every energy since . . . Cleveland to bring on open warfare between the Order and the Trades Unions." The Home Club fired the first shot in a resolution ordering "all cigar makers who are members of the Knights and also members of the International Union, to withdraw from said Union or leave the Order." What followed, however, more closely resembled massive retreat than war, as scores of unionists stormed out. They immediately capitalized on the breach by calling a conclave for early December at Columbus, Ohio, that would give birth to the American Federation of Labor.

For their part, employers made the most of the discord and the antilaborism that lingered in the wake of the Haymarket incident. "Since last May," wrote John Swinton the following fall, "many corporations and employers' associations" redoubled efforts "to break up labor organizations." This offensive began soon after Haymarket with isolated lockouts accompanied by court injunctions against picketers as well as patrols of police and militia. Mid-fall brought a rash of lockouts and also what Swinton aptly called the "obtrusive incompetency" of Powderly and his lieutenants. Through the lockouts and incompetency rank-and-filers suffered an unbroken string of defeats beginning in Chicago packing houses. Butchers had been forced into the streets by a lockout; they were clearly on the verge of preventing an extension of their workday when in early November they were unexpectedly ordered back to their jobs by a very nervous Powderly. Two months later the Home Club called off a walkout by Jersey City and New York dockers that had turned into a general strike. In Philadelphia, Knights who went on strike had the support of their leaders, but they were no match for employers in six leading industries, who prepared for open season on the Order as the New York general strike came to an end. Over the next eighteen months a succession of lockouts dispatched the Knights in their hometown.

Employers also picked off Knight strongholds in the South. In Augusta, Local Assembly 5030, a direct outgrowth of the Great Upheaval, had 3,000 members by mid-1886. It was dominated by white textile workers who rebelled against the familiar paternalism in the city's mills and factories. A June strike at the Algernon mill to force the dismissal of a despotic foreman was prelude to a summer of job actions for wage increases, shorter hours, and an end to the "pass system," which prevented workers from changing employers in the vicinity of Augusta. The job actions energized the local branch of the Southern Manufacturers' Association, which scheduled a lockout for August 10 if the 1,300 operatives on strike did not report back to work. The three-month lockout broke the strike and uprooted Local Assembly 5030. Police had guarded strikebreakers but refrained from force, perhaps because the strikers were white. Whites who lined up with blacks and blacks themselves were not so fortunate. In May 1887, H. F. Hoover, a white organizer for the Knights of Labor working in the Black Belt, was slain while addressing a racially mixed audience of cotton pickers. Black sugar plantation hands farther west went on strike in November following months of fruitless discussions with area planters over wages. Militiamen, called in to arrest leaders, evict strikers, and protect scabs imported to complete the fall harvest, shot four workers. This was followed by an even bloodier episode outside Thibodaux, Louisiana, where evicted cane workers huddled in shanties were attacked by white vigilantes in a reign of terror that took thirty black lives.

With or without armed force, employer repression broke Knight lodges. As 1887 drew to a close, assemblies that had boasted hundreds and even thousands of members were shells of their former selves. Survivors of the onslaught had second thoughts about an organization that would expel its own for no greater a transgression than belonging to a craft union. Powderly soon realized the mistake of banishing the cigar makers and in February 1887 prevailed upon the General Assembly to repeal the Richmond ruling. But it was too little, too late. Disgruntled craftsmen were leaving the Order as individuals or en bloc for national trade unions and the American Federation of Labor. As desertions continued, Powderly turned against the socialists, natural enemies of craft unionists and his own sometime allies who demanded clemency for the "Haymarket Eight." Why Powderly took an uncompromising stand against clemency is unclear. Perhaps it was his way of distancing himself from the left, improving the public image of his flagging movement, and relaxing employer opposition. Whatever the motive, he took more than a little satisfaction in being sustained by a two-thirds vote against a resolution of clemency at the Minneapolis General Assembly in October 1887. What remained of the left packed up and, following an abortive attempt by Tom Barry to form a rival brotherhood, either withdrew from unionism or joined unions affiliated with the AF of L.

So it went into 1888. Union busting, stupid leadership, and defections to the AF of L lowered Knight rosters to 220,000 in July 1888 and to a mere 100,000 by 1890, from the peak of nearly 750,000 in 1886. Urban lodges emptied at a blinding speed, plummeting to under a third of the membership in 1888 and then to under a fifth in 1890. What had begun as an urban workers' movement had become the preserve of rural labor and small-town mechanics. This demographic change, moreover, made Powderly even more conservative. It enhanced the provincialism that lurked in the Grand Master Workman but had occasionally slipped out in such heated moments as the contretemps over the cigar makers in which he defamed Gompers as a "drunk." Three years later in 1889 he wrote a longer and more bigoted brief in a tirade to an intimate, damning craft unionists as "a lot of . . . gin guzzling, pot bellied, red nosed, scab faced, dirty shirted, unwashed, leather assed, empty headed, two-faced, itch[y] palmed scavengers in the field of labor reform." The chain of epithets is as revealing of the state of the movement culture as of Powderly's cast of mind at the end of the 1880s. He and his associates finally broke the historic link between unionism and social reform. Having jettisoned the first with all it implied, they proceeded to dilute the second. The new Knights, said Powderly, would captivate "the country in an educational way," an empty threat at best that translated into innocuous homilies on behalf of temperance and cooperation, on the one hand, and a search for support outside the working class, on the other. In this context, it is fitting that Powderly first cultivated the Women's Christian Temperance Union and then began a typically irresolute romance with the Farmers' Alliance. He went to the founding convention of the Southern Alliance in 1889, a year later he urged the General Assembly to go on record in favor of a third party, and in 1891 Powderly joined with Alliancemen in calling the meeting that spawned the Populist party. But the Knights hardly mattered by then. Reduced to fewer than 100,000 members, the Knights was a weak but no less divided force. In 1893 a partnership of convenience between socialists and Populists deposed Powderly and elected Populist stalwart James Sovereign as Grand Master Workman.

Radicalism followed Knighthood into the countryside, where it crossed organization lines to help stimulate the agrarian uprising of the 1890s before expiring for good. It dwindled to an echo in the halls of labor; it spoke an arcane language, softly, and for the few. It had enjoyed an illustrious career as a source of inspiration but a frustrating one as a program for reform. Through all its transmutations since the 1820s, radicalism had fallen short of emancipating manual labor from the thrall of "accumulators," as Jacksonian proponents would have put it, or from "wage slavery," in the diction of the Knights. It could prompt self-improvement and collective struggle but in the end it failed to transcend its own limitations. Its tradition of cooperation was anachronistic. The essential ingredient of public support was not part of the political concern of late radicalism. At the same time the radicalism of Knighthood left a dual legacy in the political and in the economic realm. In spite of the republican heritage of restricted government, Knight activists had come around to a more positive view of government not only regarding public ownership of banks and utilities but also with respect to public regulation of the workplace. At the end of the 1880s lady Knights were part of a lobby which produced the first factory inspection acts in Pennsylvania, Illinois, and other industrial states. The Knights also left a model of industrial unionism responsible to a central authority. It was up to the American Federation of Labor, the new bearer of the torch, to adapt to these legacies or find its own way.

6.

The Prudential Unionism of the American Federation of Labor

As the Knights of Labor staggered from crisis to crisis through 1886, at the end of the year it faced a challenge for the loyalty of the American worker from the American Federation of Labor. Organized in December 1886 at a meeting of the Federation of Organized Trades and Labor Unions, the AF of L had more staying power than the Knights. By the late 1890s it could point to the major achievement of having withstood ferocious attacks from employers and government as well as the deepest and most prolonged recession of the nineteenth century. In its formative years the AF of L was no more cohesive than the Knights of Labor. It inherited the political factionalism that had shaken the Order, but had a dominant structure and strategy that set it apart from the Knights. The AF of L was a confederation of local, national and international unions and state labor councils rather than a centralized organization with a forceful executive. It came to accept the permanence of industrial capitalism and strove to find a place for unionism within the economy and the polity. Two fundamental forces shaped the federation, a Marxist intellectual tradition as understood by Samuel Gompers, Adolph Strasser, and other leading trade unionists, and the anti-union climate of the Gilded Age.

• • •

Samuel Gompers was not destined to be mistaken for a middle-class reformer; he would not cringe before a paternalist or bear the hoary banner of radicalism. Unlike the fastidious and reclusive Powderly, he was stocky and unkempt and liked hand-rolled cigars and shots of stiff whiskey with "the boys" in the union hall and corner tavern. He was an immigrant and a product of an urban working-class culture at once socially parochial and intellectually cosmopolitan. He was also a thinker, a street-wise intellectual, and a serious student of history and political economy. Above all, Gompers was the chief architect of an activism built on the reinforcing pillars of "pure and simple unionism," "voluntarism," and what we shall call "prudential unionism." Pure and simple unionism scorned social reform for the here and now, and sought to better conditions in the workplace within the framework of the existing order. Voluntarism taught unionized workmen to look to their own organizations rather than to reformers or the government to defend their class interests. Prudential unionism went beyond the narrow craft unionism and political pragmatism of pure and simple unionism and voluntarism; it was calculated to preserve trade unionism in an unfriendly environment. It argued strongly for turning away from unskilled and semiskilled factory workers inclined to engage in mass strikes or general work stoppages that activated the repressive machinery of government. It also encouraged unionized labor to restrict its struggles on the shop floor in the hope of reducing the possibility of government intervention. These became guiding principles of the American Federation of Labor, the house that Gompers helped construct.

Gompers's journey to the AF of L began in the slums of East London. The grandson of Dutch Jews who left Amsterdam for London in 1845, Gompers was born in 1850, a year after Powderly, to a poor cigar maker. At ten he was working at odd jobs in a tobacco factory. Not until the Gompers family left for New York in 1863 did the aspiring tradesman pursue his craft in a serious way, this time in the family shop under the tutelage of his father. The next decade held nothing out of the ordinary for a young craftsman. He married at seventeen, a bit younger than his peers; typical of newlywed workers with mounting responsibilities and the need for security, he looked to fraternalism and joined the International Order of Odd Fellows and Ancient Order of Foresters. But in 1873 when Gompers went to work in New York City for David Hirsh and Company he met working-class intellectuals in the European tradition who made a lasting impression.

No paternalist in the mold of William Scranton or Riley McKeon, the patrons of Powderly and Debs, German émigré David Hirsh was an "autocrat" with a penchant for hiring "fellow Socialist exiles." Socialism was not a foreign language to Gompers. It was the politics of the German cigar makers who dominated his craft and of the legendary street orators on the Lower East Side. By his own admission Gompers was "already familiar with the vocabulary of revolutionists" when Hirsh took him on. It was there, however, that his political education began in earnest, for Hirsh's payroll read like a who's who of socialist New York.

Gompers became friendly with Louis Baer and Karl Laurrell, leading German socialists and members of the Marxist International Working-men's Association (IWA). Laurrell became Gompers's tutor and trans-lator, a patient mentor who read Marxist tracts to him in local beer gardens and during dull spells at the workbench until the eager student learned German well enough to pore through the texts on his own. On the advice of Laurrell, Gompers never joined the International but did attend meetings and became an avid "fellow traveler." Laurrell, Baer, and others followed him into the Economic and Sociological Club, a political forum gathering regularly at the Tenth Ward Hotel, headquarters of the International as well. Theirs was not debate for its own sake. Gompers recalled them "groping their way" toward "the language, the methods, and the fundamentals of trade unionism." They read Marx and contem-porary socialist intellectuals, none more approvingly than Carl Hillmann, the labor journalist and member of the Social Democratic Workingmen's party in Saxony. Hillmann argued that it would be a "fatal error to subordinate the trade union movement directly to the purely political party movement" in Germany. In the United States, of course, there was a weak tradition of labor politics and by the Gilded Age there were no workers' parties of much stature. Nonetheless, Gompers and his com-rades appreciated the distractions of partisan politics and social mobility that faced the working-class activist in the United States. Having seen American labor leaders sidetracked by politics or entrepreneurial activi-ties, they resolved "under no circumstances will we accept public office or become invested in any business venture or accept any preferment outside the labor movement."

This novel pledge derived as much from Marxism as from the insularity of life on the Lower East Side. Marxism imparted a tough-minded materialism, what the left would later call "economism," that distinguished Gompers and his friends from American radicals. It assumed, as radicalism did not, that the march of capitalism concentrated more wealth and power into fewer hands. It was futile to seek a reversal of this natural process or mourn the passing of the small businessman as radicals did. Gompers told Senate probers in 1883 that modern society was divided into classes of employers and employees, "one incessantly striving to obtain the labor of the other . . . for as little as possible, and to obtain the largest amount and number of hours; and the members of the other . . . naturally resort to combinations in order to improve their conditions." He proceeded along the basic Marxist line that "so long as the competitive system lasts . . . the employer is entitled to a return. That is, if he is willing to pay a living wage. And if he does not . . . he ought to be crushed out as a manufacturer and forced to take the field as a laborer." Manufacturers who paid decent wages and treated labor fairly were entitled to respect but were not to be admired or admitted to the organizations of the working class. Ownership of the means of production in and of itself created an unbridgeable divide. Radicalism, polite reform, and other viewpoints that overlooked this fundamental difference were dismissed in Marxist circles. To Gompers, cooperation was an expedient, monetary reform an irrelevance, and land redistribution a dated wish unworthy of serious consideration. "It is not the ownership of land that we should fight," Gompers once shot back at an American radical, but "the doings of capitalists."

Marx, of course, looked forward to overthrowing capitalism. Few of his followers believed, however, that capitalism sowed the seeds of its own destruction. "If poverty alone could make converts to socialism, the starving millions of India . . . should be the most rabid and pronounced socialists," said a prominent socialist in answer to those who believed "worse is better," and that revolutionary consciousness naturally welled up from below. This was very much in keeping with Marx's conception of a two-pronged struggle in the economic and political spheres conducted jointly by unions and a workers' political party. Trade unions or "centers of resistance" weaned labor from capital, built class cohesion, and improved the quality of life to prevent workmen from slipping into the paralysis of poverty or the despondence of overwork. The party was less electoral instrument than political apparatus for coordinating union activity and transforming class feeling into revolutionary consciousness. That apparatus was the International Workingmen's Association, which Marx founded in 1864; it quickly spread throughout Western Europe before crossing the Atlantic in 1866. Discord over tactics, however, troubled the International both in Europe and in the United States.

Members of the International were riven into several factions, two of which concern us here. Followers of Ferdinand Lassalle religiously observed the "iron law of wages," which held that workers' earnings would inevitably sink to subsistence levels. This proposition led Lassalleans to emphasize politics over trade unionism. In so doing they antagonized the Marxists, who continued to advocate both politics and trade unionism. Disagreements among themselves and disappointments with the performance of socialist parties, however, gradually turned some Marxists away from using direct political means and toward trade union work, just as Carl Hillmann had urged. As a result, in the late 1870s the left sundered into a group of Lassalleans who stressed independent politics and a group of former Marxists who stressed trade unionism. The career of Adolph Strasser, Hungarian immigrant and Gompers's colleague in the Economic and Sociological Club and Cigar Makers' International Union, testifies to the transforming force of factionalism on the left. Strasser arrived in New York in 1872 by way of London, where he had probably become familiar with the "new model unionism" and most certainly joined the International. He sought out the IWA in New York but was expelled in 1874 for participating in an unauthorized demonstration for the unemployed in Tompkins Square, which was broken up by mounted policemen. Strasser then linked up with Lassallean Peter J. McGuire to unite the left under the auspices of the Social Democratic Workingmen's party. Two years of talks and the collapse of the IWA in 1876 gave rise to the Social Labor party (soon to be renamed the Workingmen's party of the United States and later the Socialist Labor party) around a program borrowed from the IWA. The party would concentrate on union work and refrain from electoral politics except where strong enough to "exercise a perceptible influence." But Midwestern Lassalleans read this proviso as a license to enter local elections in 1876. When Strasser objected, he was banished from the very party he had helped found, a cruel paradox, to be sure, for a man whose demeanor caused people to call him "the Prussian."

Not a little discouraged, Strasser pitched into union work with renewed fervor. By 1877 he was head of the Cigar Makers' International Union and by 1880 he was in the thick of efforts to firm up union discipline and secondly to outlaw tenement work. Both causes pitted him against Lassalleans, and the second would eventually embroil the Knights of Labor. The tenement controversy generated incisive debate that revealed different conceptions of the American experience. Lassallean polemicists insisted that unions could be agents of liberation only if they adapted to indigenous conditions. Unionism came naturally to European workmen because they could not vote and thus had no other outlet for protest. Unions were also stronger in Europe than in the United States because the working class was larger and class divisions sharper. Different conditions, it was argued, obtained in the United States with its great agricultural sector, numerous petty property holders, and relatively small working class that qualified to vote and freely exercised the franchise. American unions, in fact, were British imports grafted onto a working class more accustomed to political mobilization. Lassalleans therefore proposed to meet American workers on their own ground by forming unions that could gain strength by operating as the political arms of the Socialist Labor party and then build bridges to Grangers, Greenbackers, and other homegrown movements. Strasser answered by charging his detractors with badly misreading the American scene. In his view, independent parties, not unions, were organizations in the front lines of the fight for republican government in Europe but out of place in a nation whose wage earners already enjoyed rights of citizenship. Voting workers were incorporated into the political system and strongly attached to bourgeois parties but estranged from employers at the workplace, which is why they were such avid unionists. To convert unions into "socialist political club[s]," as Lassalleans proposed, was to invite the obstreperous who had crippled socialist politics and would surely cripple unionism if given the chance. Neither Strasser nor Gompers would inject partisan politics into unionism.

By the early 1880s, then, Strasser and Gompers had settled on a strategic and tactical course. Nearly a decade of intense reflection and personal experience with disruptive political factionalism made them shy away from socialist politics and indeed from socialism itself, if not from politics altogether. Strasser was too shrewd an observer, too aware of the limitations of unionism and the superior power of capital, to reach such a drastic course. The struggle against tenement work suggested that some form of state regulation was essential, just as it indicated that working with conventional parties could be effective. Strasser and Gompers, however, kept their political demands modest, partly because neither party was particularly sympathetic to labor and partly because lobbying required tailoring political objectives. In addition, they thought trade union pressure to be a more effective tool.

What has come to be called "pure and simple unionism" accompanied the development of voluntarism. The two were inextricably bound together: if less was asked of government, more was required of unions. The craft unions of Gompers's adolescence, however, were shabby affairs, fleeting groups whose ranks ebbed and flowed with strike activity. Gompers remembered there "was no sustained effort to secure fair wages through collective bargaining. The employer fixed wages until he shoved them down to a point where human endurance revolted. Often the revolt [was] started by an individual . . . who rose and declared [in the shop], 'I am going on strike. All who remain at work are scabs.' Usually the workers went out with him," but then drifted back to work and away from the union. The development of paid officers, collective bargaining committees, and other reforms during Reconstruction placed unions on

sounder footing, but progress was slow, uneven, and cut short by the
Long Depression of the 1870s. After the economy recovered, Gompers
and Strasser worked to remake the CMIU in the image of the "new model
unionism," a model first discussed by Hillmann and then practiced in
Great Britain. By the early 1880s they hiked dues, strengthened the
position of national officers by lengthening their terms of office, and
authorized the executive board to sanction or prohibit work stoppages
conducted by locals. The Cigar Makers also established unemployment
and health benefits, a centralized strike fund, and an equalization pool
that could be funneled into weaker affiliates at the discretion of the
president. Other craft unions gradually adopted some or all of these
measures, which helps account for the rising frequency of authorized
strikes after 1885 and the increased stability of craft unions. What
Gompers called "benefit unionism" gave workers a bigger stake in their
combinations, fortified bonds between worker and organization, and
reduced the likelihood of collapse during economic downturns and after
failed strikes.

By the first half of the 1880s, then, voluntarism and pure and simple
unionism, two essential features of Gompersism, had at least a tenuous
hold on the Cigar Makers' International Union. Voluntarism renounced
third-party politics along with the ambitious agendas of political insurgency. Pure and simple unionism meant not only investing dues to
provide social benefits but exerting disciplined union power to raise
wages, reduce hours, and protect craft traditions. Taken together, these
policies amounted to a kind of cautious syndicalism, cautious because of
the acceptance of the established order and syndicalism because of the
primacy of unionism. Well-invested dues and negotiated settlements
would provide the American worker with the benefits and security that
European workers extracted partly from employers and mostly from
government.

The building of an organization encompassing different trades provides
yet another piece of this picture. Neither Gompers nor Strasser, of
course, created the Federation of Organized Trades and Labor Unions or
its successor, the American Federation of Labor. Ever since the days of
the General Trades' Unions and the National Trades' Union in the 1830s,
workers had joined in citywide and national unions. The coming of
national labor and capital markets after the Civil War, however,
invigorated the search for collaboration, but agreement on the suitable
structure was not easy to reach. As the experience of the Knights of Labor
would suggest, some workers favored administrative centralism. This

aroused opposition because of Powderly's ineptitude and dictatorial rule; friction between local and district assemblies was another cause. Craft unionists and socialists who organized on their own outside the Knights were jealous of their power and accustomed to freedom of action. These instincts were so strong that the founders of the AF of L coined the term "trade autonomy" and enshrined it in a constitutional provision guaranteeing "strict recognition of the autonomy of each trade." Gompers observed the letter of this article throughout the late nineteenth century and scrupulously refrained from intervening in the internal affairs of constituent bodies. To be sure, the very existence of a president and other national officers gave the AF of L more shape than the amorphous FOTLU, which was more of a clearinghouse than a federation. Gompers and lesser officers sat as the Executive Council, but its powers were circumscribed: it could not even levy emergency assessments for affiliates in need until 1890. Gompers was simply a spokesman and the Executive Council a weak coordinating committee well into the 1890s. "Trade autonomy" was the order of the day.

Tradition was not the only brake on centralization. In 1886 the AF of L, after all, had only a dozen unions representing about 50,000 members. Not until 1890, when the number of affiliated unions increased to thirty-six and members to 200,000, did the federation eclipse the Knights of Labor. Even then Gompers could not help but look over his shoulder at the Knights with grudging envy. He desperately needed numbers and spared no effort courting workers of all political persuasions and occupations in what one historian aptly calls his "heroic period." "There is room enough," he told P. M. Arthur of the Brotherhood of Locomotive Engineers in 1890, "for the most radical as well as the most conservative." The relentless assaults on socialists would come later; for the moment he put out the welcome mat and flung open the doors of the house of labor to what proved a heterodox membership with several cultural tendencies.

One of the most important of these was craft conservatism. This subculture, Francis Couvares tells us, had "a rougher side" of young and single workers who crowded the bars, jammed the bawdy minstrel shows, and ruled the street corners of working-class districts. Bellicose gangs harassed intruders into their neighborhoods and committed petty crimes, just as they had in the antebellum years. William Z. Foster, the early-twentieth-century syndicalist and future Communist, recalled the raucous street life of his youth in late-nineteenth-century Philadelphia. Each neighborhood had a gang named after "animals, rivers, streets, districts, parks, etc., as for example: 'Lions,' 'Park Sparrows,' 'Reed-ies,' 'Schuylkill Rangers,' '' which were in a ''constant state'' of competition and ''warfare.'' The ''Bulldogs,'' Foster's own gang, had a social club, a fife and drum band, and a baseball team but also lived on the dark side of the law. ''Younger 'Bulldogs' broke street gas lamps, pilfered hucksters' trucks and stoned 'horseless carriages' that ventured into our lawless neighborhood. Many refused to attend school,'' he continued, ''and grew up to manhood unable to read and write.'' The older members of the gang would ''sometimes . . . do a day's work, but they were always ready to 'roll' a drunk or commit burglary or a stickup.'' The sons of better-paid workers were educated in schoolrooms rather than in the mean streets, but even some of Foster's reprobate friends hid their shady pasts. Marriage usually induced adult responsi-bility and a quest for respectability, the highest social aspiration of the industrial workman. Respectability carried a tacit code of social conduct often seen by historians as emulation of the middle class. Outward appearance would suggest social emulation: rough gangs gave way to polite fraternal societies and noisy street corners to quiet hearth and home. The industrial worker was slowly being domesticated. He began to have additional income that made possible the decorous furnishings and household technologies that slowly appeared in the homes of better-paid workmen after the Civil War. Home ownership became the goal of the respectable workman, a place of one's own that denoted economic improvement along with freedom from the gouging landlord. Middle-class America could hardly ask for more.

Industrial craftsmen, however, were not only mimicking social supe-riors. Some features of respectability were embedded in manual labor that distinguished the working class. Temperance exemplified respectable behavior. Generations of agitation against drinking, recent prohibition statutes, and rising standards of living had a broad impact. Indeed by the 1880s even the Catholic clergy became a force for abstinence, sponsoring parish-based branches of the Father Matthew Total Abstinence Society. More affluent workmen came to see drinking as destroying respectability and a menace to health and steady income. The shop drunk was no longer the butt of amusement but a threat to the safety and earnings of workmates who tended complicated equipment requiring great attentive-ness and coordination. This was very much on the minds of the Window Glass Workers' Association in Pittsburgh, prototypical labor aristocrats and autonomous craftsmen, who banned spirits at the workplace in 1883 and three years later conceded to management the right to sack members caught drinking on the job.

The nondrinking worker improved his employment prospects and job security but needed stronger medicine to protect his status. He could rely on government for tariffs, the restriction of immigration, and other legislative measures, or on the union to bring the boss to heel. As the 1880s progressed some craft conservatives became increasingly disillusioned with government, if not politics. At first blush this seems ironic because of the achievements of labor lobbyists and the rise of urban political machines powered by working-class votes. The machines, however, cemented the loyalty of workmen by substituting the politics of favor and patronage for the politics of issues and ideology. The patronage system in turn disturbed many workers. A leading labor journalist assailed state government as a nest of "dead beats" and "political shysters." He also reminded his readers that strong government trained its guns on workers in the bloody summer of 1877. Weaker government was far preferable.

Strong unionism, the mainstay of voluntarism, was more promising. A "manly bearing toward the boss" by the workman, to borrow David Montgomery's phrase, also helped measurably. The manly worker was the industrial cousin of the republican yeoman, a vigilant spirit unafraid of standing up to boss or foreman. He was more effective in a group, a collective of workmen faithful to an ethic of mutualism and individual sacrifice for the common good. Indeed maverick tradesmen earned the contempt of fellow workers expressed with a rich vocabulary of epithets suggesting they were selfish or unmanly sycophants. Peer pressure worked best to fortify trade unions; it did more than provide fatter pay envelopes and shorter hours. Trade agreements insulated labor markets and preserved laboring traditions by specifying training requirements or recruitment rights and carefully fixing work rules. Small wonder that tradesmen leaned so heavily upon their unions. The Homestead strikers in 1892, said an observer, "knew from experience that their organization was the only thing, in the first place, that enabled them to accumulate sufficient [income] to build their homes" and by extension enjoy a standard of living worthy of respectability.

Socialist culture, on the other hand, eludes easy summary. Sectarianism, feuds, and disaffection mark its ideological diversity and variability. It suffered rifts between Marxists and Lassalleans during the late 1870s, a split between English- and German-speaking Lassalleans in 1880, and defections to pure and simple unionism throughout the Gilded Age. After 1878 the arrival of Lassalleans forced out of Bismarck's Germany, whom Gompers understandably described as "zealots and visionaries," replenished the ranks of the Socialist Labor party. As if this were not enough, Midwestern Lassalleans deserted the party for the anarchist International Working People's Association, the Black International, in the first half of the 1880s. Through all this turmoil, however, socialists and anarchists shared other cultural customs. Because many were sweated workers earning subsistence incomes, few saw much point in pursuing respectability. And because they worked by hand without the din and drive of machines, it was still possible for them to talk with their fellow workers. They argued politics among themselves or listened to a "reader," a brother designated to read aloud from a text or the labor press while his fellows worked. Even an agnostic like Gompers confessed there was something special about New York's East Side sweatshops, those industrial barracks of the nation's Red armies. "I had a real joy in living," he would recall, "and loved the daily intercourse with fellow-workman." German neighborhoods were honeycombed with debating clubs and meeting rooms and the streets were lively with soap-box orators and party workers hawking socialist sheets. No group on the labor left had a greater capacity for self-organization than the anarchists of the Midwest. Chicago anarchists had at least eight newspapers run as collectives, along with scores of lecture halls, libraries, and reading rooms as well as Sunday schools, singing societies, and drama clubs. There were even armed militias organized to respond to police action in the railway strikes of 1877; they headed parades in observance of the anniversary of the Paris Commune and other "Black" spectacles.

Anarchism, as we have seen, did not preclude unionism, not in Chicago or any other Midwestern city. The boundary between anarchism and unionism was as porous as that separating anarchism from Lassalleanism. Anarchists taunted "pure and simple unionists," scolded bourgeois politicians, and unnerved everyone with talk of "dynamite" and "propaganda by deed." Devotees of the "Chicago idea" of anarcho-syndicalism, however, endorsed unionism, albeit unionism of a revolutionary kind, and pointed the way to the eight-hour strikes of 1886 in city after city. But the repression in the wake of the Haymarket bombing and the hanging of the four martyrs a year later, the historian Paul Buhle observes, sent a chill through anarchists everywhere. Robert Reitzel, editor of the Detroit *Der Arme Teufel,* "perhaps saw how an era had closed for the German-American left." Following the frightful executions in 1887 Reitzel wrote, "With the best skill one must still ask the question: why?"

According to Hartmut Keil, German workers asked themselves the same haunting question and drew different lessons. In Chicago, where repression was especially fierce, anarchists pulled back. Militiamen put aside their arms, orators toned down the provocative rhetoric of "bombs and bullets," and party activists in general went underground to form secret education groups and debating societies. Other Midwesterners and many comrades in the East preferred what a Philadelphian called "covered retreat into a more fortified position to await reinforcements." This meant finding allies within the labor movement. Powderly's betrayal of the eight-hour movement and dogged opposition to clemency for the martyrs tainted the Knights of Labor. The American Federation of Labor, on the other hand, looked appealing and proved even more hospitable because of Gompers's "heroism" and the federation's official policy of trade autonomy. His 1888 campaign to resume the struggle for the shorter workday dispelled any remaining doubts. As the 1880s drew to a close, German- and English-speaking radicals entered locals of national and international unions affiliated with the AF of L.

The inclusion of the left increased the cultural pluralism of the federation. The socialists were no longer so strident, but they were hardly quiet church mice. Some took to needling craft conservatives, while others maligned Gompers and satirized his unionism as "pure and simpledom." Even so, Gompers held his peace. He had to respect trade autonomy and was not about to risk a replay on a larger scale of the internecine war that had nearly decimated his own union in the early 1880s. Lassallean foes, who had committed the cardinal sin of dual unionism, had returned to the CMIU in 1886, prefiguring the socialist swing back to the internationals. He would proceed more cautiously this time to keep the peace and maintain the federation. As he told a socialist detractor who had advised a firmer hand in 1890, national leaders "disposed to be dictatorial" would "soon find none to dictate to."

A form of this caveat extended to other federation matters. Unlike the Knights, the AF of L never developed the activities of a movement culture. The national office had an organ, the *American Federationist;* however, as a rule it did not hold lectures or publish didactic literature. Paid field staff appeared occasionally, less to convey a coherent political message than to advocate in the late 1880s such specific causes as the eight-hour day or, a few years later, women's unionism. Executive officers bent energies toward answering correspondence and issuing charters, managing the Washington lobby, and mediating jurisdictional squabbles. But it was not always so tedious. In the early 1890s the socialists gave Gompers the political fight of his life.

Recrudescent socialism reflected widespread disaffection with conservative political orthodoxy of the late Gilded Age. Beleaguered yeomen and dirt farmers crowded Populist lecture halls. Literate city folk, weary of disruptive strikes and lockouts, scrambled for copies of Edward Bellamy's *Looking Backward,* a major best-selling novel published in 1888. In it genteel Bostonian Julian West falls asleep and awakens in the year 2000 A.D. to find himself in a bountiful but sterile and orderly socialist utopia brought about by a peaceful revolution. Shadowy factories lavish consumer goods on contented people organized in an "Industrial Army" and paid in credit redeemable for commodities. Here was a utopia that eliminated exploitation, social disorder, and even a working class, and struck such a resonant chord that Bellamy became an overnight hero of middle-class America and leader of a Nationalist movement based on his novel.

However, workers in the real world at Homestead, Pennsylvania, in 1892 and then on the railways west of the Mississippi in 1894 faced not only intractable employers but also intimidating militiamen and antilabor judges. The financial panic of 1893 dragged the economy into the steepest trough of the century, idling some 3 million by the end of the year. "Benefit unionism" covered the unionized few, but its treasuries were bare within a few months; there were demands for more drastic measures. Some 10,000 workingmen converged on Washington in May 1894 under the leadership of Jacob Sechler Coxey, an eccentric Ohio businessman, to clamor for public works funded by government-issued currency. Even Gompers cast voluntarism to the winds and endorsed Coxeyism. The *American Federationist* editorialized that " 'On to Washington' is the best evidence that hundreds of thousands of our fellow human beings are suffering the pangs of hunger and smarting under the lash of injustice.'' "Coxey's Army" reached Washington on schedule on May 1, 1894, and secured permission to parade through town. But when Coxey and his command defied a law prohibiting demonstrations on the Capitol grounds, they were jailed for twenty days and then fined $5.00 each for walking on the grass. Their leaderless army soon fell apart.

It was the socialists, however, who exploited the unrest. Indeed, the early years of the depression provided the socialists within the AF of L with real opportunity to launch a third party with an explicitly socialist manifesto drafted by the workers themselves. The significance of this occasion has been overshadowed by undue scholarly attention to the colorful feud between Gompers and Daniel DeLeon, putative voice of socialism, who was at the helm of the Socialist Labor party in the early 1890s. A lawyer by training and former professor of law at Columbia University, DeLeon went through "polite reform," the Knights, and Bellamyite Nationalism in rapid succession before latching on to Lassallean socialism. He bore the marks of the quick convert. More of a sloganeer than an original thinker or compelling leader, he made a habit of insulting Gompers and deriding his union. He minced no words in branding Gompers a "labor faker," and the federation a "tape worm," an "aggregation of links with no cohesive powers worth mentioning." Gompers returned a shower of insults no less personal, once charging that DeLeon "came from a Venezuelan family of Spanish and Dutch Jewish descent with a strain of colored blood. That makes him a first-class son-of-a-bitch." Whatever the truth about DeLeon's lineage, the fact is that the SLP was larger than he, just as the AF of L was larger than Gompers. His jaundiced views of Gompers may have been shared by the labor left, but his mercurial tactics were often ignored. Very few of the party faithful thought much of his courtship with the Knights of Labor in 1893, though more of them appreciated the Socialist Trades and Labor Alliance, the industrial arm of the SLP founded in 1895 and modeled after DeLeon's "New Unionism." In fact, the STLA was not very new at all. Its structure reproduced that of the Knights and it never reached beyond the crafts to the industrial workers DeLeon pretended to represent. Nor did it depart significantly from the conventional wisdom of Lassalleanism. DeLeon may have diverted the SLP from labor's mainstream into a backwater, as Philip Foner maintains, but most party members carried on the fight for socialism from within the AF of L.

While DeLeon attacked Gompers and bored from within the Knights, socialist trade unionists went to the 1893 convention of the AF of L with the "Political Programme." Inspired by British labor's attempt at independent politics, the Programme included a preamble written by Chicago machinist Thomas Morgan calling for a third party and an eleven-part platform highlighted by plank ten, which demanded "collective ownership of all the means of production and distribution." It was put to only one vote on the convention floor, in the form of a resolution that each member union give it "favorable consideration" before the 1894 meeting. The resolution lost by a mere 71 votes out of 2,400 cast, and the Programme was circulated to each constituent union without recommendation for straw votes before the 1894 meeting. The votes ended on an encouraging note for socialism. Only the bakers rejected the Programme in its entirety; the printers and web weavers expunged plank ten and the carpenters passed an amended version of it. Virtually every other union, including Gompers's own cigar makers and the major state federations, voted in favor of the Programme.

The showdown came at the Denver convention in 1894. Gompers and his allies, chastened by the defeat in the precincts, regrouped and lobbied the delegates very hard. They picked up vital support from Peter McGuire, longtime leader of the carpenters and joiners, co-founder of the federation, and influential socialist who nevertheless welcomed the opportunity to humiliate the SLP and DeLeon's "political disturbers in New York City misnamed Socialists." The anti-Programme alliance handily won a tactical vote to consider each plank separately and went on to defeat the preamble (1,345–861) and then pass a flabby substitute for plank ten (1,217–913). The remaining planks, which included a proposal for municipal ownership of public utilities, cleared easily but meant very little without the preamble. Socialists took revenge by electing miner John McBride president for the coming year, the only such defeat suffered by Gompers in thirty-eight years, but this was small consolation for the socialists. Their moment had passed.

Socialists scattered in every direction following Denver. New England organizer Charles Rawbone took the defeat so hard that he tendered his resignation and withdrew from the labor movement. Some New Yorkers, convinced of the hopelessness of "boring from within," bolted to the Socialist Trades and Labor Alliance, only to be upbraided by the brewers for such "disgraceful treachery." The brewers and unions centered in the Midwest remained within the federation but pursued an abortive "labor-Populist" coalition.

More significant still, growing numbers of socialists backslid to pure and simple unionism. John T. Elliott, the Baltimore painter elected General Secretary of the International Workingmen's Association in 1871–72, former Knight leader, and then secretary of the Brotherhood of Painters and Decorators of America, became a crusty labor bureaucrat and faithful friend of Gompers. Other former socialists did not fall so far. New York Lassalleans Henry L. Weissman and Charles Ibsen had derided Strasser's reform unionism and opportunist politics in 1886 when they inaugurated the Bakers' and Confectioners' International Union. In an early edition of the *Bakers' Journal,* the union's organ, Ibsen editorialized that "nothing short of a radical re-organization of production can bring us deliverance from injustice." Within four years, however, such socialist élan dissipated. Why is still unclear. Perhaps leaders and followers came around to Strasser's view of the dangers of mixing socialism with unionism. Possibly the rapid monopolization of biscuit baking exposed the futility of fighting large corporations with slogans and unions more suited to political education than economic action. One infers as much from Weissman's warning that if "workers fail to organize more successfully, then indeed they will be unable to offer organized resistance through . . . the Boycott, [union] Label, or Strike." For whatever reason the union did an abrupt about-face. In the early 1890s it adopted reform unionism and in 1892 repealed a resolution passed the previous year formally endorsing the Socialist Labor party. A year later the bakers voted down the Political Programme.

If the transformation of the Boot and Shoe Workers' Union is any indication, the ravages of the depression also cooled socialist ardor. Formed in 1895 from three separate unions, the Shoe Workers was one of the few socialist unions with a native-born and Irish constituency. The BSWU never went on record for the SLP. However, it was so closely identified with the party that an unbroken string of lost strikes in the mid-1890s substantiated the Lassallean doctrine that worse is better and failure really success. Socialist Labor activist and union president James Tobin assured his members that "we will not surrender our Union and give up hope but keep on gaining recruits and new strength with each succeeding failure of the old weapons." Instead of strengthening socialist resolve, however, successive defeats sapped spirits, gutted membership rolls, and ultimately cleared the way to pure and simple unionism. The return of prosperity at the end of the decade found Tobin holding forth like a pure and simple unionist. "Economic organization based upon high dues, and the payment of sick, death, and strike assistance, would produce much better results. . . ," he told a receptive audience, "than a union whose only source of solidarity is the class conscious sympathy of its workers." Strasser could not have said it better.

Just as federationists moved toward pure and simple unionism, so did they disown the heroism of the late 1880s that had left the door ajar for semiskilled and unskilled labor. One would not glean this from the historical literature, which continues to depict the AF of L as a club of Yankee and first- and second-generation Old Stock (Irish and German) immigrants plying skilled trades. The ethnicity of federation men is not in dispute; their social pedigree, however, was not so lofty as we have been led to believe. The confusion stems in part from equating craft unionism with craftsmen—that is, from conflating a jurisdictional term with a social category. All AF of L units were called "craft" unions but were not confined to skilled workmen. Unions of unskilled hod carriers and street railway workers were attached to the federation along with societies of semiskilled factory hands from a range of industries. In an occupational sense the federation was more diverse than has been appreciated.

The AF of L was more uniform in gender and racial terms, but even here one must be wary of facile generalization. Women and blacks were urged to join and some did at first. Female shoe workers and textile operatives in New England and Philadelphia, as well as Troy laundry workers, held membership either through national unions or more typically through federal labor unions chartered directly by the Executive Council. Women federationists in Chicago were the vanguard of their gender. There a group of socialists and former Knights headed by Elizabeth Morgan, wife of Thomas Morgan, who would write the Political Programme, formed Federal Labor Union No. 2703 in 1888. Within a year Morgan and her associates assembled the Illinois Women's Alliance, a broad coalition of temperance activists, club women, suffragists, consumer advocates, and settlement workers including Jane Addams and Florence Kelley. The union and the Alliance worked out a loose division of labor, with the former concentrating on workplace issues and the latter on educational projects and social reform. Alliance women reported cases of police brutality and child abuse, publicized deplorable conditions in factories and sweatshops, and worked feverishly for protective legislation. They could take much of the credit for an 1889 state law which reduced child labor by making elementary school education all but compulsory.

The Alliance's great achievement, however, was the Factory Inspection Act of 1893. Patterned after similar statutes adopted in Pennsylvania and New York, this act barred children under fourteen from factories, regulated the labor of children between fourteen and sixteen, legalized the eight-hour day for women and youths, and ordered state inspection of workplaces to ensure compliance. The Alliance had submitted two bills, one written by Elizabeth Morgan and the other by Florence Kelley. Morgan's proposal, which had the support of the Chicago Trades and Labor Assembly, was the weaker of the two: it simply outlawed tenement work and contained the provisions on child labor that appeared in the act. Kelley's draft was more ambitious than Morgan's, for it contained the eight-hour clause and the provision for enforcement by paid factory inspectors that were included in the law. The historian Kathryn Kish Sklar speculates that the differences owed to Kelley's "greater education and familiarity with the American political system" and her contacts with "the larger community on which she could rely for the law's passage and enforcement." While Kelley and the reformers did have such advantages, they also had a background of involvement in social and moral causes that enlisted government as a regulatory instrument. The reformers applied this tradition to labor relations by demanding a legal eight-hour day and state enforcement of it. Possibly they were also aware of the weakness of women's unionism, that unorganized women workers had nowhere to turn except to government for amelioration of conditions on the job. Morgan's group, in contrast, reflected the voluntarist strategy of the AF of L that looked to unions rather than government both to initiate and to enforce reform. This was a flawed and ineffective model for working women and it made the AF of L increasingly irrelevant to female workers. As so often happened in the Gilded Age, however, the court had the last word. In 1895 the supreme court of Illinois struck down the eight-hour provision in the law on the ground that "labor is property and an interference with the sale of it by contract or otherwise is an infringement of a constitutional right to dispose of property."

The successes of black workers were largely confined to the workplace. The major bright spot came in New Orleans in October 1892 when black teamsters collaborated with scalesmen and packers in a biracial Triple Alliance in a bid for a ten-hour day, overtime pay, and a preferential union shop. By early November their strike swelled into a general work stoppage of forty-nine unions. White and black stood as one against vicious race-baiting by the press and a ploy on the part of the Board of Trade to split the Alliance by settling with the white packers and scalesmen but not "the 'n----r' teamsters." The board compromised within a week and New Orleans labor celebrated the nation's first successful biracial general strike.

There were more mundane examples of AF of L support for black and women workers. Gompers himself had spoken out for recruiting the two groups out of idealistic and practical motives. It was Gompers, after all, who chartered FLU No. 2703 in Chicago and who in 1892 persuaded the Executive Council to appoint Mary Kenney, leader of the Chicago union, National Organizer for Women. In private correspondence he had also reprimanded racist field staff and rarely let an early AF of L convention pass without a lecture on reaching across the racial divide. "If we fail to eliminate the color line. . . ," he told the 1894 gathering. "If we fail to make friends of [black workers] the employing class won't be so short-sighted. . . . If common humanity will not prompt us to have their cooperation, enlightened self-interest should.''

Yet the federation never came close to rivaling the Knights' position on race and gender. There is no simple explanation of this. The traditional argument that the division of labor pushed women and blacks into unskilled work beyond the jurisdiction of the AF of L is based on a false premise. As we have already seen, unskilled workers were eligible for admission as long as they organized along "craft" lines. The resistance of white males, though substantial, was not insurmountable, as the experiences in Chicago and New Orleans would suggest.

On the other hand, traditional obstacles to organizing women and blacks continued to impede progress. The number of women gainfully employed rose by 1.4 million during the 1880s, but this great increase did not shake the old pattern of rigid job segregation by gender. In 1890 nearly a million women, fully a fourth of the total at work, were domestic servants, and nearly 700,000 worked in a few industries—clothing, laundry and cleaning, textiles, and shoes. Their occupational distribution in 1890 had not changed much since the antebellum period. Indeed, even as more men worked in factories many women still toiled at home under the domestic system. Over half the women needle workers in 1890 were outworkers, not factory operatives or shop employees. Women workers, moreover, were still young. Nearly 10 percent were under fifteen and the vast majority were under twenty-four and single. Marriage continued to spell withdrawal from employment outside the home in 1890, just as it did in 1830.

Ever since the first scholarly studies of women workers in the opening decades of the twentieth century, historians have cited the peculiar work experiences of women as explanations for the absence or weakness of women's unions. Abbreviated employment, crowded labor markets, subsistence wages, to list the most frequent factors, deterred women's unionism. In her study of working women in the early twentieth century, Leslie Tentler discusses a phenomenon that may have defeated women in the Gilded Age. Because young women at work had to hand over their earnings to mothers and fathers, they were often more at odds with parents over "social freedom" than with employers over wages and working conditions. The Knights of Labor, of course, had made major inroads into the women's work force, but their ultimate failure had a profound impact on working women. In the excitement of the Great Upheaval in 1886, for instance, a leading Philadelphia shoe manufacturer discharged the entire shop committee and executive board of Garfield Assembly, but the "membership took up the fight . . . and after a bitter struggle succeeded in reinstating every one of their members." This proved to be merely a stay of execution, for the manufacturer broke the Garfield Assembly and fired its leaders in the lockout of 1887. Lockouts and sackings hit textiles and other Knight strongholds throughout the nation and such recrimination probably had a lingering effect. It may have convinced most working women that aggressiveness on the job could be counterproductive and that the political action being pursued by women's labor advocates was not only safer but potentially more fruitful.

Black workers were severely hobbled by racism. Employers fomented racial hatred by using blacks as strikebreakers, and the racism of white workers sometimes came back to haunt them. In 1886, for instance, white steelworkers at Steelton, Pennsylvania, founded a Jim Crow benevolent society, then turned around five years later and solicited black support in a strike, but were told by the blacks that "we were not wanted at first, and will not join under any circumstances." The vast majority of blacks, however, were still in the South and on the land. The relatively few black industrial workers were not only set back by the rising tide of racism but also by the aftermath of the Great Upheaval.

The repression that followed 1886 in the South took black lives as well as black jobs and unquestionably discouraged black unionism. Combinations of black workers persisted or revived largely in communities with histories of black and white unionism, sympathetic white labor leadership, or political regimes friendly to organized labor. All these conditions prevailed in New Orleans, but even there race relations were ever so tenuous. Within a year of the general strike of 1892 blacks driven off the land in the depression flooded labor markets on the docks with nonunion hands, touching off racial strife that split unions and eventually brought down the Cottonmen's Executive Council, the umbrella group that had worked for racial harmony on the waterfront. In Savannah black dockers previously affiliated with the Knights of Labor were also in the forefront of black unionism and labor militancy during the late 1880s and early 1890s. Threats to discharge "negligent workers" in late summer 1891 produced the Longshoremen's Union and Protective Association and at the end of September the longshoremen went on strike for a wage increase. Expecting to confront strikebreakers, the union men resolved not to "allow others to take their places except by walking over their bodies," but quickly backed off when the mayor strengthened the police and put the militia on alert. Indeed, the dockers did their best to avoid a confrontation. They placed advertisements in the press assuring the public that they were "not prepared for war, but . . . for work," and took up positions out of harm's reach. Strike meetings were held well away from the waterfront at Odd Fellows' Hall, and instead of picketing the docks, strikers distributed circulars in the countryside to warn prospective strikebreakers away, and "walking delegates" were quietly dispatched to persuade those who did take jobs to leave town. It was an impossible situation. The Longshoremen's Union might have been more effective at preventing strikebreaking had it picketed the docks, but this would have brought in the police. By the end of the week middle-class blacks were advising a return to work, and the union was sharply split over a resolution introduced by militants demanding union recognition. While the longshoremen squabbled, strikebreakers streamed in and undermined the strike. Of the nearly 2,000 men who had participated in the strike, only 100 were taken back in early October by the waterfront employers.

The influence of Savannah's black bourgeoisie is hard to evaluate. It is very possible, however, that episodes like the Savannah strike lent greater credence to the strategy of shunning unionism or alienating white employers that had been followed by most free blacks in antebellum times and at least some freedmen after emancipation. William Councill and other middle-class blacks in Birmingham had advocated as much during the 1880s, beseeching black labor to "maintain peaceful and friendly relations with the best white people of the community . . . who give our race employment and pay their wages." It remained for Booker T. Washington to codify this form of accommodation in his famous "Atlanta Exposition Address" in 1895. Washington, of course, was no Councill. While in his own subtle way he was far more critical of segregation and disenfranchisement than Councill, both men were in agreement on the labor question and their advice seems to have gained wider acceptance in the black community as the 1890s wore on.

Given these constraints, it would have been surprising indeed if women and blacks answered the call of the AF of L in any numbers. That call, moreover, was never loud or persuasive enough to overcome resistance from constituent unions. Women were still perceived as keepers of hearth and home in spite of their steady increase in the labor force. Indeed, the more women went to work, the more they aroused the anxieties of workmen who considered it their birthright to be the sole support of the household. The *Coast Seamen's Journal,* the newspaper of a union that had no women members, expressed this well in an 1893 editorial. "Mentally and physically, women are incapable as a sex of achieving great things, but they are capable of being instrumental in making it impossible for men . . . to be the providers . . . of women and children." "The labor movement . . . ," it continued, "has the special responsibility of giving every man a chance to earn sufficient income to provide for a wife and family." A year earlier Gompers had failed to persuade the Executive Council to extend the commission of women's organizer Mary Kenney, and in early 1894 the Council rejected his proposal to appoint four additional women's organizers. When the 1894 convention met later in the year, the AF of L had no women's organizers on staff.

Racism in the 1890s was a vicious fact of life and growing uglier in the upsurge in antiblack vigilantism and the rash of segregationist legislation in the South. White workers who saw blacks as a "servile people" regarded Eastern European immigrants taking jobs in mines and factories across the nation in the same light. John Jarrett, head of the Amalgamated Association of Iron and Steel Workers, snickered at such "foreigners—Hungarians, Poles, Italians, Bohemians . . . [who] really don't know the difference between light work and heavy work, or between good wages and bad." A colleague of Jarrett's called them "beaten men of beaten races"—that is, something less than men.

This hardening of white male chauvinism, racism, and xenophobia in the context of trade autonomy all but slammed shut AF of L doors to women, blacks, and Eastern Europeans. As Alexander Saxton observes, the federation followed a kind of "right hand–left hand arrangement by which national unions made their practical decisions in the field," while the Executive Council "lacked any coercive power over them." Gompers could coax and cajole but could not prevail on members who belonged to autonomous unions not to be bigoted and prejudiced. Only two unions, the cigar makers and printers, joined by the United Garment Workers and the Boot and Shoe Workers in the mid-1890s, admitted women at all, and usually consigned them to separate locals. The few that did induct blacks maintained Jim Crow locals that had to accept inferior pay scales. Unions with "white only" constitutional provisions were at first denied charters. The National Association of Machinists, a Southern union for whites only, was refused admission in 1890 by vote of the convention. Gompers then encouraged the formation of a rival union the following year, which, as he doubtless expected, merged with the NAM into the International Association of Machinists in 1893 and applied for a charter in 1894. The application was accepted and the IAM was admitted even though everyone knew that it had removed the color bar from the constitution but adhered to its ritual that bound members to propose whites only for membership. Several later entrants followed the same subterfuge. Even as he welcomed the IAM, Gompers reaffirmed the federation's blindness to "color, creed, sex, nationality, or politics." But this was meaningless rhetoric. The 1894 convention marked his capitulation to racism.

• • •

The prejudices that animated AF of L men did not simply limit membership mainly to white males. The federation's view of benighted workers also informed the emerging strategy of prudential unionism, a strategy that repudiated mass strikes and general work stoppages for fear of inciting labor violence. Members of the federation held ambiguous and contradictory views of less privileged workmen: the same workers considered to be slavish were also seen as hotheaded and impetuous, susceptible to spasmodic outbursts that activated the repressive machinery of government. Gompers had been introduced to police violence at a New York demonstration for the unemployed in 1874 at Tompkins Square when a policeman's billy whizzed past his ear. This seemingly trivial incident made such a vivid impression on Gompers that he recounted it in his autobiography nearly fifty years later. By then a rabid antisocialist, he wrote that his brush with the law was a signal lesson in the "dangers of entangling alliances with intellectuals," by whom he meant the Marxist organizers of the rally. He seems to have drawn a different conclusion, not immediately after the riot, but in the wake of the railway strikes in 1877 and the successively brutal encounters with authority during the 1880s and 1890s. It was the unwashed masses, not the armchair radicals, who were to blame. It was the unwashed who brought out the bully in the state that crushed unions as readily as it beat and bruised individuals. Such workers lacked what Gompers, McGuire, and others were fond of calling "civilization," or patience, self-discipline, and a realistic sense of the possible. To them, civilization derived not from asceticism and restraint, as Powderly like to think, but from personal responsibility born of material improvement and a rising standard of living. "It is only . . . the enlightenment gotten from material prosperity," said Gompers, "that makes it . . . possible for mental advancement."

This outlook deepens our understanding of the AF of L's retreat from heroism. That retreat cannot be attributed exclusively to the withering of the Knights and the "craft consciousness" of skilled workmen. The materialistic perspective of the AF of L leadership, which associated the unskilled and underprivileged with barbarism, played an important role. As unskilled labor came to mean Eastern Europeans, moreover, the better the excuse to write them off. "New immigrants," after all, lived in volatile bachelor communities, worked for slave wages, and would rather save than buy modern comforts; they had less at stake than the settled, respectable family man. In addition, unskilled and semiskilled workmen were not strategically located in the production process and did not enjoy the leverage of industrial craftsmen. They could not prevail on the shop floor without force of numbers—that is, without large strikes. The bloody battles of 1877 and 1886 indicated, however, that such actions antagonized duly constituted authority. It seemed prudent to contain the activities of federationists and, if need be, work against rival unions that represented industrial workers.

Three episodes in the first half of the 1890s—the renewed drive for the eight-hour day, the Homestead strike, and the Pullman boycott—reflected and reinforced prudential unionism. The first began with the ballyhoo of earlier struggles to cut the length of the workday. In 1887 and again in 1888, Gompers aroused conventions with electrifying speeches on the ramifications of overwork. "As long as there is one man who seeks employment and cannot get it," Gompers intoned at his rhetorical best in 1887, "the hours of work are too long." His call for "steps . . . [that] would lead to practical action and results" laid the groundwork for a resolution adopted the following year that scheduled job actions for the eight-hour day on May 1, 1890. An energized Executive Council dutifully distributed pamphlets, commissioned the federation's first paid field workers, and planned demonstrations on Washington's Birthday, Independence Day, and Labor Day. Eight Hour Leagues instigated rallies and parades and unfurled banners with the venerable slogan: "Eight Hours for Work, Eight Hours for Rest, Eight Hours for What We Will." For a moment it looked very much like 1886 in the making, a prospect that upset many and drove an apprehensive brother in early 1889 to write Gompers about his concern. Gompers responded with a calming letter that partly disclosed his intentions. First, he averred that the "agitation will do us much good. It will wake up the millions of workers from their past lethargy. All men of labor, however much they may disagree on other matters, can unite upon" the issue. This was another way of describing the campaign for the eight-hour day as an extension of the effort to upstage the Knights, a rallying point to foster unity and bolster membership. It succeeded admirably in that respect, creating the largest increase in membership before the upsurge of the late 1890s. The hemorrhage that followed Haymarket stopped, as new unions emerged and many affiliates doubled in size. Second, Gompers assured his nervous colleague that "it did not necessarily follow that because we are agitating the subject . . . all workers must strike on May 1st 1890." It was not until the convention later in 1889, however, that Gompers finally tipped his hand. Instead of a general work stoppage, there would be strikes by individual national or international unions over several years. Each union would poll its members to assess the strength of eight-hour sentiment and report back to the Executive Council, which would select the first to go on strike. In March 1890, the Council chose the United Brotherhood of Carpenters and Joiners, the largest union in the federation. On May 1, carpenters packed up their tools in nearly 150 cities and towns, often with the support of kindred construction tradesmen in big cities. These tightly organized and planned strikes, a far cry from what David Montgomery calls the "contagious uprisings" of the past, won the eight-hour day only for building workers. Plans to continue the struggle were shelved when in 1891 the United Mine Workers, the next in line, proved too weak to take its turn. The Executive Council considered it "inopportune" to designate a substitute, and the movement petered out.

By this point all eyes were riveted on Homestead, the steel-making community of 11,000 east of Pittsburgh on the Monongahela River. Nearly all adult males were employed at the Homestead works, one of twelve subsidiaries of the Carnegie Company. Just about two-thirds of Carnegie's payroll of 3,800 performed unskilled tasks and were not welcome in the Amalgamated Association of Iron and Steel Workers. One of the oldest AF of L unions, the Amalgamated represented labor aristocrats who parlayed the proficiency required to make iron plate, hardware, and rails into an empire of industrial craftsmen. Puddlers, rollers, and others hired and trained their own help, set the stint, and divided wages among themselves. But the fantastic pace of technological change and the rapid development of managerial hierarchies that accompanied the shift from iron to steel loosened the Amalgamated's grip. "The steel mills," said Amalgamated leader J. T. Schaeffer, "are getting away from us." Anti-unionism was "becoming worse in the steel mills."

That was an understatement. Amalgamated lodges were either broken in unsuccessful strikes or depleted by technological innovation during the first half of the 1880s. Bessemer converters for purifying molten iron hastened the displacement of puddlers with chargers, regulators, and other specialists, severely weakening or destroying key lodges. Skilled crews that had worked the puddling furnaces and the rail-mill train at the

Edgar Thomson works, another Carnegie satellite, were decimated and two lodges closed their doors. Membership dipped to an all-time low of 6,000 in 1885 and lodges struggled to hang on. Weak bargaining teams had allowed work rules to be relaxed, relinquished hiring rights, and abandoned coordinated negotiations that had established region-wide wage standards. The iron and steel boom at the end of the 1880s had, however, breathed new life into the flagging union. Membership jumped to a historic high of 24,000 and lodges won major concessions from management. The new agreement reached at Homestead in 1889 had a sliding scale that pegged wages to market prices but with a floor, and fifty-eight lengthy footnotes spelled out work procedures. A Homestead manager muttered that "the method of apportioning the work, of regulating the turns, of altering machinery, in short, every detail of working the great plant was subject to the interference of some busybody representing the Amalgamated." The tangle of rules tied the hands of a management team driven by Carnegie to cut costs to the bone. The union, said a Carnegie partner, "placed a tax on improvement, therefore the Amalgamated had to go."

Before leaving for a European vacation in spring 1892, Andrew Carnegie instructed newly hired superintendent Henry Clay Frick to sever ties with the union. A coal magnate who had rooted out the United Mine Workers from southwestern Pennsylvania, Frick preferred the more devious course of going through the motions of negotiating while plotting a lockout. In April, three months before the expiration of the 1889 contract, he terminated negotiations and issued an ultimatum: if the men did not accept a wage cut (of about 20 percent) and a change in the expiration date of their bargaining agreement from June back to January, the plant would be run nonunion. Last-minute talks broke down and in late June the workers were locked out.

The Amalgamated men lost no time preparing their ranks. On June 30 an Advisory Committee with delegates from each of the eight lodges orchestrated strike activity and exercised civil authority for its duration. Units organized like regiments policed the streets and bars, picketed the huge plant, and patrolled the waterfront to intercept strikebreakers. The manpower for such comprehensive tasks was not supplied by the union alone; indeed only 800 held Amalgamated membership. The 2,400 unskilled and semiskilled hands not in the union voted to walk out in solidarity with its members. The 600 Eastern Europeans among them elected representatives to the Advisory Committee and did their share of picket duty.

Homesteaders picketed without incident until July 6, the day Frick intended to resume production with strikebreakers protected by Pinkerton guards. He had erected what the community facetiously called "Fort Frick" by enclosing the gigantic works with a fence topped with barbed wire and equipped with battle stations for sharpshooters. The plan went awry when worker patrols spotted a steamboat towing two barges of armed guards up the Monongahela at dawn. A timely alarm summoned thousands of Homesteaders to the riverbank for a furious battle that raged intermittently for twelve hours. Some strikers and townsfolk along the shore crouched behind scrap-iron bunkers and rained bullets and hurled sticks of dynamite at the barges; others fired at the barges from squadrons of small boats and tried to burn out the Pinkertons by igniting an oil slick. The Pinkertons eventually surrendered, but both sides took heavy casualties. Nine workers and seven Pinkerton guards were killed; forty strikers and half that number of Pinkertons were wounded; and hundreds of the guards were punched and kicked when forced to run a gauntlet following their surrender. The tattered Pinkertons were then held in a local arena before being shipped out of town. The tide turned four days later, when Governor Robert Pattison ordered out the state militia under the command of Major General George Snowden. By July 12, 8,000 troops, about two for each worker on strike, took charge of the streets and plant gates, much to the relief of the Advisory Committee, who greeted Snowden as the representative of the people's government out to restrain corporate lawlessness. But Snowden wasted no time breaking up picket lines and guarding strikebreakers quartered in huts inside Frick's compound. At the end of July company lawyers had the leaders of the Advisory Committee arrested for murder of the Pinkertons and in September a grand jury, which had been empaneled in midsummer, returned 167 true bills for murder, aggravated riot, and conspiracy against scores of strikers. Several union heads were later indicted for treason. However, no one was convicted. But while the arrests and prosecutions took leaders out of circulation and drained resources and dampened spirits, they did not weigh very much in the outcome. The turning point had come with the arrival of the troops and the strikebreakers, who got the plant converters running by late July. A month later the mill was turning out some steel even though the Amalgamated did not formally call off the strike until early November.

To the historian Melvyn Dubofsky, Homestead represents "a perfect fit into the pattern of late-nineteenth-century industrial conflict." The essential parts of that pattern were indeed there, from the plebeian sympathies of the community to the corporate partisanship of the governor and an alien military force. The strike also laid bare the vulnerability of the Amalgamated and its parent body, the AF of L. Their adversary was a mighty corporation with unlimited resources and wide latitude for maneuver. The new technology allowed Frick to replace union crews with green hands, and the multi-plant structure of the firm permitted him to shift production to another site and wait out the union. Even without the militia, it would have taken a herculean union effort to overcome such corporate power.

As for the federation, it was no Hercules. The historian Philip Taft wrote that its "efforts at Homestead dramatically demonstrated the value of the organization to constituent unions." This is improbable. Gompers, it is true, kept in close touch with the battlefront and tried to assist the strikers. He first threw up pickets at the offices of Frick's labor recruiters in New York, then helped arrange for the legal defense of the indicted, and in December declared "Homestead Day," a time for federationists to ante up for hungry brothers bracing for a cold Pittsburgh winter. He could do no more. Sympathy strikes made no sense because no affiliate was positioned to do much given the federation's narrow base. And besides, wider action would have run the risk of further antagonizing a hostile state. That is what troubled Gompers as he mulled over the meaning of Homestead. He considered the grisly event a "premonition of what is yet to come. Sometimes my heart almost sinks," he confessed, "at the thought of what we . . . may yet witness as the results of the overweening greed of the corporate and capitalist class." Gompers knew that Homestead was different. The federation had tussled with individual employers ever since its inception, but seldom with a corporation and none on the scale of Carnegie. Homestead, its first collision with really big business, provided a sobering baptism that confirmed apprehensions over taking on basic industry. The price was simply too high.

Homestead was not the only trouble weighing on Gompers. As he reflected on the strike, small employers went on a robust offensive against sympathy strikes. A rash of lockouts along with injunctions, prosecutions for conspiracy, and police interventions knocked craftsmen back on their heels. Over half the strikes in 1892 went down to defeat, compared with fewer than 40 percent in 1888–90. As a result, writes David Montgomery, "trade unionists began to shy away from sympathetic strikes." The sharp economic downturn of 1893 filled the streets with jobless demonstrators demanding public works and strikers demanding cancellations of wage reductions, as well as corresponding police actions. In April 1894 a miners' strike broke out in United Mine Worker collieries in Pennsylvania and then strikes erupted in nonunion fields throughout the nation. Coal reserves were quickly depleted but the scarcity didn't help to restore wage scales as the miners had expected. Repeated clashes with local police and militiamen ended the strike and nearly brought down the UMW. By summer 1894, wrote a sullen Gompers, there were "probably not more than two national unions affiliated with the American Federation of Labor, which have not had their resources greatly diminished and their efforts largely crippled by reason of trade struggles." It was in this sorry state that the federation faced the Pullman boycott, the epic labor war of the age.

Two circuitous paths led to Pullman. One was taken by Eugene V. Debs and the other by George M. Pullman. Debs, the son of a Terre Haute, Indiana, grocer, became a locomotive fireman at age seventeen in 1873 and within four years was elected secretary of the Vigo Lodge of the Brotherhood of Locomotive Firemen. By the end of the decade, he was secretary-treasurer of the BLF and editor-in-chief of its journal, the *Firemen's Magazine*. The young labor journalist espoused conciliation and outflanked Powderly on the right as late as the mid-1880s. He still believed that the highest expression of civic and social responsibility lay in honoring the Protestant work ethic and its strictures of "honesty, manhood, and hard work." The true man deferred to his betters on the job and in the community, just as Debs himself had deferred to the Terre Haute railway owner Riley McKeon. It comes as no surprise that Debs, who tongue-lashed railway strikers in 1877 and 1885, could not find a good word for the Knights in 1886. But as Powderly grew more moderate in the aftermath of Haymarket, Debs moved toward militant radicalism and eventually socialism. The pivotal moment came in 1888 during a strike against the Chicago, Burlington, and Quincy Railroad, the first brotherhood work stoppage he endorsed and one fraught with disaster. It dragged on for a year but was lost within the first two months, as brotherhood members walked through firemen's pickets, Knights of Labor strikebreakers took their jobs, and judges stymied leaders and rank-and-filers with a flurry of injunctions. The strike diminished Debs's faith in bringing order and reconciliation through the goodwill of conservative railway unionism. He redefined manhood as an affirmation of self, of individual and collective rights on the job, and questioned the utility of organizational structures that not only divided labor against itself but also snubbed the unskilled majority. He first experimented with a federation of the brotherhoods in the Supreme Council, and when it collapsed in 1891 after two years, he gave up completely on craft unionism. Resigning from the Firemen in 1892, he spearheaded the American Railway Union, the first industrial union on the railways since the abortive Trainmen's Union of 1877.

The Railway Union had a phenomenal beginning. It had yet to hold its first convention when in April 1894, James J. Hill, principal owner of the Northern Pacific, ordered the third wage cut in eight months. Strikes hit the northern tier and within two weeks the ARU stepped in to take credit for forcing Hill to back down. The notorious victory not only thrust Debs to national prominence, it also set off a headlong rush into ARU lodges that recalled the resurgence of the Knights of Labor in 1885–86. "The officers," Ray Ginger wrote, "were unable to pass out charters fast enough to keep up with applications. Entire lodges of Railway Carmen and Switchmen transferred to the ARU Firemen, conductors, even engineers, joined the industrial union. But the great majority . . . came from previously unorganized men." Scarcely a year old in summer 1894, the union had 150,000 members, just about as many as the American Federation of Labor.

George M. Pullman, a self-made millionaire, poured a fortune accumulated from his famous "palace car" into a model company town outside Chicago. Tidy tree-lined streets and gardens framed churches, a library in "advanced secular Gothic," and rows of yellow brick cottages with indoor plumbing and other conveniences. There were public squares and spacious athletic fields for a work force pruned of malcontents and dissidents. Pullman preferred the rosy-cheeked "buckwheats" from village America and blond Northern Europeans, who had a relatively high standard of living but not the rights and freedoms enjoyed by other citizens. Pullman ran his town like a fiefdom. He personally conducted local government but delegated the management of labor to loyal underlings. His complex of workshops and assembly rooms had over 4,000 employees. In the early 1890s he ran one of the largest industrial establishments in the nation. The complaint of an early-twentieth-century worker that "when we begin our day's work, we never know what our day's pay will be" also applied to the Pullman works during the 1880s. About half the hands were paid by the piece but the rates varied widely because foremen freely invented scales and played favorites. Other Pullman workers were paid daily wages by inside contractors who were as capricious as the foremen. It did not take long for unrest to surface. A purge of Knights of Labor activists in 1886 only deferred the inevitable. Workers grumbled about being treated like "slaves" by "tyrannical and abusive'' managers and foremen. They reached their limits in the spring of 1894, when Pullman imposed wage reductions of 33 to 50 percent but refused to cut rents or dividends. A committee representing a lodge of the ARU complained in early April to Pullman vice president T. H. Wickes, who turned a deaf ear and three weeks later summarily dismissed three of the committeemen, precipitating a walkout on May 11.

Donations of money and other assistance from working-class Chicago helped the Pullman men hold out for a month. The fourth week of the strike coincided with the first national convention of the American Railway Union; four hundred delegates gathered in Chicago full of fight from the Northern Pacific victory. Pullman strikers told moving tales of woe and appealed for a national boycott of all Pullman rolling stock. Delegates roared support of a resolution ordering a boycott should Pullman reject eleventh-hour arbitration. When Pullman snorted that there was ''nothing to arbitrate,'' the Executive Committee scheduled the boycott for June 25.

Eugene Debs was not pleased. Visions of the regiments that had smashed the Burlington strike, we are told, flashed through his mind. Indeed, immediately after that debacle he had editorialized on the government's ''shot-gun policy,'' prophesying that trainmen would one day see phalanxes of federal troops breaking strikes on the pretext of delivering the mails. Mass action was especially dangerous to a new union as fragile as an eggshell that would shatter as surely as the Knights had in similar circumstances. Debs thus found himself in the uncomfortable position, as Ray Ginger once put it, of leading a job action that ''he tried to avoid'' and that spun out of control. It engulfed rural depots and municipal terminals of the transcontinental roads and trunk lines throughout the Mississippi Valley and the Far West. By one estimate over a quarter of a million railway workers in twenty-seven states honored the boycott by uncoupling Pullman cars and sending trains on their way without them, or simply quitting when station managers insisted on running the boycotted stock. Supportive crowds cheered wildly and non-railway workers marched in solidarity or served employers with demands of their own. On July 2 a spokesman for the General Managers' Association in Chicago acknowledged that the railroads had been ''fought to a standstill.''

The General Managers' Association, the trade group of the twenty-four lines serving Chicago, flexed its economic and then political muscle. Threats to sack all participants had no effect, so the GMA connived to involve the federal government by alleging that strikers disrupted interstate commerce and prevented mail delivery. It did not take much to sway the Cleveland administration to its side. President Cleveland was sympathetic, and Attorney General Richard Olney, who had spent over thirty years as a railway lawyer, was still on the executive board of several lines, including one involved in the strike, when he became the nation's .chief law enforcement officer. Olney strongly disapproved of unions and harbored special animus for combinations of railway workers. On June 30, 1894, he confided to a friend in Chicago that if the federal government "vigorously asserted" itself at "the origin and center of the demonstration, the result would be to make it a failure everywhere." On that day Olney appointed GMA lawyer Edwin Walker Special Federal Attorney for Chicago. Three days later he instructed Walker to request a court order, and on July 3 the federal district court issued a blanket injunction ordering the strikers back to work and restraining their leaders from communicating with union locals. The next day Olney used a minor disturbance outside Chicago as the excuse for sending in troops despite assurances from the governor and mayor that local forces had the situation under control. As a GMA spokesman gloated, it "was now a fight between the United States government and the American Railway Union and we shall leave it to them to fight it out."

Chicagoans were not in a festive mood when on the Fourth of July some 12,000 federal troops arrived in their city. Most Railway Union members, a federal investigation of the strike would conclude, heeded the appeals of their leaders for calm. But the myriad unemployed and at least some union men went after the railways with a vengeance. On the night of the Fourth of July crowds destroyed track and ceremoniously over-turned boxcars. The next day roving bands jammed railway switches, sacked rolling stock, and set a fire that spread to the World's Columbia Exposition. On the morning of July 6 mob action escalated following the shooting of two civilians by an official of the Illinois Central. The Illinois Central's yards were burned and the Panhandle's depot was completely wrecked. Over the next few days eleven more rioters were killed and over fifty were wounded by the federal troops or state militia. Forty more civilians were shot down and scores were injured in clashes with troops and militiamen in six other states. As the worst of the tumult ended in Chicago on July 10, Debs and fellow ARU officers were hauled off to jail and charged with conspiracy to obstruct interstate commerce. They were released within a day, and rearrested a week later, this time for contempt of court. In between these legal ensnarements, Debs moved to cut his losses in hopes of salvaging the union. What transpired revealed both the tragedy that had befallen him and the nature of Gompers's prudential unionism.

The interventions of troops and judges convinced Debs that the strike was a lost cause. But rather than surrender or pursue the impossible, he decided upon tactical retreat in order to save face for the union. He sounded out area unionists for a general strike to enforce the reinstatement of ARU men fired during the strike. The walkout that followed on the day Debs was whisked off to jail was something of a disappointment, partly because there were so many police and ARU officials were rounded up. In addition, Chicago unionists were reluctant to jump in without sanction from national headquarters and demanded an emergency meeting with their leaders. The historic meeting at the Briggs House, a Chicago hotel, on July 12 and 13 brought together the Executive Council and the heads of nearly all federation members with brotherhood spokesmen and ARU officers. Debs's proposal for a sympathy strike got an icy reception. Gompers and his lieutenants not only rejected it out of hand but issued a statement urging an immediate and unconditional return to work. Debs would later charge Gompers with betrayal, but as Nick Salvatore argues, this was unfair since Debs had already declared the strike a failure. Salvatore goes on to observe that Gompers had spurned sympathetic action of any kind because he sought to curry favor with the brotherhoods and because he was "searching for stability within the labor movement and for its acceptance by . . . corporation[s]." There is something to this. It was an open secret that Gompers had been trying for years to lure the brotherhoods into the federation. Pullman presented an irresistible opportunity for ingratiating the railway unions by embarrassing Debs and perhaps even discrediting the ARU. It is also true that Gompers craved stability in a time of crisis; a competitor was the last thing he needed.

The decision reached at Briggs House, however, had a much deeper meaning that penetrates to the core of the dilemma faced by organized labor in Gilded Age America. Such workers confronted an American peculiarity, a difference that distinguished their experience from that of Western Europeans and is best understood as the paradox of state power. English, French, and German workers were, for example, citizens of nations with strong governments and deeper traditions of the exercise of state power. With the obvious exception of insurrections and revolutionary moments, however, they rarely felt the official repression that came down against American workers in the last third of the nineteenth century. Indeed, as Gerald Friedman observes, when French elective officials did intervene in major strikes, they either sided with labor or acted as mediators but in either instance refrained from the overt use of force. In many German states and principalities before 1860 trade unions were illegal and between 1878 and 1890 socialist organizations were outlawed in the unified German state. Yet German authorities seldom shot down unionists or strikers in the last quarter of the nineteenth century. Britons continue to look upon the Peterloo Massacre of 1819—one of the first and last massacres, in which hundreds of workers and townsfolk were either killed or injured by the Yeomanry Cavalry while attending an open-air meeting—as something of a national calamity.

The American case was as ironic as it was distinctive. A nation that thrived on limited government turned out to be singularly intolerant of organized labor. Mass actions and even sectional strikes tripped the hair triggers that brought not only injunctions but violence against workers who took to the streets not for revolution but for better wages, shorter hours, union recognition, and job control. What Debs aptly called "shot-gun policy" stiffened the resistance of an already intransigent class of employers. No Americans were more acutely aware of this than leading labor spokesmen. Better than anyone, they knew that unpopular work stoppages brought government interventions that beat union men into submission. The wider the effect of the job action, the greater the probability of repression. Gompers and his colleagues had denounced the Pullman strike as an "impulsive vigorous protest" that cast organized labor into "open hostility to Federal authority. This is a position we do not wish to be placed in. . . . Against this array of armed force and brutal moneyed aristocracy," it asked rhetorically, "would it not be worse than folly to call men out on a general strike in the days of stagnant trade and commercial depression?" The leaders of the AF of L were not simply looking to win the favor of capital, if indeed that was a consideration before the late 1890s; they were also out to stay the hand of the state.

The ARU did not survive Pullman in its original form. The enfeebled union became the Social Democracy of America that sought to resettle workers fired during the strike in a utopian community in the Far West. Debs may not yet have been, as biographer Salvatore argues, fully converted to socialism during his six-month stretch in a Woodstock, Illinois, jail cell. The precise dating of his conversion matters less than the profound impression left by the cumulative experiences beginning with the Burlington strike. As Salvatore tells us, Debs concluded that the Knights were right after all, "an injury to one was indeed the concern of all." At the same time, the collusion between capital and government rendered remedial action taken only through industrial unionism a treacherous course. True enough, he would flirt with an industrial union base for the Socialist party in the opening decade of the twentieth century, but for the rest of his life Debs hewed closely to his own maxim that "the ballots of workingmen emancipated from the [old] parties would bring a higher plane of prosperity." His kind of trade unionism did not stand much chance without a check on the police power of government. Workers had no choice but to erect their own cover by organizing politically and seeking to control the state.

For his part, Samuel Gompers could only associate the slogans of the Knights of Labor with the nightmares of 1877, 1886, 1892, and 1894. It was more prudent not only to refrain from mass strikes but also to turn away from the industrial workers who fueled them. He readily accepted Debs's realization of the intimate relationship between unionism and state power, but drew precisely the opposite conclusion. Gompers maintained that it was self-defeating to enter the political arena under a single standard, socialist or otherwise. He also believed that partisanship was pointless as long as unionists operated in the shadows of big business and organized the shops of entrepreneurial employers who did not have the cozy relations with the state enjoyed by the heads of corporations. "I have insisted, and I do now insist," said Gompers in 1898, "that the only power capable of coping with and (if necessary) smashing the trusts, is that much abused and often ridiculed force known . . . [as] 'The Trades Union Movement' as understood and practiced by the American Federation of Labor." This was not a little disingenuous. Gompers had about as much appetite for taking on the trusts as he did for organizing their workers. The federation found safer harbor in smaller business—building construction, printing, and other sectors not a part of corporate America. He chose the line of least resistance for the sake of surviving a hostile age. Given the realities of the period, survival was no mean achievement, if hardly a model for all labor in the future.

Epilogue: Radicalism, Unionism, and the State

"The problem of to-day, as of yesterday and tomorrow," wrote the labor reformer George McNeill in 1887, "is how to establish equality between men. The laborer who is forced to sell his day's labor to-day, or tomorrow, is not in equitable relations with his employer." Here was the ongoing dilemma of the labor partisan and labor radical who built the working-class movements in nineteenth-century America. But all working people were not so critical of emergent industrialism. Some never thought inequality was a problem, and others, a larger number perhaps, believed it would eventually take care of itself or somehow be resolved through conventional politics. Workers did not respond to the industrial revolution of the nineteenth century in unison or with a single voice.

One source of this diversity was the economy's uneven growth. That industrialism was retarded in the antebellum South is a truism; that it was patchy in the North before the Civil War cannot be stressed enough. For every wage earner at midcentury bent over a whirring machine in a grimy factory or using hand tools in a squalid garret, there were equal numbers who still owned their own tools and worked at home or in farmhouses at night and during the down side of the rural work cycle for manufacturers or merchant capitalists. Many urban journeymen remained in an old-fashioned artisan shop. They earned better wages than factory hands, often approached the living standard of their employers, and could save enough to buy a home or set up shop on their own. The world of the journeyman diverged sharply from the world of the early factory hand typified by young women fresh from the American farm and later from the Irish tenant plot. Neither group of mill operatives brought skills to their jobs, learned proper skills while at work, or worked very long, gainful employment outside the home being a brief interlude that ended with marriage. While in the factory female operatives experienced the ambiguity of the industrial revolution, a grueling work routine that grew harsher in time but eased somewhat under paternalistic management.

Evangelical Protestantism, a frequent companion of paternalism, could also soften early industrialism. Evangelicalism, to be sure, offered a contradictory message. The 1840s found workers invoking the injunction "in the sweat of thy brow shalt thou eat bread" to attack selfishness and inequality; they quoted passages from Genesis to assail mandatory labor on the Sabbath and excessive hours during the week. At the same time, evangelicalism imbued workers with the individualistic spirit of the entrepreneur, with distrust of collective action to redress job-related grievances and with suspicion of nonbelievers as well as virulent anti-Catholicism. The church was also a social center, a place where employee and employer met as equals in the eyes of God and sometimes worked out mutually beneficial arrangements to serve Mammon. Poorer churchgoers patronized the shops of wealthier parishioners who hired fellow congregants or helped ambitious journeymen establish their own businesses.

Few antebellum workers, however, were evangelicals. Only a fraction of working people in the North or the South regularly attended church before the popular revivals during the economic slump of the late 1830s. These outbursts of holiness were followed by a great influx of European immigrants that fundamentally changed the composition of the working class in both regions. Some English and German newcomers, refugees from Chartism and revolution, mixed easily with American radicals. Many more, and the "Famine Irish" especially, were former peasants and an underclass forced into menial jobs and Catholics in a sea of Methodists, Baptists, and Presbyterians. They counted themselves fortunate to have work at all and were more aggressive at first in defending their culture than in pursuing economic justice. They displaced native-born Americans as leaders of the rough urban street culture—the gangs and fire companies that made the city dangerous for blacks and Irish Protestants. The late 1840s spelled the end of a once ethnically homogeneous white working class.

Politics was received culture at its most potent. One hesitates to describe political democracy as the "nail in the coffin of class consciousness," but in the context of the two-party system, white male universal suffrage was a strong force for social and ideological integration. From the birth of the "second party system" in the 1830s the Whigs and Democrats mirrored and aggravated the cultural conflicts caused by popular religion. The Whigs' call for a "Christian party in politics" meant as much to evangelicals as the Democratic hue and cry for "freedom of conscience" did to nonevangelicals. Each party, moreover, broadcast versions of free laborism that differed in particulars but emphasized economic improvement for ordinary people. Even the Whigs, the party of wealthy merchants and rising manufacturers, pitched their "American System" of banks, tariffs, and internal improvements as the infrastructure of opportunity for the workingman and yeoman farmer. Northern Democrats outdid the Whigs and their Southern fellows in courting the "producing classes" with such popular blandishments as the abolition of imprisonment for debt and mandatory militia duty, programs to expand public schools, and, of course, the politics of antimonopoly and hard money. In the South, Democrats relied heavily on the promise of "white egalitarianism" to solidify their electoral base.

These received cultures, however, were only beginning to take hold during the late 1820s. Indeed, the comparative ethnic cohesiveness of the working class, the weakness of evangelicalism, and the formlessness of party politics opened a moment of opportunity for organized labor. The intensification of economic change, marked by the rise of the sweating system and expansion of factory production, set off the first sustained attacks on the industrial revolution and systematic programs for equality drafted by artisans for artisans. The radical essayists and pamphleteers of the 1820s brought together two strands of thought, an older political convention and a new economics. The first was rooted in the traditional republican wisdom that vilified government as oppressive and exploitative and entrusted mechanics and small farmers with preserving equality and republican rule. The political vigilance of the plain people grew out of their economic autonomy and self-sufficiency, which inculcated a fierce sense of independence and deep distrust of those who depended on government, whether for subsistence or for economic advantage. This link between politics and economic well-being invested political radicalism with a critical perspective on the commercial and industrial revolutions, but not with concepts that grasped economic affairs in economic terms. The economic strand of radicalism, as espoused by William Heighton and others, rested on a cooperative ethic and the labor theory of value. The first taught that competitive capitalism worked to the detriment of the artisan, the second that the artisan was the creator of all wealth and entitled to the full product of his labor. Both principles located exploitation in economic relationships and not simply in the abuse of political power.

The politics and economics of radicalism had different implications.

Political radicalism told the artisan he was a citizen and, within the context of political democracy, the peer of every (white) man. It asserted that as a citizen and a voter he could eliminate economic inequality through political action that would clear the field of privilege and favoritism. Since this was not qualitatively different from the rhetorical goals of the Democrats, and later the American Republicans or indeed the Republicans, political radicalism was at all times susceptible to being incorporated by mainstream parties or insurgent groups headed by middle-class dissidents. The economics of radicalism, on the other hand, told the worker he was an economic being, a producer with interests separate and distinct from such parasitic accumulators as merchants, financiers, and large employers (if not necessarily from the small employer who hired labor but still worked with his men). Economic radicalism pointed the worker toward unionism in a more emphatic way than political radicalism. The union hall was labor's ground, one of the few socially autonomous places in a society with an awesome capacity for proliferating social organizations—churches, fraternal orders, beneficial societies, and so on—that brought different classes together.

Unions were the foundation of the movement culture that arose in the major cities of the North during the 1830s. The General Trades' Unions of those years combined cultural with economic functions, supporting labor papers, debating societies, reading rooms, and other cultural resources while standing behind union men seeking better pay and shorter workdays. They were remarkably successful on the economic front, perhaps more so than any other union movement in the century. The vast majority of the general strikes in 1835 either achieved the ten-hour day or ended in compromise settlements, and most of the strikes for wage increases in 1836 won their demand. But radicals were not content with workplace militancy that left competitive capitalism intact. The logic of their economic outlook required institutional reform that restructured the relations of production. The logic of their politics determined how far they would go and what form institutional reform would take. This interaction between the economics and politics of radicalism produced the drive for cooperative production in the second half of 1836. Insofar as cooperation was a voluntarist project without government participation, it satisfied economic radicalism's tenet that labor had just rights to the full product of its toil and the political radical's passion for impartial rule. Political radicalism thus set the limits of economic radicalism.

It is an idle exercise to suppose what might have been had the panic of 1837 not stopped the momentum for cooperation in its tracks and then brought about the collapse of the labor movement itself. We can be certain that the destruction of unions and cooperatives gave the initiative to the politics of radicalism. In the immediate aftermath of the panic, labor advocates fell back on the politics of hard money; they lampooned bankers and speculators in language consistent with the received politics of the Democratic party. By midpoint in the depression labor had leaders without a movement; with few exceptions the leaders had become minor functionaries in the Democratic party.

Recovery from the panic was not free from class conflict. Some workers spent the late 1840s and the 1850s struggling to recover losses suffered during the protracted depression. Their unions, however, were hobbled by periodic economic recessions and by a deluge of immigrants who disrupted labor markets and turned trade after trade into parochial ethnic colonies. The fragility of trade unionism also reflected the diversions of emotionally charged cultural politics. The great revivals of the depression years, followed by stepped-up immigration, brought on eruptions of nativism that reoriented worker politics. American Republican party associations and nativist fraternal societies, patriotic clubs, and temperance groups spread ominously through Protestant neighborhoods, exploiting the American worker's latent fears of "foreign domination." The native-born mechanic felt under siege as citizen and as producer, and responded enthusiastically to nativism's tirades against Catholics. Nativism pushed in two directions simultaneously. It set Protestant worker against immigrant and bridged the class divide within the native-born community by galvanizing a political bloc of journeymen, master craftsmen, and entrepreneurs. Republicans touched an even more sensitive nerve by raising the specter of an expansionist "slave power" in the South, a more immediate threat to republican liberty and economic independence. Even as labor unrest shook Lynn and other urban centers in the North and class tension rose in the South, workers called a class truce to fight on the battlefields of civil war for free labor or white egalitarianism.

The fabric of the received culture frayed badly in the years after the war. Machine-driven production eclipsed the hand labor of the sweating system, all but completing the transformation of artisans into industrial workers. Except for the building trades and pockets of industrial craftsmen in the old crafts and newer industries, the typical wage earner in manufacturing was turned into a semiskilled machine operative without much discretion on the job. The supple artisan culture of the small shop was swept to the industrial periphery and paternalistic management declined or fell apart. No one referred to the employer as a master craftsman any longer; he was an industrialist or "captain of industry." He was a wealthy man who consorted with the elite, lived in a gaudy mansion that copied the European château, and spoke the spiteful language of Social Darwinism, not the common idiom of free labor. The Gilded Age industrialist could not always rely on local lawmakers. But just as economic power shifted to the national corporation so did political power gravitate to state and federal government increasingly responsive to business interests. Small wonder that the Gilded Age witnessed flare-ups of progressively intense class warfare.

Working-class customs were slower to change and working-class language especially seemed stuck in the past. The dissident worker still thought of himself as a "producer," continued to talk of accumulating a "competency," and still referred to capitalism as "wage slavery." While such radical terminology died hard, radicalism strained to adjust to the industrial order. It developed a definition of class more in line with economic realities, with the division of labor and destruction of skill. The labor movement in antebellum America, after all, had been the bailiwick of the white male journeyman partly because of deep-seated prejudice against women and blacks and partly because of pervasive disdain for factory operatives and unskilled laborers. During Reconstruction such labor advocates as William Sylvis argued strongly for the inclusion of women and blacks in the house of labor but were rebuffed by both local and national leaders. Many members of the Knights of Labor were equally chauvinistic. They were pushed aside, however, by an idealistic leadership that took seriously the motto "An injury to one is the concern of all" regardless of race, sex, national origin, or level of skill. The active recruitment of women, blacks, and unskilled whites into the Order scarcely signified the forging of one out of many but did mark a historic breakthrough.

The Knights of Labor also strove to adapt the traditional radical program to industrial society. They took a small step by calling for government inspection of mines and factories, and a larger one by demanding government ownership of the banks and the railways. Nationalizing these businesses promised to narrow the historic gap between radicalism's stated objective of equality and the means to achieve it. Public ownership would have proscribed private accumulation in the very businesses that spawned the richest Americans and limited the distribution of wealth. But innovation ended there; it stopped at the factory gates, for the Knights flinched at public ownership of manufacturing enterprise. Like the Jacksonian radicals, they believed that worker-owned cooperatives privately financed would produce social equality. This privatistic emphasis set them apart from the labor left in the Gilded Age, notably the followers of the Socialist Labor party, who advocated public support for cooperatives through a nationalized banking system. Publicly owned banks would become the servants of the cooperative commonwealth. It was a daring and inventive stroke that infused a traditional radical solution with new relevance, and had the potential of solidifying the alliance of convenience between the radicals and socialists within the Knights of Labor. But it was simply too adventurous for an old political culture with an enduring belief in the wickedness of active government. Radicalism in the Gilded Age was as incapable of envisioning a public means of credit for collective activity as it had been in the Jackson years. The dualism in the radical tradition persisted: political radicalism continued to restrain economic radicalism.

Another tension within radicalism confounded Knighthood. This had to do with balancing direct workplace action with the nostrum of social reconstruction. It was an old problem that had been handled in two ways. The leaders of the General Trades' Unions and of the National Labor Union took a flexible approach that combined trade union work with agitation for social reform. The National Reformers of the 1840s, though former trade unionists sensitive to workplace issues, first paid lip service to unionism and then acted as if it was antithetical to labor reform. For their part, the Knights of Labor followed the former course during the 1870s, then inched toward the latter, and by the mid-1880s wound up taking a stiff anti-union stance in the midst of the Great Upheaval. The factionalism that ensued from the huge increase in membership in 1885–86 threw the Knights into turmoil, but Powderly and the moderate radicals turned an understandably difficult situation into a disaster by digging in their heels and pushing what a critic called the "rule or ruin policy." Their uncompromising positions on strikes, craft unionism, and even amnesty for the Haymarket martyrs led to expulsions and defections to the AF of L, weakening the Order and leaving it easy prey for employers.

Powderly's dispute with Gompers was not grounded only in antipathy to craft unionism. Following Haymarket, Powderly and his faction were set against unionism of any kind. Some local assemblies, to be sure, conducted strikes and declared boycotts well into the 1890s, but for all practical purposes the "new" Knights of the post-Haymarket period abandoned union work. They scrapped unionism and went through the

motions of political reform, first by launching what proved to be a
feckless educational campaign and then by nurturing ties with middle-
class women's groups before seeking a formal alliance with agrarian
rebels.

The American Federation of Labor moved in precisely the opposite
direction. By the early 1880s Gompers and Strasser reflected the
disillusionment with socialist politics felt by a growing and influential
group of union men. They threw themselves into trade unionism and
gradually perfected the conservative syndicalism that would become the
hallmark of the AF of L. When they entered the political arena, they did
so as lobbyists and members of a pressure group plying legislators from
the established parties for ameliorative laws. By the second half of the
decade the cumulative impact of the police actions during and after
Haymarket, the highly publicized trials and executions of the anarchists,
and the collapse of third-partyism strengthened the appeal of pure and
simple unionism. Haymarket momentarily removed the socialist thorn in
Gompers's side by intimidating and scattering the left. Some anarchists
and socialists went into hiding; others retired from political affairs or
dashed for cover into the AF of L. Socialism was at a low ebb as the
1880s drew to a close, only to revive a few years later and make a serious
if ultimately unsuccessful bid for control of the federation. Socialism was
not simply outmaneuvered by a wily band of craft unionists at the 1894
convention of the AF of L. It was also a casualty of the depression and
the victim of its own tendentiousness. The socialist consciousness that
SLP stalwarts believed would return in hard times never materialized.
When it did not, some socialists saw nowhere to turn but to pure and
simple unionism.

If the political orientation of the AF of L was unsettled in the early
1890s, so too was the scope of its unionism. There was still a chance for
something other than narrow craft unionism. Two tendencies vied for
influence, craft unionism centered on entrepreneurial business and a
vaguely defined if more democratic unionism that was craft oriented in
name only and reached beyond small firms. Craft union sentiment was
older, stronger, and rested on a firmer foundation. Its advocates were
either untouched by mechanization or strong enough to exercise some
control over the production process. They were native-born Americans
and "old immigrants" and among the best-paid workmen, the labor
aristocrats of the day. These workmen saw women as a threat to the
"family wage," viewed blacks with contempt, and scorned the hordes of
Eastern European immigrants streaming into mines and factories. The

advocates of more democratic unionism, on the other hand, were socialists and former Knights based in baking, furniture making, urban transportation, and other industries that relied on semiskilled and unskilled labor. They were not friendly to women, blacks, or the maligned "new immigrants" but did support Gompers's "heroism" at the turn of the 1890s. Had it not been for that campaign, it is doubtful that such workers would have found a home in the federation at all.

The "heroism" that had expanded the base of the AF of L was not simply defeated from within. It was also beaten back by the ferocious anti-unionism of government and corporate America. This enmity requires an explanation. If Homestead is any guide, leading businessmen were determined to wrest control of the labor process from highly skilled and tightly organized industrial craftsmen. But as the Pullman strike and other large work stoppages would suggest, employers of semiskilled and unskilled workers were equally implacable anti-unionists. Both groups shared an acute sense of economic self-interest, an abiding belief in the ideology of Social Darwinism, and the insecurity and jealousy of power common to the parvenu. Never before had manufacturers and industrialists accumulated such vast fortunes so quickly, and rarely was there a class so unsure of itself or so quick to call upon government in a crisis. Government, or to be more accurate, presidents, governors, and judges, responded more favorably to capital than labor because the former had more access to the centers of power and the latter lacked a strong political party or enough informal influence to stay the repressive arm of the state. Labor paid dearly for its declining political might. It wound up with a movement committed to prudential unionism, to studied cautiousness at the workplace, and to a political strategy that virtually ceded the political terrain to capital. Politics and unionism were closely related, for without a friendly state, labor was unable to extend the frontiers of unionism.

Looked at differently, the received culture of electoral politics remained consistently co-optive, while the received culture of government was both co-optive and repressive. The same state and federal governments that sometimes approved labor legislation did not flinch from coming down hard against worker activity in the economic sphere. The AF of L was made as much by the peculiarities of American government as it was by the peculiarities of American electoral politics.

What was lost and what was gained in the transition from radicalism to prudential unionism? The latter was not without its achievements. Comparative studies of the standard of living in Europe and the United States in the early twentieth century indicate that wage differentials between the skilled and the unskilled were much greater on this side of the Atlantic. In large part it was the strength of craft unionism that helped preserve the skills that brought these better incomes. The federation was effective at the point of production but only for a fraction of the work force. What the AF of L had in strength, it lost in vision and larger purpose. In spite of its failures, radicalism impressed workers with the belief that they had a right to the fruits of their toil and, by the late nineteenth century, with the notion that all who worked were part of one great class. It also armed workers with a sense of mission, the conviction that theirs was to change the world, not simply improve their station within it. That radicalism did not realize its transcendent vision should not tarnish its principles.

Bibliographic Essay

This bibliographic essay does not pretend to be comprehensive. It lists books and articles as well as government studies, printed collections of primary materials, and works by nineteenth-century labor advocates that I have found especially useful. Students who wish an exhaustive bibliography of works in the field of labor history should consult Maurice F. Neufeld, Daniel J. Leab, and Dorothy Swanson, *American Working Class History: A Representative Bibliography* (New York, 1983), and Swanson's annual compilation of published works and doctoral dissertations in *Labor History*.

GENERAL WORKS

The standard institutional history of American labor is John R. Commons, et al., *History of Labour in the United States*, 4 vols. (New York, 1918–35). Philip S. Foner, *History of the Labor Movement in the United States*, 7 vols. (New York, 1947–87), is also an institutional history but is written from a conventional Marxist perspective and predictably vilifies the pragmatic labor leaders lionized by Commons. Unlike Commons, however, Foner does not slight women workers or black workers. Indeed he is the first labor historian to pay any attention to race and gender relations. The most comprehensive history of black labor is Philip S. Foner, *Organized Labor & the Black Worker, 1619–1973* (New York, 1974). William H. Harris, *The Harder We Run: Black Workers Since the Civil War* (New York, 1982), is a spotty survey with helpful statistical information. Jacqueline Jones, *Labor of Love, Labor of Sorrow: Black Women, Work, and the Family from Slavery to the Present* (New York, 1985), is more of a social history than a labor history but is the only available synthesis of black women. Philip S. Foner, *Women and the American Labor Movement*, 2 vols. (Garden City, N.Y., 1979–80), focuses on organized women workers. Far more expansive is Alice Kessler-Harris, *Out to Work: A History of Wage-Earning Women in the United States* (New York, 1982). No historian of labor in America can do without collections of documents. Several such works are noted in the pages that follow, but the standard one is John R. Commons, et al., *A Documentary History of American Industrial Society*, 10 vols. (Cleveland, 1910–11).

INTRODUCTION

Werner Sombart raised the question of socialism in *Why Is There No Socialism in the United States?* (White Plains, N.Y., 1976, orig. pub. 1906). Selig Perlman, *A Theory of the Labor Movement* (New York, 1928), paralleled Sombart but curiously enough overlooked Sombart's argument that higher living standards also stunted socialism in the United States. There is no dearth of subsequent scholarly work on reasons for the failure of socialism in the United States. Much of this literature, however, deals with the twentieth century. Two helpful works are Seymour Martin Lipset and John H. M. Laslett, eds., *Failure of a Dream? Essays in the History of American Socialism* (Garden City, N.Y., 1974), and John H. M. Laslett, *Reluctant Proletarians: A Short Comparative History of American Socialism* (Westport, Conn., 1964). One of the more arresting interpretations of the uniqueness of politics in the United States during the nineteenth century is Mike Davis, *Prisoners of the American Dream: Politics and Economy in the History of the U.S. Working Class* (London, 1986). For a fine summary of the literature on ''American exceptionalism,'' see Eric Foner, ''Why Is There No Socialism in the United States?'' *History Workshop Journal*, 17 (1984): 57–80. The version of the debate discussed in this chapter is reflected in Sean Wilentz, ''Against Exceptionalism: Class Consciousness and the American Labor Movement''; ''Response'' by Nick Salvatore; and ''Response'' by Michael Hanagan in *International Labor and Working Class History*, 26 (1984): 1–36, and Wilentz, ''Wilentz Answers His Critics,'' *International Labor and Working Class History*, 28 (1985): 46–55. For contrasting views of the politics of nineteenth-century labor leaders, see Norman J. Ware, *The Industrial Worker, 1840–1860: The Reaction of American Industrial Society to the Advance of the Industrial Revolution* (Boston, 1924), and Gerald Grob, *Workers and Utopia: A Study of Ideological Conflict in the American Labor Movement, 1865–1900* (Evanston, 1961), on the one hand, and on the other, David Montgomery, *Beyond Equality: Labor and the Radical Republicans, 1862–1872* (New York, 1967). The first book in the ''new labor history'' is David Brody, *Steelworkers in America: The Nonunion Era* (Cambridge, Mass., 1960). The first major community study in this genre is Alan Dawley, *Class and Community: The Industrial Revolution in Lynn* (Cambridge, Mass., 1976). Other community studies are cited below and especially in Chapter 3. The first and most influential mobility study is Stephan Thernstrom, *Poverty and Progress: Social Mobility in a Nineteenth Century City* (Cambridge, Mass., 1964). For an admiring review of this literature, see Thernstrom and Peter Knights, ''Men in Motion: Some Data Speculations about Population Mobility in Nineteenth-Century America,'' *Journal of Interdisciplinary History*, 1 (1970): 7–35. For a skeptical interpretation, see Charles Stephenson, ''A Gathering of Strangers? Mobility, Social Structure, and Political Participation in the Formation of the American Working Class,'' in Milton Cantor, ed., *American Workingclass Culture: Essays in Labor and Social History* (Westport, Conn., 1979): 31–60, and by the same author, '' 'There's Plenty Waitin' at the Gates': Mobility, Opportunity, and the American Worker,'' in Stephenson and Robert Asher, eds., *Life and Labor: Dimensions of American Working-Class History* (Albany, 1986): 72–91. Herbert G. Gutman's early essays and seminal essay ''Work, Culture and Society in Industrializing America, 1815–1919,'' are collected in Gutman, *Work, Culture, and Society in Industrializing America: Essays in American Working-Class and Social*

History (New York, 1976). For critical views of the new labor history, see David Brody, "The Old Labor History and the New: In Search of an American Working Class," *Labor History*, 20 (1979): 111–26, and Michael Kazin, "Struggling with the Class Struggle: Marxism and the Search for a Synthesis of U.S. Labor History," *Labor History*, 28 (1987): 497–514. For a more sympathetic treatment, see David Montgomery, "To Study the People: The American Working Class," *Labor History*, 21 (1980): 485–512.

1. HOUSEHOLD TO FACTORY

Few historians accept the image of the completely self-sufficient yeoman farmer first depicted in Percy Wells Bidwell and John I. Falconer, *History of Agriculture in the Northern United States, 1620–1860* (Washington, D.C., 1925). Contemporary scholars instead fall into two schools of thought. One of these, which closely follows Bidwell and Falconer, argues that the typical farmer in Colonial and early-nineteenth-century America was embedded in a kind of "moral economy" and motivated by the modest objectives of living a decent life and securing land for his children. For vivid portraits of such farmers, see James Henretta, "Families and Farms: *Mentalité* in Pre-Industrial America," *William and Mary Quarterly*, 3rd Ser., 35 (1978): 3–32, and Michael Merrill, "Cash Is Good to Eat: Self-Sufficiency and Exchange in the Rural Economy of the United States," *Radical History Review*, 4 (1977): 42–71. Steven Hahn, *The Roots of Southern Populism: Yeomen Farmers and the Transformation of the Georgia Upcountry, 1850–1890* (New York, 1983), offers the clearest view of this "security first" strategy in the South by showing that yeomen were reluctant to engage in market exchange and when they did raise cash crops, their aim was to secure independence. This literature is in part a reaction to Richard Hofstadter, "The Myth of the Happy Farmer," *American Heritage*, 7 (April 1956): 43–53, which depicted the farmer as entrepreneur; it still has its advocates. Two recent studies in the Hofstadter tradition are Charles S. Grant, *Democracy in the Connecticut Frontier Town of Kent* (New York, 1961), and James T. Lemon, *The Best Poor Man's Country: A Geographical Study of Early Southeastern Pennsylvania* (Baltimore, 1972). On the other hand, Charles Danhof, *Change in Agriculture: The Northern States, 1820–1870* (Cambridge, Mass., 1969), implies, and I believe, that we need not choose between the subsistence farmer and the entrepreneurial yeoman if we imagine farmers on a continuum of market orientations. Danhof also offers a rich description of work routines on the farm. John Mack Faragher, *Sugar Creek: Life on the Illinois Prairie* (New Haven, 1986), and Joan Jensen, *Loosening the Bonds: Mid-Atlantic Farm Women, 1750–1850* (New Haven, 1986), stress the sexual division of labor on the farm. The classic study of the "household factory" is Rolla Tryon, *Household Manufactures in the United States, 1640–1860* (Chicago, 1917). Thomas Dublin, "Women and Outwork in a Nineteenth-Century New England Town: Fitzwilliam, New Hampshire, 1830–1880," in Steven Hahn and Jonathan Prude, eds., *The*

224 BIBLIOGRAPHIC ESSAY

Countryside in the Age of Capitalist Transformation (Chapel Hill, 1985): 51–69, examines the rise and decline of the domestic system. George R. Taylor, *The Transportation Revolution, 1815–1860* (New York, 1951), remains the most thorough treatment of transportation improvements and the general erosion of self-sufficiency. A more specialized but important study of the development of the market economy is Christopher Clark, "Household Economy, Market Exchange, and the Rise of Capitalism in the Connecticut Valley, 1800–1860," *Journal of Social History,* 13 (1979): 169–89. Helpful studies of rural-urban migration include John Modell, "The Peopling of a Working-Class Ward: Reading, Pennsylvania, 1850," *Journal of Social History,* 5 (1971): 71–95, and Peter Knights, *The Plain People of Boston, 1830–1860: A Study in City Growth* (New York, 1971). For figures on immigration, I relied on Leonard Dinnerstein and David M. Reimers, *Ethnic Americans: A History of Immigration and Assimilation* (New York, 1975); U.S. Bureau of the Census, *The Seventh Census of the United States, 1850* (Washington, D.C., 1853); and by the same bureau, *Population of the United States in 1860* (Washington, D.C., 1864). Caroline Ware, *The Early New England Cotton Manufacture* (Boston, 1931), is the standard work on the first textile mills and the recruitment of their work force. Thomas Dublin, *Women at Work: The Transformation of Work and Community in Lowell, Massachusetts, 1826–1860* (New York, 1979), stresses the middling origins of the early mill women and their desire to achieve independence. Jonathan Prude, *The Coming of Industrial Order: Town and Factory Life in Rural Massachusetts, 1800–1860* (New York, 1983), a study of the "Rhode Island system," uncovers worker resistance to early industrialism without unions. Barbara M. Tucker, *Samuel Slater and the Origins of the American Textile Industry, 1790–1860* (Ithaca, N.Y., 1984), traces the rise and fall of paternalism. Anthony F. C. Wallace, *Rockdale: The Growth of an American Village in the Early Industrial Revolution* (New York, 1978), attributes the adaptation of millhands in southeastern Pennsylvania to evangelical religion. The voice of the early millhand has been preserved in Philip S. Foner, ed., *The Factory Girls* (Urbana, 1977), and Benita A. Eisler, ed., *The Lowell Offering: Writings by New England Mill Women, 1840–1845* (Philadelphia, 1977), both of which reprint material from the labor press. These editions should be supplemented by Thomas Dublin, ed., *Farm to Factory: Women's Letters, 1830–1860* (New York, 1981), a splendid collection of heretofore unpublished letters by Lowell women to family and friends. For Southern textiles, I have used Ernest McPherson Lander, Jr., *The Textile Industry in Antebellum South Carolina* (Baton Rouge, 1969); Bess Beaty, "Lowells of the South: Northern Influences on the Nineteenth Century North Carolina Textile Industry," *Journal of Southern History,* 53 (1987): 37–62; and David C. Ward, "Industrial Workers in the Mid-19th Century South: Family and Labor in the Graniteville (SC) Textile Mill, 1845–1880," *Labor History,* 28 (1978): 328–48. David A. Hounshell, *From the American System to Mass Production, 1800–1932: The Development of Manufacturing Technology in the*

United States (Baltimore, 1983), is an informative narrative history of technological change in woodworking and machine building. Brooke Hindle and Steven Lubar, *Engines of Change: The American Industrial Revolution, 1790–1860* (Washington, D.C., 1986), is one of the few histories of technology that discuss hand tools as well as machines. Peter Temin, *Iron and Steel in Nineteenth-Century America: An Economic Inquiry* (Cambridge, Mass., 1964), is a sound introduction to the subject that slights the role of labor. Merritt Roe Smith, *Harpers Ferry Arsenal and the New Technology: The Challenge of Change* (Ithaca, N.Y., 1977), is a fine analysis of worker resistance to new technology. The standard study of industrial slavery is Robert S. Starobin, *Industrial Slavery in the Old South* (New York, 1970), and the basic work on slave labor in tobacco manufacturing is Joseph Clarke Robert, *The Tobacco Kingdom: Plantation, Market, and Factory in Virginia and North Carolina, 1800–1860* (Gloucester, Mass., 1965, orig. pub. 1938). More sophisticated accounts that emphasize the skilled slave's struggle for autonomy include Ronald L. Lewis, *Coal, Iron, and Slaves: Industrial Slavery in Maryland and Virginia, 1715–1865* (Westport, Conn., 1979), and Charles B. Dew, "Disciplining Slave Iron Workers in the Antebellum South," *American Historical Review,* 79 (1974): 393–416. The laboring traditions of early artisans are described in Carl Bridenbaugh, *The Colonial Craftsman* (New York, 1950). A good if positivistic account of the erosion of the artisan system can be found in John R. Commons, "American Shoemakers, 1648–1895: A Sketch of Industrial Evolution," *Quarterly Journal of Economics,* 24 (November 1910): 23–84. David Montgomery, "The Working Classes of the Pre-Industrial American City, 1790–1830," *Labor History,* 9 (1968): 3–22, is richer and more convincing. The most thorough history of apprenticeship is W. J. Rorabaugh, *The Craft Apprentice: From Franklin to the Machine Age in America* (New York, 1986). The footnotes in this intelligent study are studded with references to autobiographies and other first-person accounts of masters and journeymen. Sean Wilentz, *Chants Democratic: New York City and the Rise of the Working Class, 1788–1850* (New York, 1984), and Christine Stansell, *City of Women: Sex and Class in New York, 1789–1860* (New York, 1986), provide the best modern accounts of the sweating system. Alan Dawley, *Class and Community,* provides a first-rate analysis of the mechanization of shoemaking. I have also drawn on Edwin T. Freedley, *Leading Pursuits and Leading Men* (Philadelphia, 1854), and by the same author, *Philadelphia and Its Manufactures* (Philadelphia, 1858), for descriptions of the labor process in the handicrafts.

2. Free Labor and Radical Labor

Mechanics' institutes are only beginning to find their historians. Gary John Kornblith, "From Artisans to Businessmen: Master Mechanics in New England, 1789–1850," 2 vols. (Ph.D. diss., 1983), is a superior study of such groups and their leaders. Howard B. Rock, *Artisans of the New Republic: The Tradesmen of*

New York City in the Age of Jefferson (New York, 1979), and Charles G. Steffen, *The Mechanics of Baltimore: Workers and Politics in the Age of Revolution, 1763–1812* (Urbana, 1984), are also helpful, as are the autobiographies and reminiscences of socially mobile mechanics. I especially recommend Henry Brokmeyer, *A Mechanic's Diary* (Washington, D.C., 1910), as well as John B. Gough, *Autobiography and Personal Recollections* . . . (Springfield, Mass., 1871), and by the same author, *Sunlight and Shadow; or, Gleanings from My Work* . . . (Hartford, 1884). The debate over republicanism in the historical literature is summarized in Robert Shalhope, "Republicanism in Early America," *William and Mary Quarterly*, 38 (1982): 334–56. The *American Quarterly*, 37 (1985), is devoted entirely to this debate. The magisterial study of classic republicanism is J. G. A. Pocock, *The Machiavellian Moment: Florentine Republican Thought and the Atlantic Republican Tradition* (Princeton, 1975). Joyce Appleby, *Capitalism and a New Social Order: The Republican Vision of the 1790s* (New York, 1984), argues that republicanism adapted to the emerging market economy, as does Drew R. McCoy, *The Elusive Republic: Political Economy in Jeffersonian America* (Chapel Hill, 1980). John P. Diggins, *The Lost Soul of American Politics: Virtue, Self-Interest, and the Foundations of Liberalism* (New York, 1984), is more impressed by the enduring influence of Lockean self-interest. My understanding of Jacksonian politics closely follows Richard P. McCormick, *The Second American Party System: Party Formation in the Jacksonian Era* (Chapel Hill, 1966). More narrowly focused but quite useful are Michael Wallace, "Changing Concepts of Party in the United States: New York, 1815–1828," *American Historical Review*, 74 (1968): 453–91, and Ronald P. Formisano, *The Transformation of Political Culture: Massachusetts Political Parties, 1790s–1840s* (New York, 1983). Marvin Meyers, *The Jacksonian Persuasion: Politics and Belief* (Stanford, 1957), wears rather well, and Jean H. Baker, *The Affairs of Party: The Political Culture of Northern Democrats in the Mid-Nineteenth Century* (Ithaca, N.Y., 1983) is a marvelous fusion of political, intellectual, and cultural history that includes a particularly compelling analysis of popular racism. For the Whigs I have relied mostly on Lee Benson, *The Concept of Jacksonian Democracy: New York as a Test Case* (Princeton, 1961), and Daniel Walker Howe, *The Political Culture of the American Whigs* (Chicago, 1979). Douglas T. Miller, *Jacksonian Aristocracy: Class and Democracy in New York, 1830–1860* (New York, 1967), is a workmanlike treatment of the antebellum upper class. Far more satisfying is Edward Pessen, *Riches, Class, and Power Before the Civil War* (Lexington, Mass., 1973). Ronald Story, *The Forging of an Aristocracy: Harvard & the Boston Upper Class, 1800–1870* (Middletown, Conn., 1980), is a model study of the making of an elite. William G. McLoughlin, Jr., *Modern Revivalism: Charles Grandison Finney to Billy Graham* (New York, 1959), is a good introduction to the subject from a biographical perspective. Whitney R. Cross, *The Burned-Over District: The Social and Intellectual History of Enthusiastic Religion in Western New York,*

1800–1850 (Ithaca, N.Y., 1950), cannot be ignored. More recent work on the Second Great Awakening underlines its class and gender aspects. Paul E. Johnson, *A Shopkeeper's Millennium: Society and Revivals in Rochester, 1815–1837* (New York, 1978), argues that the middle class was the chief audience of evangelicalism. Nancy A. Hewitt, *Women's Activism and Social Change: Rochester, New York, 1822–1872* (Ithaca, N.Y., 1984), is an exceptional study of class, gender, and holiness religion. Mary P. Ryan, *Cradle of the Middle Class: The Family in Oneida County, New York, 1790–1865* (New York, 1981), sees evangelicalism as a force both for social reform and domesticity for middle-class women. Donald G. Mathews, *Slavery and Methodism: A Chapter in American Morality, 1780–1845* (Princeton, 1965), is useful. The outstanding analysis of planter paternalism and hegemony is Eugene D. Genovese, *The Political Economy of Slavery: Studies in the Economy and Society of the Slave South* (New York, 1966), and *Roll, Jordan, Roll: The World the Slaves Made* (New York, 1974). Fred Siegel, "The Paternalist Thesis: Virginia as a Test Case," *Civil War History*, 25 (1979): 246–61, shows why paternalism is inadequate to account for the politics in a single state, and James Oakes, *The Ruling Race: A History of American Slaveholders* (New York, 1982), persuasively demonstrates that after 1830 Southern planters were self-made men of an entrepreneurial cast of mind. William L. Barney, *The Road to Secession: A New Perspective on the Old South* (New York, 1972), draws attention to class tensions and discusses Southern free laborism. Philip Scranton, *Proprietary Capitalism: The Textile Manufacture at Philadelphia, 1800–1885* (New York, 1983), exposes the aspirations of the small master craftsman. Several studies investigate the careers of such employers. Two of the better ones are Stuart Blumin, "Mobility and Change in Ante-Bellum Philadelphia," in Stephan Thernstrom and Richard Sennett, eds., *Nineteenth-Century Cities: Essays in the New Urban History* (New Haven, 1969): 165–208, and Clyde and Sally Griffen, *Natives and Newcomers: The Ordering of Opportunity in Mid-19th Century Poughkeepsie* (Cambridge, Mass., 1978). The figures on wages come largely from Stanley Lebergott, *Manpower in Economic Growth* (New York, 1964). Ira Berlin, *Slaves Without Masters: The Free Negro in the Antebellum South* (New York, 1974), is simply outstanding. Berlin and Herbert G. Gutman, "Natives and Immigrants, Free Men and Slaves: Urban Workingmen in the Antebellum South," *American Historical Review*, 88 (1983): 1175–1200, presents startling demographic data, but in my view overstates the antislavery sentiments of the Southern workers. Frederick Douglass, *Life and Times of Frederick Douglass* (New York, 1968, orig. pub. 1898), vividly reports encounters with hostile white workers on the Baltimore waterfront. Similar incidents are described in Earl F. Niehaus, *The Irish in New Orleans, 1800–1865* (Baton Rouge, 1965), and Leonard P. Curry, *The Free Black in Urban America, 1800–1850: The Shadow of the Dream* (Chicago, 1981). The best quantitative study of the free black man's loss of status is Theodore Hershberg, "Free Blacks in Antebellum Philadelphia: A Study of

Ex-Slaves, Freeborn, and Socioeconomic Decline," *Journal of Social History*, 5 (1971–72): 183–209. The development of working-class radicalism is skillfully handled in Eric Foner, *Tom Paine and Revolutionary America* (New York, 1976). The leading radical thinkers are discussed in David Harris, *Socialist Origins in the United States: American Forerunners of Marx, 1817–1832* (Assen, Neth., 1968), and Paul K. Conkin, *Prophets of Prosperity: America's First Political Economists* (Bloomington, 1980). Arthur Bestor, *Backwoods Utopias: The Sectarian Origins and the Owenite Phase of Communitarian Socialism in America, 1663–1829* (Philadelphia, 1950), examines the transatlantic passage of Owenism and its practice. The best study of radicalism and gender is Mary Blewett, "Work, Gender, and the Artisan Tradition in New England Shoemaking, 1780–1860," *Journal of Social History*, 18 (1984): 221–48. There is still no substitute for the writings of the early radicals themselves, many of which are accessible. I highly recommend Langton Byllesby, *Observations on the Sources and Effects of Unequal Wealth* . . . (New York, 1826), and Thomas Skidmore, *The Rights of Man to Property!* (New York, 1829), as well as [William Heighton], "An Address to the Members of Trade Societies, and to the Working Classes Generally . . . by a Fellow Laborer" (Philadelphia, 1827); "An Address Delivered Before the Mechanics and Working Classes Generally, of the City of Philadelphia . . . by the 'Unlettered Mechanic' " (Philadelphia, 1827); and "The Principles of Aristocratic Legislation, Developed in an Address . . . by an Operative Citizen" (Philadelphia, 1828). What we know of Heighton's background comes from Louis H. Arky, "The Mechanics' Union of Trade Associations and the Formation of the Philadelphia Working Men's Movement," *Pennsylvania Magazine of History and Biography*, 76 (1952): 142–76. For sketches of other prominent labor advocates in this era, see Walter Hugins, "Ely Moore: The Case History of a Jacksonian Labor Leader," *Political Science Quarterly*, 55 (1950): 105–25; Edward Pessen, "Thomas Skidmore, Agrarian Reformer in the Early American Labor Movement," *New York History*, 25 (1954): 280–94; and Lewis Hartz, "Seth Luther: The Story of a Working Class Rebel," *New England Quarterly*, 13 (1940): 401–18.

3. MOVEMENT CULTURE AND RECEIVED CULTURE

The concepts "movement culture" and "received culture" are discussed more fully in Lawrence Goodwyn, *Democratic Promise: The Populist Moment in America* (New York, 1976). The historical literature of the first labor parties is voluminous. The best overview is Edward Pessen, *Most Uncommon Jacksonians: The Radical Leaders of the Early Labor Movement* (Albany, 1967). For more specialized studies, see Walter Hugins, *Jacksonian Democracy and the Working Class* (Stanford, 1960); William A. Sullivan, "Did Labor Support Andrew Jackson," *Political Science Quarterly*, 62 (1947): 569–80, and by the same author, "Philadelphia Labor During the Jackson Era," *Pennsylvania History*, 15 (1948): 1–16; Edward Pessen, "Did Labor Support Andrew Jackson? The Boston

Story," *Political Science Quarterly*, 64 (1949): 262–74; Arthur B. Darling, "The Working Men's Party in Massachusetts, 1833–1834," *American Historical Review*, 29 (1923): 81–87; and Milton Nadworny, "New Jersey Working Men and the Jacksonians," *Proceedings of the New Jersey Historical Society*, 67 (1949): 185–98.

Two recent works that cast popular politics in a larger political and cultural framework are Amy Bridges, *A City in the Republic: Antebellum New York and the Origins of Machine Politics* (New York, 1984), and Paul Goodman, *Towards a Christian Republic: Antimasonry and the Great Transition in New England, 1826–1836* (New York, 1988). Several community studies follow workers from labor movements of the 1830s through the disorganization of the 1840s and 1850s. Susan E. Hirsch, *Roots of the American Working Class: The Industrialization of the Crafts in Newark, 1800–1860* (Philadelphia, 1978), stresses the development of status distinctions based on skill and income. Paul G. Faler, *Mechanics and Manufacturers in the Early Industrial Revolution: Lynn, Massachusetts, 1786–1860* (Albany, 1981), underlines the "industrial morality" of the middle class and the radicalism of the working class. Steven J. Ross, *Workers on the Edge: Work, Leisure, and Politics in Industrializing Cincinnati, 1788–1890* (New York, 1985), is one of the more detailed accounts of the selective decomposition of the handicrafts. Ross also deals with worker efforts to overcome the ethnic and cultural divisiveness of the 1840s. Ethnic contentiousness within the context of class conflict is also the theme of David Montgomery, "The Shuttle and the Cross: Weavers and Artisans in the Kensington Riots of 1844," *Journal of Social History*, 5 (1972): 411–47. For a detailed history of the riots, see Michael Feldberg, *The Philadelphia Riots of 1844: A Study of Ethnic Conflict* (Westport, Conn., 1975). My *Working People of Philadelphia, 1800–1850* (Philadelphia, 1980), discusses the transition from the secular radicalism of the 1830s to the evangelical radicalism of the 1840s and 1850s. Jama Lazerow, "Religion and Labor Reform in Antebellum America: The World of William Field Young," *American Quarterly*, 38 (1986): 265–86, is easily the most subtle analysis of working-class Protestantism in the late antebellum period. John Allen Krout, *Origins of Prohibition* (New York, 1925), has withstood the test of time. W. J. Rorabaugh, *The Alcoholic Republic: An American Tradition* (New York, 1979), is a lively general study of drink and its opponents, and Jed Dannenbaum, *Drink and Disorder: Temperance Reform in Cincinnati from the Washingtonian Revival to the W.C.T.U.* (Urbana, 1984), is a sound social history of the topic. My own analysis of temperance and prohibition draws heavily on Ian Tyrrell, *Sobering Up: From Temperance to Prohibition in Antebellum America* (Westport, Conn., 1979). Oscar Handlin, *Boston's Immigrants: A Study in Acculturation* (rev. ed., Cambridge, Mass., 1968), associates the Old World experience with poverty alone and seems to foreshorten the assimilation process. Oliver Macdonagh, "The Irish Famine Emigration to the United States," *Perspectives in American History*, 10 (1976): 357–488, recognizes the fatalism of this beleaguered generation but argues that it coexisted with the peasant tradition of "white boyism" that encouraged group solidarity and collective action to redress economic grievances in industrializing America. Kerby A. Miller, *Emigrants and Exiles: Ireland and the Irish Exodus to North America* (New York, 1985), an exhaustive transatlantic history, argues that Irish immigrants thought of themselves as "exiles" and harbored a profound sense of nationalism that shaped their institutional life and politics in America. The study of German immigrants had a promising beginning with Carl Wittke, *The Utopian Communist: A Biography of Wilhelm Weitling, Nineteenth-Century Reformer* (Baton Rouge, 1950), and by the same author, *The German Forty-eighters: Refugees of Revolution in America* (Philadelphia, 1952), but scholarly interest quickly fell off. It has revived in the last decade or so. Kathleen Neils Conzen, *Immigrant Milwaukee, 1836–1860: Acculturation and Community in a Frontier City* (Cambridge, Mass., 1976), is a readable social history but is weak on politics. Hartmut Keil and John B. Jentz, eds., *German Workers in Industrial Chicago, 1850–1910: A Comparative Perspective* (De Kalb, Ill., 1983), contains essays on occupational profiles, neighborhood life, generational conflicts, and political activity. Bruce Carlan Levine's essay "Free Soil, Free Labor, and *Freimänner*: German Chicago in the Civil War Era," 163–82, reveals the strength of antislavery sentiment among German radicals. Clifton K. Yearley, Jr., *Britons in American Labor: A History of the Influence of United Kingdom Immigrants on American Labor, 1820–1914* (Baltimore, 1957), and Ray Boston, *British Chartists in America* (Manchester, U.K., 1971), provide biographical sketches of the leading British-born trade unionists in America. Charlotte Erickson, ed., *Invisible Immigrants: The Adaptation of English and Scottish Immigrants in Nineteenth-Century America* (Coral Gables, 1972), reveals the perceptions and aspirations of ordinary farmers and workers. Not a few of these immigrants seem to have been taken by land reform in the 1840s. Land reform itself has no modern historian. The basic works are Helene S. Zahler, *Eastern Workingmen and National Land Policy, 1829–1862* (New York, 1941), and Norman J. Ware, *The Industrial Worker, 1840–1860* (Boston, 1924), though the latter also deals with mechanization, living standards, and the ten-hour movement. Two conventional histories of nativism are Ray Allen Billington, *The Protestant Crusade, 1800–1860: A Study of the Origins of American Nativism* (New York, 1938), and John Higham, *Strangers in the Land: Patterns of American Nativism, 1860–1925* (New Brunswick, N.J., 1955). More recent work either roots nativism in the rough-and-tumble street culture of antebellum America or emphasizes its radical strain and consonance with Republicanism. A fine example of the first is Elliott J. Gorn, " 'Good-Bye, Boys, I Die a True American': Homicide, Nativism, and Working-Class Culture in Antebellum New York City," *Journal of American History*, 74 (1987): 388–410. For examples of the second, see David Brion Davis, "Some Themes of Countersubversion: An Analysis of Anti-Masonic, Anti-Catholic, and Anti-Mormon Literature," *Mississippi Valley Historical Review*, 47 (1960): 205–24, and William E. Gienapp, "Nativism and the

Creation of a Republican Majority in the North Before the Civil War," *Journal of American History,* 72 (1985): 529–59. Two excellent studies of the emergence of the Republican party are Ronald P. Formisano, *The Birth of Mass Political Parties: Michigan, 1827–1861* (Princeton, 1971), and Michael F. Holt, *Forging of a Majority: The Formation of the Republican Party in Pittsburgh, 1848–1860* (New Haven, 1969). W. Darrell Overdyke, *The Know Nothing Party in the South* (Baton Rouge, 1950), is the only book-length study of its kind. While Overdyke ignores the class character of nativism, a number of Southern historians have recently found evidence of popular opposition to slavery that stopped short of abolitionism. Ronald T. Takaki, *A Pro-Slavery Crusade: The Agitation to Reopen the African Slave Trade* (New York, 1971), contains glimpses of worker and yeoman opposition to resuming the transatlantic slave trade. Michael P. Johnson, *Toward a Patriarchcal Republic: The Secession Crisis in Georgia* (Baton Rouge, 1977), also analyzes internal strife over class and slavery. Fred Siegel, "Artisans and Immigrants in the Politics of Late Antebellum Georgia," *Civil War History,* 27 (1981): 221–31, demonstrates that suspicions of free white labor were so strongly felt that some planters and manufacturers attempted to strip white workers of their right to vote. Michael P. Johnson and James L. Roark, eds., *"No Chariot Let Down": Charleston's Free People of Color* (Chapel Hill, 1984), is an artfully edited collection of the letters of a free black family that not only reveals the interior life of freedmen but also shows how small employers used appeals to class and race to solidify the loyalty of white workers in the midst of the secession crisis.

4. Coming Apart

The mechanization of production and the rise of the national corporation are the themes of such basic overviews of Gilded Age industrialism as Edward C. Kirkland, *Industry Comes of Age: Business, Labor, and Public Policy, 1860–1897* (New York, 1961), and Thomas C. Cochran and William Miller, *The Age of Enterprise: A Social History of Industrial America* (rev. ed., New York, 1961). I believe that David M. Gordon, Richard Edwards, and Michael Reich, *Segmented Work, Divided Workers: The Historical Transformation of Labor in the United States* (New York, 1982), overlooks the division of labor that took place under the sweating system, but I tend to agree with its interpretation of the causes of mechanization. Alfred D. Chandler, *The Visible Hand: The Managerial Revolution in American Business* (Cambridge, Mass., 1977), argues that the integrated corporation was designed to capture control of product markets—that is, to substitute the "visible hand" of business for the "invisible hand" of the market. A useful guide to machinery and its proliferation is Siegfried Giedion, *Mechanization Takes Command: A Contribution to Anonymous History* (London, 1948). The most influential analysis of the social relations of production in this period is David Montgomery, "Workers' Control of Machine Production in the Nineteenth Century," *Labor History,* 17 (1976): 486–509. Dan Clawson,

Bureaucracy and the Labor Process: The Transformation of U.S. Industry, 1860–1920 (New York, 1980), is an informative study of inside contracting. For a different understanding of this system, see Ernest J. Englander, "The Inside Contract System of Production and Organization: A Neglected Aspect of the History of the Firm," *Labor History,* 28 (1987): 429–46. Philip Scranton, "Varieties of Paternalism: Industrial Structures and the Social Relations of Production in American Textiles," *American Quarterly,* 36 (1984): 235–57, is an absorbing inquiry. Daniel Nelson, *Managers and Workers: Origins of the New Factory System in the United States, 1880–1920* (Madison, 1975), covers everything from plant design to welfare work and is especially revealing on the development of the "foreman's empire." Herbert G. Gutman, "The Reality of the Rags-to-Riches 'Myth': The Case of Paterson, New Jersey, Locomotive, Iron, and Machinery Manufacturers, 1830–1880," in Thernstrom and Sennett, *Nineteenth-Century Cities,* 98–124, is one of the better treatments of local, self-made manufacturers. For a view of the social origins of national elites, see Frances W. Gregory and Irene D. Neu, "The American Industrial Elite in the 1870s: Their Social Origins," and William Miller, "The Business Elite in Business Bureaucracies: Careers of the Top Executives in the Early Twentieth Century," in Miller, ed., *Men in Business: Essays on the Historical Role of the Entrepreneur* (rev. ed., New York, 1962), 193–211 and 286–308. An excellent but ignored study of urbanization is Adna Ferrin Weber, *The Growth of Cities in the Nineteenth Century: A Study in Statistics* (Ithaca, N.Y., 1963, orig. pub. 1899). I have also used U.S. Census Office, *Census of Population,* vol. 1 (Washington, D.C., 1883). On the occupational improvement of the sons of immigrants, see Bruce Laurie, Theodore Hershberg, and George Alter, "Immigrants and Industry: The Philadelphia Experience, 1850–1880,"*Journal of Social History,* 9 (1975): 219–48. Daniel J. Walkowitz, *Worker City, Company Town: Iron and Cotton-Worker Protest in Troy and Cohoes, New York, 1855–1884* (Urbana, 1978), shows that chronic labor shortages made it possible for some first-generation Irish immigrants to move into skilled positions. The most provocative study of Irish working women is Hasia R. Diner, *Erin's Daughters in America: Irish Immigrant Women in the Nineteenth Century* (Baltimore, 1983). The varied occupational configurations of Germans in different cities are disclosed by Hartmut Keil, "Chicago's German Working Class in 1900," and Nora Faires, "Occupational Patterns of German-Americans in Nineteenth-Century Cities," in Keil and Jentz, *German Workers,* 19-51. C. Vann Woodward, *Origins of the New South, 1877–1913* (Baton Rouge, 1951), has been superseded by a number of studies that stress the continued economic backwardness of the South. Roger L. Ransom and Richard Sutch, *One Kind of Freedom: The Economic Consequences of Emancipation* (New York, 1977), attributes industrial underdevelopment largely to rural poverty. Gavin Wright, *Old South, New South: Revolutions in the Southern Economy Since the Civil War* (New York, 1986), doubts that debt peonage was as pervasive as we have been led to believe and refutes the argument that economic development in the South was slow following the Civil War. Eric Foner, *Nothing But Freedom: Emancipation and Its Legacy* (Baton Rouge, 1983), marks the first effort to analyze the aftermath of emancipation in a comparative framework, and by the same author, *Reconstruction: America's Unfinished Revolution, 1863–1877* (New York, 1988), is the best synthesis of the period. Freedmen and women speak for themselves in Ira Berlin, et al., eds., *Freedom: A Documentary History of Emancipation, 1861–1867*, Ser. I and II (New York, 1982–85). Nor should one overlook U.S. Senate, *Report of the Committee upon the Relations Between Labor and Capital*, 5 vols. (Washington, D.C., 1882–87); vol. 4 contains interviews with a number of black workers and preachers. Paul B. Worthman, "Working-Class Mobility in Birmingham, Alabama, 1880–1914," in Tamara Hareven, *The Anonymous Americans: Explorations in Nineteenth Century Social History* (Englewood Cliffs, N.J., 1974), 172–213, is excellent. Lee Soltow, *Men and Wealth in the United States, 1850–1870* (New Haven, 1975), is a trying read. I recalculated the figures on wealth gathered by Horace Wadlin, "The Distribution of Wealth—Probates," *Twenty-fifth Annual Report of the Massachusetts Bureau of the Statistics of Labor* (Boston, 1895), 51–302. Nell Irvin Painter, *Standing at Armageddon: The United States, 1877–1919* (New York, 1987), has helpful information on the standard of living of the different social classes. A rich original source on working-class living standards is "The Condition of Workingmen's Families," *Massachusetts Bureau of the Statistics of Labor Sixth Annual Report* (Boston, 1875), 191–450. This pioneering investigation was later duplicated by nearly every state bureau of labor statistics in the 1880s and 1890s. For an outstanding study of unemployment, see Alexander Keyssar, *Out of Work: The First Century of Unemployment in Massachusetts* (New York, 1986). The basic works on Gilded Age industrialism cited above discuss the various collusive tactics of businessmen. Naomi R. Lamoreaux, *The Merger Movement in American Business, 1895–1904* (New York, 1985), takes a fresh look at their methods. For all their moralizing, the standard works on the Gilded Age industrialists still have a lot to offer the discriminating reader. I relied on Charles F. Adams, Jr., and Henry Adams, *Chapters of Erie* . . . (New York, 1967, orig. pub. 1871); Gustavus Myers, *History of Great American Fortunes* (New York, 1936, orig. pub. 1907); and Matthew Josephson, *The Robber Barons: The Great American Capitalists, 1861–1901* (New York, 1934). Useful modern studies include Frederic Cople Jaher, "Nineteenth-Century Elites in Boston and New York," *Journal of Social History*, 6 (1972): 32–77, and John Ingham, *The Iron Barons: A Social Analysis of an American Urban Elite, 1874–1965* (Westport, Conn., 1978). For the high life in the Gilded Age, I used Maury Klein, *The Life and Legend of Jay Gould* (Baltimore, 1986), as well as John Burchard and Albert Bush-Brown, *The Architecture of America: A Social and Cultural History* (Boston, 1966). Lally Weymouth, ed., *America in 1876: The Way We Were* (New York, 1976), is a fine popular history with revealing graphics as well as spicy excerpts from the social columns of the mainstream press. The ideology of industrialists has lost its appeal to historians. A notable exception is Robert C. Bannister, *Social Darwinism: Science and Myth in Anglo-American Social Thought* (Philadelphia, 1979). I still prefer Richard Hofstadter, *Social Darwinism in American Thought* (rev. ed., New York, 1955), and Edward C. Kirkland, *Dream and Thought in the Business Community, 1860–1900* (Ithaca, N.Y., 1956). The "Gutman Thesis" is stated in Herbert G. Gutman, "The Workers' Search for Power," in H. Wayne Morgan, *The Gilded Age* (rev. and enlgd. ed., Syracuse, 1970). See also Gutman, "Protestantism and the American Labor Movement: The Christian Spirit in the Gilded Age"; "Class, Status, and Community Power in Nineteenth-Century American Industrial Cities: Paterson, New Jersey: A Case Study"; and "Trouble on the Railroads: Prelude to the Crisis of 1877?" in Gutman, *Work, Culture, and Society*, 79–117, 234–59, and 295–320. While Gutman emphasizes community solidarities and the clash between preindustrial values of working people and the exigencies of the industrial system, David Montgomery, *The Fall of the House of Labor: The Workplace, the State, and American Labor Activism, 1865–1925* (New York, 1988), focuses on the shop floor and on the activities of workers with a growing store of industrial experience. Morton Keller, *Affairs of State: Public Life in Late Nineteenth Century America* (Cambridge, Mass., 1977), argues that the energetic government promoted by the Civil War eventually gave way to the traditional values of localism and individualism. Steven Skowronek, *Building the New American State: The Expansion of National Administrative Capacities, 1877–1920* (New York, 1982), offers a convincing explanation for the relative impotence of the national government before the Civil War and of the role of the courts and political parties in the context of limited government. By narrowing his analysis to three case studies in the Gilded Age, however, Skowronek misses a great deal of government activity. I continue to think highly of Sidney Fine, *Laissez Faire and the General-Welfare State: A Study of Conflict in American Thought, 1865–1901* (Ann Arbor, 1956). I also depended on James Willard Hurst, *Law and Markets in the United States* (Madison, 1982), and Robert Green McCloskey, *American Conservatism in the Age of Enterprise, 1865–1910* (New York, 1951). Arnold M. Paul, *Conservative Crisis and the Rule of Law: Attitudes of Bench and Bar, 1887–1895* (Ithaca, N.Y., 1960), is a very fine history of the development of legal conservatism. Christopher L. Tomlins, *The State and the Unions: Labor Relations, Law, and the Organized Labor Movement in America, 1880–1960* (New York, 1985), is the most impressive work of its kind.

5. THE RISE AND FALL OF THE KNIGHTS OF LABOR

The outstanding work on organized labor during the Civil War and Reconstruction is David Montgomery, *Beyond Equality*. Several biographies of prominent labor leaders are also worth reading. Obadiah Hicks, *Life of Richard Trevellick, the Labor Orator, or the Harbinger of the Eight-Hour System* (Joliet,

Ill., 1896), remains the only book-length biography of this important figure. Jonathan P. Grossman, *William Sylvis, Pioneer of American Labor* (New York, 1945), tells much about Sylvis and the development of the International Molders' Union. George E. McNeill, ed., *The Labor Movement: The Problem of To-Day* (Boston, 1887), is a collection of essays written by McNeill and contemporary labor activists. As Montgomery points out, however, we desperately need studies of labor during Reconstruction at the local level; at this moment none has appeared, though several are in the works. One of the more rewarding investigations of the relationship between the suffragists and the labor movement is Ellen Carol DuBois, *Feminism and Suffrage: The Emergence of an Independent Women's Movement in America, 1848–1869* (Ithaca, N.Y., 1978). A serviceable narrative of the New York draft riots is Adrian Cook, *Armies of the Streets: The New York City Draft Riots of 1863* (Lexington, Ky., 1974). Until recently the literature on the Knights of Labor was surprisingly thin. Selig Perlman, author of the section on the Knights in Commons, *History of Labour,* vol. 2, presents a far more sympathetic and balanced picture of the Order than that which appears in his *Theory of the Labor Movement.* Gerald Grob, *Workers and Utopia,* is of a piece with Perlman's later interpretation. Vincent Falzone, *Terence V. Powderly: Middle-Class Reformer* (Washington, D.C., 1978), is hopelessly traditional but does contain useful information on Powderly's early years and tenure as mayor of Scranton. Powderly's two autobiographies, *Thirty Years of Labor* (New York, 1967, orig. pub. 1940), and Harry J. Carman, Henry David, and Paul N. Guthrie, eds., *The Path I Trod: The Autobiography of Terence V. Powderly* (New York, 1940), are self-serving and often inaccurate, but the former provides a feel for the depth of the crisis in the mid-1880s. Samuel Walker, "Terence V. Powderly, Machinist: 1866–1877," *Labor History,* 19 (1978): 165–84, corrects Powderly's own account of his conversion to radicalism. Richard Oestreicher, "Terence V. Powderly, the Knights of Labor, and Artisanal Republicanism," in Melvyn Dubofsky and Warren Van Tine, eds., *Labor Leaders in America* (Urbana, 1986), 30–61, is a distinguished intellectual biography that has strongly influenced my view of the man and his movement. The most satisfying national history of the Knights is Norman J. Ware, *The Labor Movement in the United States, 1860–1895: A Study in Democracy* (New York, 1929). Except for Powderly we still know very little about the leading figures in the Order. Short sketches of Uriah Stephens, Frederick Turner, and John W. Hayes can be found in Gary M. Fink, ed., *Biographical Dictionary of American Labor Leaders* (rev. ed., Westport, Conn., 1984). A rare in-depth look at a local labor chieftain is Oestreicher, "The Limits of Labor Radicalism: Tom Barry and the Knights of Labor" (unpublished paper, 1978). Jonathan Garlock, *Guide to the Local Assemblies of the Knights of Labor* (Westport, Conn., 1982), is an indispensable quantitative study that lists each local assembly in the Order and provides its founding date and membership. More recent work treats the Knights in local communities. Gregory Kealey and Bryan Palmer, *Dreaming of What Might Be:*

The Knights of Labor in Ontario, 1880–1900 (New York, 1982), is a superior analysis of the culture and politics of the Order. Leon Fink, *Workingmen's Democracy: The Knights of Labor and American Politics* (Urbana, 1983), a study of political activity of the Knights in five communities, concludes that the republican legacy of limited government and urban-rural conflicts hobbled the Knights. Oestreicher, *Solidarity and Fragmentation: Working People and Class Consciousness in Detroit, 1875–1900* (Urbana, 1986), carefully examines the Knights on the shop floor as well as in the political arena and demonstrates that the Great Upheaval intensified the factionalism that ultimately collapsed the Order from within. Judith L. Goldberg, "Strikes, Organizing, and Change: The Knights of Labor in Philadelphia, 1869–1890"(Ph.D. diss., 1985), likewise moves back and forth between the worlds of work and politics. Goldberg paints the most detailed picture of the Knights in the 1870s and offers an original interpretation of the tensions between the rank and file and the leadership over trade union matters. It is hard to find a more probing account of the Molly Maguires than Wayne G. Broehl, Jr., *The Molly Maguires* (Cambridge, Mass., 1964). Anthony F. C. Wallace, *St. Clair: A Nineteenth-Century Coal Town's Experience with a Disaster-Prone Industry* (New York, 1987), draws attention to the hazards of mining and how workers dealt with it. The railway strikes of 1877 do not lack for historians. Two good narratives are Robert V. Bruce, *1877: Year of Violence* (Indianapolis, 1959), and Philip S. Foner, *The Great Labor Uprising of 1877* (New York, 1977). Walter Licht, *Working for the Railroad: The Organization of Work in the Nineteenth Century* (Princeton, 1983), is an important investigation of working conditions on the railroads and labor's efforts to restrain corporate power. Shelton Stromquist, "Enginemen and Shopmen: Technological Change in an Era of Railroad Expansion," *Labor History*, 24 (1983): 485–99, is a first-rate study of railway labor's response to the reorganization of work. The best short history of the Great Upheaval can be found in Jeremy Brecher, *Strike!* (San Francisco, 1972). I also used Samuel Yellen, *American Labor Struggles, 1877–1934* (New York, 1936), and Jama Lazerow, "The Workingman's Hour: The 1886 Labor Uprising in Boston," *Labor History*, 21 (1980): 200–20. The standard work on the Knights in the South is Melton Alonza McLaurin, *The Knights of Labor in the South* (Westport, Conn., 1978). Peter S. Rachleff, *Black Labor in the South: Richmond, Virginia, 1865–1890* (Philadelphia, 1984), is a superb study that roots the Knights in the culture of the local black community and shows the enduring significance of white racism. William B. Hine, "Black Organized Labor in Reconstruction Charleston," *Labor History*, 25 (1984): 504–17, is a good investigation of black dockworker militancy. For Southern textile labor, I have depended on McLaurin, *Paternalism and Protest: Southern Cotton Mill Workers and Organized Labor, 1875–1905* (Westport, Conn., 1971), and Merl Reed, "The Augusta Textile Mills and the Strike of 1886," *Labor History*, 14 (1973): 228–46. Susan Levine, *Labor's True Woman: Carpet Weavers, Industrialization, and Labor Reform in the Gilded Age*

(Philadelphia, 1984), looks at women textile workers in two Northern communities and the Knights' conception of womanhood. Paul Buhle, "The Knights of Labor in Rhode Island," *Radical History Review,* 17 (1978): 39–74, opens a window on the cultural activities of lady Knights. Edwin Gabler, *The American Telegrapher: A Social History, 1860–1900* (New Brunswick, N.J., 1988), uses the telegraphers' strike of 1883 as a point of departure to explore the question of gender within the Knights and the self-image of women members. Two of the more illuminating studies of conflict between craft unionists and Knights apart from the well-known dispute between the cigar makers are Elizabeth and Kenneth Fones-Wolf, "Knights versus Trade Unionists: The Case of the Washington, D.C., Carpenters, 1881–1896,"*Labor History,* 22 (1981): 192–212, and by the same authors, "The War at Mingo Junction: The Autonomous Workman and the Decline of the Knights of Labor," *Ohio History,* 92 (1983): 37–51. The basic monograph on Haymarket is Henry David, *A History of the Haymarket Affair* (New York, 1936). Paul Avrich, *The Haymarket Tragedy* (Princeton, 1984), is a lively narrative with a biographical emphasis. Richard Schneirov, "Free Thought and Socialism in the Czech Community in Chicago, 1875–1887," in Dirk Hoerder, ed., *"Struggle a Hard Battle"*: *Essays on Working-Class Immigrants* (De Kalb, Ill., 1986), 71–94, demonstrates both the ethnic base of socialism and anarchism and the porous boundaries between these ideological forms. Bruce C. Nelson, " 'We Can't Get Them to Do Aggressive Work': Chicago's Anarchists and the Eight-Hour Movement," and Hartmut Keil, "The Impact of Haymarket on German-American Radicalism," *International Labor and Working Class History,* 29 (1986): 1–27, are excellent investigations of the quality of German socialism and the impact of Haymarket on working-class radicals. Paul Buhle, "German Radicals and the Roots of American Working-Class Radicalism," in Keil and Jentz, *German Workers in Industrial Chicago,* 224–35, covers similar ground.

6. THE PRUDENTIAL UNIONISM OF THE AMERICAN FEDERATION OF LABOR

Students of Samuel Gompers used to cleave neatly into two groups. Commons School scholars depicted a tough-minded pragmatist, while Marxists saw an opportunist and "misleader" of labor. H. M. Gitelman, "Adolph Strasser and the Origins of Pure and Simple Unionism," *Labor History,* 6 (1965): 71–82, may be seen as something of a departure. While Gitelman ended up in agreement with the Commons School, he was one of the first scholars to take Gompers's socialist background seriously. Stuart B. Kaufman, *Samuel Gompers and the Origins of the American Federation of Labor, 1848–1896* (Westport, Conn., 1973), is an intellectual biography that also stresses Gompers's socialist heritage and what he owed it. William Dick, *Labor and Socialism in America: The Gompers Era* (Port Washington, N.Y., 1972), is very much in this vein, but views Gompers as a syndicalist. The most recent work attempts to understand Gompers and the federation as the products not only of intellectual traditions but also of a hostile

238 BIBLIOGRAPHIC ESSAY

political environment and a parochial rank and file. The best of this new wave is John H. M. Laslett, "Samuel Gompers and the Rise of American Business Unionism," in Dubofsky and Van Tine, *Labor Leaders in America,* 62–88, and Grace Palladino, "The Ties That Bind: Samuel Gompers and the Structure of Solidarity, 1886–1895"(unpublished paper, 1987). Gerald Friedman, "Politics and Unions" (Ph.D. diss., 1986), a comparative study of the political and economic context of union development in France and the United States, is the most original and stimulating example of this new scholarship. Gompers's ghostwritten autobiography, *Seventy Years of Life and Labor,* 2 vols. (New York, 1925), must be read critically but is still refreshingly candid and especially useful for understanding early socialist culture and the quality of workers' culture in the small shop immediately after the Civil War. No student of Gompers or the AF of L can afford to ignore Stuart B. Kaufman, et al., eds., *The Samuel Gompers Papers, 1850–1886: The Making of a Union Leader,* vol. 1 (Urbana, 1986). The second volume in this projected multi-volume series was published too late to be used for this book. Though some of the documents that appear in vol. 1 are well known and accessible elsewhere, many are more obscure and provide insights into Gompers's differences with the socialists and the Knights of Labor and Adolph Strasser's view of American politics. Gompers's closest associates remain unstudied. There are no book-length biographies of Adolph Strasser or other influential figures in the AF of L. Mark Erlich, "Peter J. McGuire's Trade Unionism: Socialism of a Trade Union Kind?" *Labor History,* 24 (1983): 165–97, is a thoughtful look at this leading socialist. The standard work on the International Workingmen's Association is Samuel Bernstein, *The First International in America* (New York, 1965); it is helpful but badly in need of updating. There is no modern book on the Socialist Labor party. L. Glenn Seretan, *Daniel DeLeon: The Odyssey of an American Marxist* (Cambridge, Mass., 1979), is a critical biography of the SLP's leading light. The life of craftsmen on and off the job is sensitively treated in Francis G. Couvares, *The Remaking of Pittsburgh: Class and Culture in an Industrializing City, 1877–1919* (Albany, 1984). Roy Rosenzweig, *Eight Hours for What We Will: Workers & Leisure in an Industrial City, 1870–1920* (New York, 1983), centers on the transition from popular culture to mass culture in Worcester, Massachusetts. There are numerous monographs on craft unions. Lloyd Ulman, *The Rise of the National Trade Union: The Development and Significance of Its Structure, Governing Institutions, and Economic Policies* (Cambridge, Mass., 1955), is a dull but encyclopedic institutional history. More specialized works in recent years include Robert Christie, *Empire in Wood: A History of the Carpenters* (Ithaca, N.Y., 1956); David A. Corbin, *Life, Work, and Rebellion in the Coal Fields: The Southern West Virginia Coal Miners, 1880–1920* (Urbana, 1981); David Bensman, *The Practice of Solidarity: American Hat Finishers in the Nineteenth Century* (Urbana, 1985); Patricia Cooper, *Once a Cigar Maker: Men, Women, and Work Culture in American Cigar Factories, 1900–1919* (Urbana, 1987); and

Michael Kazin, *Barons of Labor: The San Francisco Building Trades and Trade Union Power in Progressive America* (Urbana, 1987). The political activities of working-class women and their middle-class allies have only recently attracted the attention of historians. Even then, work has centered on Chicago. Meredith Tax, *The Rising of the Women: Feminist Solidarity and Class Conflict, 1880–1917* (New York, 1979), downplays the role of Hull House activists in achieving regulatory laws, while Kathryn Kish Sklar, "Hull House in the 1890s: A Community of Women Reformers," *Signs,* 10 (1985): 658–77, stresses the importance of Florence Kelley and other middle-class reformers. For evidence of cooperation between white and black labor at the local level, see Herbert G. Gutman, "The Negro and the United Mine Workers of America: The Career and Letters of Richard Davis and Something of Their Meaning," in Gutman, *Work, Culture and Society,* 119–208; Paul B. Worthman, "Black Workers and Labor Unions in Birmingham, Alabama, 1897–1904," in Milton Cantor, ed., *Black Labor in America* (Westport, Conn., 1970), 51–85; and Eric Arnesen, "Learning the Lessons of Solidarity: Work Rules and Work Relations on the New Orleans Waterfront, 1880–1902" (unpublished paper, 1987). Several writers emphasize the enduring racism of the AF of L, none more single-mindedly than Gwendolyn Mink, *Old Labor and New Labor in American Political Development: Union, Party, and State, 1875–1920* (Ithaca, N.Y., 1986). Alexander Saxton, *The Indispensable Enemy: Labor and the Anti-Chinese Movement in California* (Berkeley, 1971), sees the "coolie question" as key to the Democratic party's appeal to labor and the making of the labor movement in California. Andrew Gyory, "Yan-kee to Yan-ki: American Workers React to Chinese Laborers in 1870" (unpublished paper, 1986), shows that Eastern workers were not unified on the issue of ending Chinese immigration. On the trade union views of black civic and political leaders, I used August Meier, *Negro Thought in America, 1880–1915* (Ann Arbor, 1963). There is no modern study of the eight-hour movement of the early 1890s. My narrative is based on Walter Galenson, *The United Brotherhood of Carpenters* (Cambridge, Mass., 1983), and the standard histories of the AF of L. For the decline of socialism in the 1890s, I used John H. M. Laslett, *Labor and the Left: A Study of Socialist and Radical Influence in the American Labor Movement, 1881–1924* (New York, 1970), and by the same author, "Reflections on the Failure of Socialism in the American Federation of Labor," *Mississippi Valley Historical Review,* 80 (1964): 634–51. Chester M. Destler, *American Radicalism, 1865–1901* (New York, 1946), is still the most thorough account of radical politics in Chicago during the 1890s. For radicalism in New York, see Eli Goldschmidt, "Labor and Populism: New York City, 1891–1896," *Labor History,* 13 (1972): 520–32, and Herbert Perrier, "The Socialists and the Working Class in New York, 1890–1896," *Labor History,* 22 (1981): 485–511. There is no dearth of work on the Homestead strike or the Pullman boycott. David Brody, *Steelworkers in America* (Cambridge, Mass., 1960), places the strike in its industrial context. Arthur G. Burgoyne, *Homestead*

(Pittsburgh, 1893), is an hour-by-hour account of the strike. Leon Wolff, *Lockout, the Story of the Homestead Strike of 1892: A Study of Violence, Unionism, and the Carnegie Steel Empire* (New York, 1965), is a readable popular history. Linda Schneider, "The Citizen Striker: Workers' Ideology in the Homestead Strike of 1892," *Labor History*, 23 (1982): 47–66, is an imaginative analysis of republican ideology in transition. Ray Ginger, *The Bending Cross: A Biography of Eugene V. Debs* (New Brunswick, N.J., 1949), has been eclipsed by Nick Salvatore, *Eugene V. Debs: Citizen and Socialist* (Urbana, 1982), which has shaped my view of the man and of the significance of paternalism. Two useful studies of Pullman and his experiment are Stanley Buder, *Pullman: An Experiment in Industrial Order and Community Planning, 1880–1930* (New York, 1967), and Almont Lindsey, *The Pullman Strike: The Story of a Unique Experiment and of a Great Labor Upheaval* (Chicago, 1971, orig. pub. 1942). William H. Carwadine, *The Pullman Strike* (Chicago, 1894), the account of clergymen sympathetic to labor, includes information on wages and working conditions as reported by Pullman workers. U.S. Strike Commission, *Report on the Chicago Strike of June–July, 1894*, U.S. Congress, 53rd. Cong., 3rd sess., Sen. Exec. Doc. No. 7 (Washington, D.C., 1895), contains the testimony of figures on both sides of the strike.

Index

abolitionists (ism), 71, 87, 161
Academy of Music, Richmond, and
    blacks, 160
Addams, Jane, 192
"Address to the Members of Trade
    Societies . . . ," 68
Adelphon Kruptos, 154
Afro-Americans, *see* blacks
agrarians, and market economy, 24
agriculture, commercial, 21, 23
Allen, Samuel Cresson, 82
Alliance movement, 153
Almy, William, 29
Altgeld, John Peter, 170
Amalgamated Ass'n of Iron, Steel,
    and Tin Workers, 164, 197,
    200–1; and Homestead strike,
    201–2
American Federalist, 187–8
American Federation of Labor (AF
    of L), 5, 14, 135, 164, 171,
    175, 198, 218; craft unions of,
    4, 13, 192, 218; progenitors of,
    5; and Knights of Labor, 5,
    174, 199, 217; and prudential
    unionism, 13, 198–9; and
    strikes, 13, 204, 209; creation
    of, 176, 182; Gompers and,
    176–7, 183, 189; guiding prin-
    ciples of, 177, 183; affiliated
    unions and numbers and types
    of members of, 183, 200, 205;
    and craft conservatism, 183–5;
    field staff and executive officers
    of, 187–8; socialists in, 187–9;
strength and weakness of, 187,
    203, 219–20; Political
    Programme of, 189–90; occupa-
    tional, race, and gender diver-
    sity of, 191–2; and blacks and
    women, 192–3, 196; and volun-
    tarism, 193; perspective of lead-
    ers of, 198–9; and corporations,
    203; and Pullman boycott, 204;
    change of policy in, 218; poli-
    tics and government and, 219;
    see also Gompers
American party, Fillmore and, 106;
    see also Know-Nothings
American Protestant Ass'n, 97
American Railway Union, 13, 138,
    205; victorious strikes of, 205;
    and Pullman boycott, 206–8;
    after Pullman strike, 209
American Republicans, 97–9, 101,
    105, 214–15
American Tobacco Co., 118
Ameringer, Oscar, 170
anarchism (ists), 186–7
Anarchist International, 169
Ancient Order of Hibernians, 96,
    143
Anderson, John, 77
Anderson, Joseph, 34–5
Anthony, Susan B., 161
antimonopoly, 4–5, 13, 90; St.
    Louis work stoppage and, 145;
    convention of, 148; rural Amer-
    ica and, 153; K of L and, 167;
    Democrats and, 213

242

Populism, American, movement culture of, 74
Populist party, spawning of, 175
Powderly, Terence and Margery, 147
Powderly, Terence V., 146–50, 154–5, 174, 176–7, 198, 204, 217; indecisive leadership of, 155, 167, 170, 173, 183; and newcomers, 157–8; and strikes, 157, 166–8; and blacks, 160–1; and women, 162; and lobbying, 164–5; and arbitration, 167; and unruly membership, 171; and eight-hour movement, 172, 187; and butchers, 173; and Gompers, 174, 217; and craftsmen, 174–5; last activities and replacement of, 175; and "rule or ruin," 217; see also Knights of Labor
Pratt, Micajab, 41–2
printing (ers), 38–9, 45; and ink and type, 45; and unions, 51, 102–3; women and strike of, 161; and women members, 197
production, cooperative, see cooperation
Progressive Cigar Makers of N.Y., 168, 171
Protestants (ism), 52, 96–7, 212
Providence Ass'n of Mechanics, 47
prudential unionism, 13, 177, 198–9, 208, 219–20
public works, demand for, 109
Pullman, George M., 204; model town of, 205
Pullman boycott, 11–12, 199, 204, 206–9
Pullman works: unrest of workers in, 205–6; ARU committee complaints in, 206; strike of, see Pullman boycott

pure and simple unionism, 177, 181–2, 186–7, 191; CMIU and, 182; anarchists and, 186; socialists and, 190; strengthened appeal of, 218

race riots, 62, 91; see also racism
Rachleff, Peter, 162
racism, 71–2, 76–7, 108, 195, 197–8
radicalism (s), 9–13, 47, 63, 66, 68–72, 79, 83–4, 92, 105, 112, 150–2, 216; and cooperation, 89–90; German, 106; weakening of, 139; Civil War and, 152; strength of, in U.S., 153; K of L and, 154; death of, 175; vs. Marxism, 178–9; and AF of L, 187; politics and economics of, 213–15, 217; and competitive capitalism, 214; and industrialization, 216; transition of, to prudential unionism, 219–20
Railway Carmen and Switchmen, lodges of, to ARU, 205
railways, 16, 23–4, 61; brotherhoods of, 10, 143; building of, 22; expansion and ownership of, 114; refrigerated cars of, 116; cooperative agreements among, 129–30; public regulation of, 132; and wage reductions, 143–4; management of, response to strikes, 146; strikes on, see under strikes
Ransom, Roger, 158
Rawbone, Charles, 190
reform unionism, 190–1
Reid, Whitelaw, 158
Reitzel, Robert, 186–7

UNIVERSITY OF ILLINOIS PRESS
1325 SOUTH OAK STREET
CHAMPAIGN, ILLINOIS 61820-6903
WWW.PRESS.UILLINOIS.EDU